JANE COUCH
FLEETWOOD ASSASSIN

JANE COUCH
FLEETWOOD ASSASSIN

by Jane Couch as told to Tex Woodward

BLAKE

Published by Blake Publishing Ltd,
3 Bramber Court, 2 Bramber Road,
London W14 9PB, England

First published in 2000

ISBN 1 85782 4350

British Library Cataloguing-in-Publication Data:

A catalogue record for this book is
available from the British Library.

Typeset by t2

Printed in Great Britain by
Creative Print and Design (Wales),
Ebbw Vale, Gwent.

1 3 5 7 9 10 8 6 4 2

Pictures reproduced by kind permission of Capital, Les Clark, Empics
and Francis Loney.

ACKNOWLEDGEMENTS

This book would never have been written if it wasn't for 'Granddad', that is Tex Woodward, my coach/trainer and manager. We travelled thousands of miles together, and as we talked, when we were hanging about places or flying or things, I would tell him stories about my life before I met him. Sometimes he would look at me as if he didn't believe me, a lot of the time he would laugh until he cried. He'd say to me, 'Jane, you're hilarious.' (He's a bit posh sometimes and uses big words.) 'The things you have done are hard to believe. You would be a great subject for a book.' So then it started, 'Talk to me Jane, tell me about this, tell me about that, I can write your story.'

For more than two years he would be asking questions. Sometimes I would co-operate. Sometimes I couldn't be bothered and then we'd argue and snap at each other: 'I can't write this book unless you tell me things to write about.'

'Oh, fuck the book! I'm bored.' He wouldn't give up though, and kept writing his notes. God knows how many pens he used — that's probably why he kept nicking them from the hotels and places we went.

It would be impossible to write about everything I've done — in fact some of the things I have done are better not written about, but I suppose that's the same for everyone. Anyway, this book isn't just about the life I had before I was a boxer, but about how I became a boxer, and the world of boxing and entertainment that I found myself involved in. It's about the bright lights of television, the camera flashes, the almost non-stop press interviews, the dinners, the boxing shows, the thousands of miles travelling. It's about the hard slog of training all the time, the hundreds and hundreds of rounds of sparring I have done with countless sparring partners, nearly all of them male and nearly all of them giving me a hard time in the ring and then telling me it's 'all for your own good'. Didn't feel much like it when I was having my eyes blackened, lips split, nose bleeding, and it definitely didn't feel like it when

Simon Stowell split my eye open with his wild thoughtless head. He didn't mean to do it — none of my sparring partners really tried to hurt me, apart from the occasional dickhead who thought he could knock me out, 'cos I'm a woman. Usually it goes the other way: I've knocked plenty of them out because they tried to be cocky.

I will always be really grateful to all those guys that helped me because without them to spar with I would never have learnt to box so well. Darren Dorrington, Dean Cooper, Eddie Hedges, Martin Hurd, Mike Loveridge, Simon (Dangerous-Head) Stowell and too many others to list. I've got to mention Ronnie Butler though. He wasn't a boxer, just a really big hard man: he did door work on clubs, minding and collecting jobs. He was about 50 years old, and looked more like a gypsy than I do. If Ronnie had come from the Fleetwood area he could well have been a relation of mine, thick black hair, swarthy features. We certainly used a lot of the same language, much to Tex's disgust, but Ronnie had got a broad Bristol accent. Like me, Ronnie had a heart of gold inside a cast-iron body. Like me, he had a sense of right and wrong that other people didn't always agree with but he got respect from those who upheld the law and those that didn't. There were all sorts of rumours and stories about what Ronnie got up to in his spare time. He told me he had been prosecuted seventy-five times but only appeared in court once, and then he got away with it. There used to be some drug dealers on Ronnie's patch but when he found them, they decided there were more comfortable ways of making a living. Ronnie was big and frightening yet he did a lot of charity work and helped the under-privileged. He often trained in the gym at the same time as me and we would wind each other up. He'd plod away with his exercising and I'd shout at him, 'Fat, lazy bastard.' He'd shout back, 'Ugly fucking useless bitch.' Tex stared and complained but at least we made each other work. Sometimes Ronnie would get in the ring with me and let me punch his body as hard as I could, non-stop for round after round. One time I did ten three-minute rounds, and Ronnie kept geeing me on — he didn't seem to feel a thing when I hit him. He even let heavyweight male boxers do it to him. Talk about hard!

When I first came to Spaniorum Farm to learn how to box, instead of brawl, Sandra Rouse had been training there for just over a year. She was a really good boxer, but only small, just over eight stone if she weighed after she had had a good meal. 'Cos she was so small I started calling her 'The Midget', and that got shortened to 'Midge'. She played a big part in my life, both in the gym and by giving me a break by taking me off shopping, or just taking me out to cheer me up if I got a bit low. Sometimes I would get a bit depressed when I thought of all my friends and family in Fleetwood who I hardly ever saw any more. The 'Midge' was good at helping Tex in the corner whenever she could get to my fights, and she was an even better drinking partner when we were celebrating. We had some laughs.

When I think back about all the people that helped me get started as a boxer in Fleetwood, especially as they thought I was mad to want to be a boxer, I'm really grateful for their help. If it hadn't been for them I would never have travelled so far, met so many famous people or done so many things. Frank Smallbone, a bit unwillingly, tried to teach me the basics of boxing but I couldn't see what all the fuss was about, having to train, skip, and keep sticking my left hand out straight. I thought I could just get in the ring and knock people out — I didn't know how much there was to learn! Anyway thanks for trying Frank, and thanks to Brent and Ray at Fleetwood's Bodyquest gym. Brent was a really good fitness adviser and Ray would take me running, even when I didn't want to run. If it hadn't been for those guys I would have probably thought a lot and talked a lot about boxing but never got in a ring

The one person who probably deserved the most thanks, for really setting me on my way to an exciting future, was Steve Presnail. It was Steve who promoted my first fights in Fleetwood, and managed the early part of my career. He would often drive me to Tex's gym for training weekends, and was always willing to help me in any way he could.

In fact everyone I knew, and a lot I didn't, supported me in Fleetwood. I even started having phone calls from one of my ex-school teachers who told me how good I was at school and that he knew I would do well. Bullshit: I wasn't and he didn't.

To me the highlight of my story was being granted my professional boxer's licence by the British Boxing Board of Control so that I could box in the UK under good organisation and medical supervision. It was Tex's idea I should apply for my licence but it was the pressure of my excellent legal team from Irwin Mitchell, Sara Leslie, Imogen and Holly, the Equal Opportunities Commission and my brilliant, brilliant, barrister Dinah Rose that made that dream come true and assured me of a place in sporting history.

Even when you're famous, you still feel lonely at times. So when I got home for a break it was really good when me mum fussed over me and cooked me smashing Sunday dinners. I liked her pampering me.

If anyone 'adopted' me it had to be Pat and Tex. It was Tex that I came west to train with. He was the one person who managed to stick with me and put up with my tantrums when I decided to become a full-time boxer. From the start of me being famous all sorts of people made promises that they never fulfilled, and then disappeared. From the time we decided that it would be just the two of us working together, things got better. 'Granddad', Pat, and all his family supported me and made me feel part of the family. Pat did all the printing out of this book on her computer, never complaining, even if she did have to make changes every two minutes. I thought she was a computer genius before she started working on this book, but she certainly got a bit of practice from it. Thanks Pat, and all those other people who have helped me. You were all brill and you have helped me to be what I am.

CONTENTS

INTRODUCTION

More than once, over the years that I coached and trained Jane Couch to become a three-times World boxing champion, the thought would come into my mind, Whatever am I doing, spending so much time with this woman who brings my normally placid nature to such a boiling point that all I want to do is drive her to the railway station, give her her fare home and get her out of my life?

In our calmer moments, I knew the answer. Obnoxious and abrasive as Jane could be on occasions (mostly before midday, or when I insisted she did something she didn't want to do like get out of bed), there was a much softer and caring side to her nature. Old people, children, street beggars, all of them treated with kindness and generosity that she couldn't really afford. In fact, whoever wrote the poem about the little girl who had the curl right in the middle of her forehead, could have written it for Jane Couch – when she was good she was very very good, but when she was bad she was horrid!

Jane was also a great asset to the running of my gym, Spaniorum Farm Gymnasium, a large and active boxing gym I had built up in an old farm building that had once been a South Gloucestershire cider factory. She was an example to the other budding boxers of what could be achieved by hard work, determination, and that degree of madness that makes physical pain sufferable.

As well as using the facilities for training, Jane took a pride in their presentation. Sweat-blurred mirrors were regularly cleaned, the sticky punch-bags wiped. If the ring was dusty or the dressing rooms untidy, forget the cleaner – the vacuum was out and the job done, especially if one of the regular flow of journalists or TV people were visiting.

The media were no strangers to my gym, even before Jane. I had promoted professional boxing shows, coached boxers and other sports people. I even promoted a wrestling show on one hilarious, if not economic, occasion. Male wrestlers, midget wrestlers, some weird, some ugly and some, like Donna Maria, very attractive. It was Donna who inspired the local TV company to film her both during training and at leisure. It was a successful piece by Graham Purches. And some months later he called me again to ask if the female wrestlers were still working out at the farm. They weren't, but I wasn't going to miss the chance of some free publicity so, slightly tongue in cheek, I said, 'No, but I do have some female boxers!'

It was sort of true. I did have some young women kick-boxers, and a delightful mother and daughter, Jane and Charlotte Leslie, who were boxing training for fitness. So back came the TV cameras and they filmed another successful piece.

Publicity snowballs. I was invited to other TV shows in

Birmingham, Manchester and Bristol to discuss women's boxing. The subject seemed to have captured the media's imagination. It was on these shows that I first met those initial stalwarts of women's boxing in the UK, Susan Atkins and Jane Johnson.

It was a TV documentary from my gym featuring Jane Johnson that caught the eye of Jimmy Finn and Barbara Buttrick, the Vice-President and President of the Women's International Boxing Federation. They came to see me. My facilities and boxing experience must have captured their imagination. Without consultation I was announced as WIBF Chairman! Unwittingly, I had been drawn into the organisation of women's boxing and I started to attend the female boxing shows in my now official capacity.

It was at a combined boxing and kick-boxing show in Wigan that I first saw Jane Couch compete. She was having the first legitimate fight that was to start her fairly short journey to becoming a world champion boxer. Her opponent was Kalpna Shah, a London policewoman. It was an irony not lost on Jane's Fleetwood fans, and one I would learn to appreciate as I came to know her and be told of the frequent brushes she had had with the law - not least the single-handed riot she had evoked when five police officers had joined forces to arrest her and put her in a van to be taken to the Fleetwood police station.

With that sort of record there was no way one off-duty policewoman in boxing gloves was going to cause her much of a problem. In the second round of the fight the referee, Eugene Valerio, rescued Kalpna from the hail of flailing arms, to the delight of the throng of vociferous fans who had vacated Fleetwood to support their new-found sporting heroine. My job, as official in charge, was to present Jane with the winner's trophy. Little did I know how this wild, extrovert, gypsy-looking woman was going to disrupt my life in the not-too-distance future.

At first Jane, like many other boxers before her, came to the gym for training sessions, and left after her workout. Then she would stay for a night, a weekend, a few days. As we both decided she was going to make a name for herself in the big-time boxing world, it made sense for her to move in with my wife Pat and me to start serious full-time training. From then on, she worked harder and achieved more than either of us could possibly have dreamt of.

Her story is an inspiring one, one that she has related in her own characteristic, no-nonsense street language. To some, the words may be offensive – but that's Jane: what you see (and hear) is what you get!

This book shows glimpses of the many aspects of Jane's nature, and how she has worked towards achieving her dreams, despite the many problems and hurdles she met along the way, some of which she inflicted on herself. It shows the warm-hearted motherly Jane, caring for an elderly woman who was travelling by train for the first time in many years. We were travelling from Fleetwood back to Bristol and, arriving at Preston, we found the trains were running late. Confusion prevailed: confusion about train times, confusion about platforms, and confusion particularly for a little old lady who was travelling alone. She had no idea what was happening, and was not a little distressed. So Jane Couch, the fearful Fleetwood Assassin, took charge, fussing around like a mother hen, making sure the lady, who was travelling to Bristol, was helped on the train (I carried the luggage!), placed in her pre-booked seat and visited regularly during the journey. When we reached Bristol, the lady was met by her sister. A few days later, Jane received a letter, thanking her for her kindness.

In contrast there is the vicious, vindictive Jane Couch who can bear a grudge, as long as it is uppermost in her ultra-active brain and not forgotten in the deluge of new thoughts that refill her mind constantly. The Jane Couch that will abuse verbally and physically with fist, head or whatever else is to hand, anyone who intrudes unwanted into her personal domain, just as she did when a loud-mouthed lout started having a go at her boyfriend at the time, while they were enjoying a quiet drink. 'Don't let him talk to you like that,' says Jane.

'What the fuck's it got to do with you?' was the lout's response. That was the end of that short argument – one right-whack and a head-butt and the would-be hardman was out cold. And that was before she even learned to box...

When Jane first came to live with Pat and me, she slept in a small attic room at the top of the house. As we realised her stay was getting more permanent, we suggested she turn a larger room that we had on a ground floor into a flat. This area had, many years ago, been built on to the side of the farmhouse, and was separated from the main house by a door we kept locked at night. At first, Jane welcomed the idea of a self-contained flatlet. She enthusiastically painted the room in startling colours, orange walls, yellow doors and beams with the furniture bright green.

But the new living quarters stayed unused for quite a while, their proposed occupant reluctant to leave the main house. She had feelings of being discarded, mixed with those of being shut away alone, even though she would be just the other side of the living room wall.

Pat provided the solution: 'Take Nipper in with you.' Nipper, a small mongrel dog of indeterminate age, that we had saved from the dogs' home many years ago, was not the epitome of a guard dog. In fact, Jane had called him Billy Blunt-Teeth for some while. That was until he bit straight through her trainers and into her toe, when she had accidentally stepped on him. Nevertheless, Nipper became Jane's nightly companion and she began to enjoy her own space, with a TV and video recorder (she could watch herself over and over again), a computer connected to the Internet, the expertise to send and receive E-mail quickly learnt: a whole new world had opened up for Jane's active and receptive mind.

With her life now fully occupied, mentally and physically, Jane matured into a far more sophisticated woman. The abrasiveness still appeared in times of stress, but the sharp edges of this once very rough diamond were gradually eroding, the daily routine of me tiptoeing through a minefield of explosive emotions was becoming less hazardous. The volatile nature still smouldering beneath the surface was controlled to a reasonably acceptable level.

So when the thought entered my head, as it often did, Would I go through all that time and energy-consuming work, the arguments and the tantrums again? Was it worth the achievements, the travelling, the many enjoyable moments, and the often hilarious times? The answer was always yes!

Tex Woodward
Spaniorum Farm Gymnasium, 2000

PART ONE

DOWN AND OUT IN FLEETWOOD AND LONDON

1

ALBERT STREET, FLEETWOOD, LANCASHIRE

Anyone who had known me when I was young, and even when I wasn't quite so young, would have said I was a right little bastard, but I wasn't! I had a good mum and a dad! Mum's name was Susan, her friends called her Sue but to my mind it was always Sioux like the Red Indians would have spelt it. I liked to think we were descended from Indians, and with my black crinkly hair I would have looked quite at home squatting outside a wigwam. Dad was Tom, or Tommy to his mates.

It was me dad I took after, in a lot of ways. He was

described as a 'lovable rogue' by a local policeman who just happened to catch me pinching lead off a roof to sell. I was eleven years old! I tried to fight him, just like my dad would've, but I was dragged home to me mum. It was the beginning of me following in my father's footsteps: he was a petty criminal, always pinching, boozing, fighting. It's little wonder his daughter should have tried to take the same path.

Mostly my dad was a fisherman and we were part of a close fishing community. The only thing with Dad was that he never stayed with a ship very long. He either didn't like the Skipper, or he'd miss the ship after spending too long in the pub. His fishing career consisted of him being on one ship for a few weeks, being sacked from that one, joining another, and so on. Dad didn't like being told what to do — something I definitely inherited from him!

His ancestors hadn't always been fishermen, but my dad's dad, Claude Harrington Couch, or 'Plymouth Jim' as everyone used to call him, actually sailed on the famous sailing ship, the *Cutty Sark*. Dad's eldest half-brother, George, died at sea, on the way back from Iceland in a trawler, the *Red Falcon*, which went down with all hands when they were coming home for Christmas.

I think that experiencing those tragedies may well have been the reason for Dad's dislike of deep-sea fishing. He'd seen what Granddad and Granny Couch had been through when told the news that they had lost a son. That's probably why he got out of fishing when he did.

Mum and Dad got divorced not long after I was born. I don't know the real reasons why and I don't fuckin' care. He would still come to see us on a Sunday, to take us to the 'Mount' where we would play on the slide and swings. Then we would visit my granny, his mum, Ethel Patricia Couch, who lived in Byron Street. Sadly, Granny was blind. She hadn't always been, but old age had caught up with her and she wasn't able to see for the last five or six years of her life, until she died at eighty-five, the same age her husband had died at some time before. She used to sit me on her knee for ages, just touching my face and asking me what I looked like. In her younger days she too had been a strong, determined woman. I suppose she had to be with nine sons and two daughters! She also had strong principles. When my mum went round to tell her she was marrying Dad in a Registry Office, and invited Granny to the wedding, Gran said, 'I'm not coming. If you get married in a Registry Office it will never work.' She got that right!

But we still used to go and see her after Mum and Dad were divorced. Mum would make her fire up and get some shopping in, and I would sit on Gran's knee just staring at her for ages, wondering why she couldn't see me. Each Sunday she would give me 10p to take to Sunday School and put in the collection pot, but more often than not it got spent on sweets! Granny kept a bowl of fruit on the table behind her chair, and sometimes I would try to pinch an apple or banana. I don't know how she knew I was going to do it, but before I had it in my hand she would shout, 'Put it back!'

Granny Couch died when I was about seven or eight years old. I did miss her and my visits. I just wish I had known her better when I was older and she was younger, so that we could have got to know more about each other.

Perhaps I wouldn't have missed her so much if my mum's parents had been around, but as she was dumped into the Fleetwood orphanage when she was a little girl, she didn't have any family to call her own. That's probably why my brother, Tom, me and Mum have always stayed so close. Tom, who is five years older than me, became my idol. I always looked up to him, and he was always there to help me when I was in trouble, and ready to comfort me when I got upset about things. We would fight like fuck at times, but I did love him more than most girls do their brothers. We looked very much alike, so much alike, in fact, that people often thought we were twins.

Getting back to me mum, her mum was a nurse in a hospital in Kennington, London, who had been made pregnant by a doctor. The doctor wasn't willing to take the responsibility for a child, and the nurse confided her problems to a patient. The patient offered to marry her and took her to Fleetwood, where he ran an electrician's shop. Somehow he managed to electrocute himself and died. Mum's mum couldn't cope on her own, which is why my mum was put in the orphanage.

When the Second World War was on, Mum got evacuated to Guildford, Surrey. She was placed with a very nice family. Auntie Hilda, as me mum came to call her, took Mum into her home, took care of her, and gave her a great start in life. Auntie Hilda and Uncle Harry had two children of their own, June and John, and Mum became like their sister. When the war was over, though, it was back to Fleetwood. Auntie Hilda really wanted to adopt Mum, but for some unknown reason her mother preferred to have her put back in the orphanage, rather than letting her live with a well-to-do family, even though Mum had become very fond of them and they always kept in touch.

When Mum and Dad got married, despite Granny's warning about the Registry Office, they first rented a bungalow in Kenilworth Avenue, then a house in Kent Street, before moving into number 16, Albert Street, which I have always thought of as my real home. That's where I was born, in the front bedroom, on August 14th 1968. The first compliment about my skin came from the midwife, as she showed me to my mum: 'Ah! She's got skin like peaches and cream.' Mum said, 'I expect that's because I've been eating a lot of peaches while I've been pregnant.' I don't know if that was the real reason — I always felt it was the fresh sea air of the small fishing town, just along the coast from the more famous Blackpool, that gave me my healthy complexion.

Mum was twenty-eight years old when I was born — at least she has always told me she was. I've got a feeling though that, like me, as she got older she may have lost a year or two. Dad was thirty-four years old and that was probably true, although he could get things mixed up at times.

Number 16 was one of a terrace of big old houses. I think

it was old enough to be Victorian. It had iron railings outside it and an iron grid in the pavement, covering an opening to the cellar through which the coal-man used to dump the coal, when Mum could afford it. She couldn't afford much in those days; nor could any of our neighbours, come to that. Many's the time there would be a knock at the door and she would say to me and Tom, 'Shush, get in the back and keep quiet, it might be the rent-man or the loan-man.' The same would happen if the TV detector van was about. The old black and white telly would be turned off, curtains drawn, and to all intents and purposes, no one would be at home.

Money was always short, even when the fishermen landed, the fish were sold off and the men paid. They would piss up all the money they had risked their lives for in a very short time. Then it was back to sea for them, and back to candlelight for us, if Mum couldn't borrow a coin for the electric meter.

Our front room didn't even have a carpet; in fact it was only used for storing toys and things. We lived in the back room which Mum tried to keep warm with a coal fire. Even with that the house was fucking freezing. I don't know which was worse, the outside toilet with its torn sheets of newspaper for wiping your bum, or the bathroom. Sunday night at about half past six was bathnight. Tom and I bathed together mostly, but if I was lucky I got in first, in the clean water. Mum would wash me, wrap a towel round me, and send me back down to the fire. Sometimes Tom and me would be in the bath together, and then there would be a right do. I'd pull his hair, he'd fight me off. What a mess! I feel sorry for my mum when I look back at the things I used to do.

I reckon she was a good mother really, and I often wonder how she managed. To say times were hard is a right understatement. With my dad gone, there was even less money. The small amount she did earn came from her part-time job working as a waitress in a Chinese restaurant called the Hoi Kin, which was just across the road from Albert Street. She could only do a few hours a week, though, as she had to look after me and Tom on her own. Sometimes she would go without food just so we would have our dinner. That was one of the best things about her: she always made sure we had at least one good meal a day. If she got any extra money from anywhere, she always used to treat us. I suppose that's why me and Tom grew up all right, because even though we never had anything, we knew that if she did get some money we would get some too. I suppose it worked out all right, because if she had been rich we might have been spoiled and we would never have seen the times she was sat without electric or heating, and going without food so she could give it to us. Seeing that sort of thing makes you realise someone must really love you.

The other thing that sticks in my mind about my mum is that she always used to make the beds, do the washing, and clean before she went out. She used to say, 'It costs nothing to be clean.' That was one thing about my first home: it wasn't much to look at, but it *was* clean. She made sure of that. I suppose one reason I became a champion is that my mum passed that strength of mind on to me. She never used to moan and groan, she just got on with life.

In a way, all the people in Albert Street were like one big family. There would be arguments but they would soon blow over. There was Toni McDermot, one of Mum's friends. Them two used to borrow off each other all the time. Toni's husband was also a fisherman, and when he was at sea and she was short, if Mum had been to the Social Security on a Monday, Toni would borrow off Mum and pay it back when her husband had landed. It's the way things were in the fishing community: everybody would help everybody else.

One time Toni got taken into Milton Lodge Hospital to have her second baby. When Mum visited her on a Sunday evening she said, 'Sue, I've got no cigarettes.' Next morning Mum drew her money, bought twenty cigarettes, then we sneaked up to the window next to Toni's bed, and passed her the fags. I suppose it was through seeing things like that made me realise you should share things and help your friends. If you help people, they will always help you back.

On one side of my mum's was old Mrs Mac's house. She used to hang her rug over the railings outside the house every day, and beat it with a big stick. She was a big fat lady that used to cook biscuits and bread, in between being a bit nosy. When my mum was getting divorced from my dad, Mrs Mac went to court and told the judge my mum was always having parties and had different men going in and out of the house. My mum fell out with her for a while, and said 'they were only landing parties, anyway.' When the fishermen who had been to sea, working like hell and freezing their bollocks off for three weeks, landed and got their money, they would be straight off to the pubs, drinking until they closed, about three a.m., then they would go to different houses around the town for a drink and a laugh before they went back to sea for another few weeks. I used to love it when they came to our house because they all used to treat us, and the more drunk they got the more money we would get. When they had money they would live like kings for three days, and anyone around them did too. They certainly knew how to enjoy themselves, and who can fucking blame them doing the job they did? They should have been millionaires. Instead they were risking their lives for the people who made the real money out of fishing, the fucking boat owners. I couldn't tell you how many fishermen have lost their lives, because I don't know, but I *do* know that sad stories of fishermen lost and boats going down were all part of my growing up. Nearly everyone in the fishing community of Fleetwood had lost a friend or relation. We lost my Granddad, my father's father. Somehow I think it's this ever present danger and uncertainty of whether you're going to see someone again, after they set sail, that gives you a different attitude to life from most people and creates a type of communal spirit that helps people to be there, to support and help each other, and create a spirit that may be special to Fleetwood, if not all fishing towns.

Mrs Mac's son, Danny, and his wife, Audrey, lived at the

end of the street. They had sons called Dave, Paul and Phil, who my brother, Tom, was good friends with. I would play with the daughter, Janice. As so often happens with kids, Tom would fall out with the lads at times and they would end up fighting. He would come home, tell my mum, and off she would go and argue with Audrey about who started the fight. After one of these disagreements, I was arguing with Phil and I just lashed out and punched him on the nose. He punched me straight back! That was the first time I had been whacked by a boy, but far from the last, as most of my childhood was spent playing with boys from the McDermott and Boswell families.

Claire Boswell, who lived next door but one to us with John, her husband, had two boys, Chris and John. Chris was a really close friend of Tom's, and they spent a lot of time together. I used to try and tag along with them but at the first opportunity they would run off and leave me. Whenever Mum went out, Claire would look after me. Albert Street was like that, a proper street, where everyone would look out for everyone else. Even after I had been away from Fleetwood for many years, it always remained a special place in my mind, somewhere I could go and feel safe, just as I had felt when I was young.

I loved Christmas, and one of the things I loved the most was 'Baby Jesus'. Albert Street is one of the spoke-like roads that run off the Rowntree Clock Tower at the centre, along with Adelaide Street, Lord Street and North Albert Street. Tram lines run along Lord Street, and just across these, opposite the top of Albert Street, looms the great big church of St Peter's. Every Christmas there would be a Nativity scene outside the church with a crib. It wasn't just the crib that fascinated me, it was baby Jesus. Joseph, Mary and the Three Wise Men I wasn't bothered about: I wanted baby Jesus, and I wanted him for my bedroom. I wanted him so much I would take a screwdriver and try to force open the glass case. It was too well made, though, and a saw didn't work, either. I was only young, nine or ten years old, but I just wanted baby Jesus.

Now I'm much older I am still obsessed with him. I would steal him now if I could.

I used to talk to him whenever I had the opportunity. I would tell him, 'I've just been to the Youth Club,' and whatever I had done there. 'I've just been suspended from school again.' 'I'm going home now, I don't know if me mum's there. If she has got any money she will be in The Ship. I'll have to go and get money off her so I can buy something to eat.' If I had to go to The Ship, looking for me mum, I would climb up to a window, about ten foot high, and knock on the glass until she, or Lenny (her boyfriend of sixteen years) heard me, then I would beckon them out. If Albert, the landlord, saw me he would bellow at me to get down. I would stick two fingers up and get ready to run.

Opposite the crib was a tree, and I would sit in the branches watching baby Jesus. When other people came to see him, some of them with their children, I would shout out things at them. 'Leave him alone you will wake him up.' 'He is asleep, don't make a noise.' I had convinced myself that he was mine and I was responsible for him. One time, though, I was up the tree for a different reason — I was hiding from my brother Tom and his friend Bozzy. Lenny had left two one pound notes on the mantelpiece at home. One was for Tom and one for me. I immediately spent mine on some toffees for myself and my friends. When I went home I could see Tom's note looking at me so I nicked it, but only so that they couldn't go swimming without me. They guessed where I would be and came and found me up the tree. I didn't think they could get at me and started taunting them: 'I've got your pound, I've got your pound,' over and over again, bouncing and waving in the tree. Suddenly I lost my grip, slipped, and fell about ten feet landing on a wall beneath. My head hit the wall and I was knocked out. Tom told me later that he and Bozzy picked me up by the arms and legs, dumped me outside our house whilst I was still unconscious, yelled for Mum, grabbed the pound and ran off. How I got to hospital I don't know, but I woke up in Casualty! I kept being sick, but they sent me home and Mum had to keep me awake for 24 hours. So much for Baby Jesus and the tree.

Just down the road from where we lived in Albert Street was a blacksmith's shop, and beyond that a large semi-derelict house occupied in part by a grubby old couple who lived there like tramps. Maybe they were the original squatters — they were certainly old enough, I'd guess they were in their late seventies. Annie, or Dock Street Annie as everyone called her, was the favourite for us to taunt, us being the gang of nine- and ten-year-old kids that regularly roamed the Dock Street area. If Annie wasn't visible we would invade the house, sneaking upstairs and yelling at her to 'come out to play'. The stairs alone were a hazard and formed a rotting trap for any small foot that fell too heavily on their crumbling boards. Another hazard was Annie's male companion, constantly drunk but, amazingly, able to propel himself quite rapidly on crutches as he tried to catch us. The smell of the filthy grey suit he must have worn for years urged us to greater speed if he managed to get too close. Miles he was called — the more miles away the better, we thought.

Annie had no crutches but matched her man for dirt and drunkenness. One day, when she was really drunk, we banged on her back door, taunting her to come out. We could smell her coming, as she stank worse than Miles, but she tried to look smart, her tiny body clothed in a small skirt worn over brown tights, the top half covered with the filthiest of patchwork coats. She answered the taunts by chasing us and swearing. Her language was bad. That day she chased us until we caught her! Six of us grabbed her and tied her to a lamppost with a washing line. We ran off and left her, but eventually the police came and let her free. When I think of her now, I think, 'Ah! what a shame.'

When she died in the old house we all really missed her — a few weeks later, Miles died in hospital. A big part of my childhood was gone. We had all seen Annie almost every day. Yeah, we messed around with her, but it was nothing vicious, it wasn't like the stories you hear of old people getting mugged and stuff. It was just teasing, and if she was still alive, as I got older, I know we would have been friends, and I would have always been around to help her out if she needed me. I would have done her shopping, and shared my money with her if she was skint. I'm just sorry she didn't live long enough for me to grow up.

What I liked most was when Lenny, whenever he wasn't at sea, took me places. I remember so well going to the ship with him to pick up fish, watching him mending nets and working and cleaning the ship for the next trip. This had to be done before the fishermen were paid, otherwise they would have been off to the pub. Tom and I used to fight to go with Lenny as the fishermen were always generous, usually giving us ten shillings each. Lenny would give me a fiver — he liked me with him best because I didn't grass him off to Mum about how much he had to drink. When she asked me if he had been to the offy I'd say 'no', even though he'd bought half a bottle of rum. I'd hide it for him in the cistern of the toilet, or the airing cupboard. In return he would write me a note for school saying I was ill. Then it was off to the Legion where he would give me money to play the one-arm bandits, and buy crisps and coke. It was dead exciting when you didn't get treats very often.

Sometimes I would go with him, about six o'clock in the morning, when he took a fry of fish to Rowey Taylor's fish shop to get money for a drink of rum. A fry of fish is a selection of fish given to the fishermen when they dock to share with their families. Often it would be too much, and what wasn't wanted would be sold to Rowey. Rowey would provide the rum and deduct the cost from the price of the fish.

When we got home later in the day, Mum would have been getting ready to go out on the town, back-combing her hair, trying on different outfits and high heels — she has a thing about shoes. It would take her about four hours to get ready. I'll never forget the smell of hairspray as I came in through the front door. Lenny and I would come back by taxi, he would be well pissed, but would always deny it: 'No, Sue, I'm all right.' She'd say, 'I'm not going out with you if you're drunk!' There would be the usual row, then off to The Ship by taxi, into the king for three days lifestyle. All the hard-earned money from another fishing trip, possibly as far away as Iceland, spent on drink. Drinking and fighting, no thought of saving their money.

Mum in particular was always fighting. Lenny would buy drinks for other women and she would be jealous, but it was what happened. The fisherman who had money would buy drinks for those that hadn't been paid, knowing their friends would do the same if it was the other way round. This was the way they were: their idea of a good life was money, drink and a woman, mostly in that order. The women were there ready for them — married or single they knew when the boats were arriving and where the fun was happening.

Often, while all this was going on, Tom and me and the neighbours' kids would be playing on the boards of the closed market behind our house. Swinging on the steel stall frames, doing somersaults, playing 'Dens Out', which was like hide and seek, where you had to hide, then get back to a can in a certain spot, kick it away, and shout 'Rally O!' Sometimes there would be as many as fourteen kids playing. It was always late when we went home. We would try to judge it to be there before Mum, but if we weren't we would pull up the cover of the coal chute on the pavement outside the front door, slide down to the cellar and creep up the stairs, hoping no one would see us. By this time, Mum would have enjoyed a few drinks anyway, so she never knew what was going on. Often she would have brought a party home for more drinking. It was quite normal for a fight to break out, the men arguing about fishing, the women about more silly things.

One night, a man came to find his wife, as it was so late.

He started to beat her up. Mum got her hairspray and sprayed it in his eyes. He fucked off. His wife went home next day and all was forgiven. In fact, all the fights were forgotten quickly — it was just the way things were.

I had so many things happen to me when I was living at Albert Street that I've forgotten a lot. One I won't forget, at least I can remember some of it — Mum must have told me the rest. How it all started I don't remember. Tom and his mate, Bozzy, and me were arguing at the top of the stairs. I was only nine years old but I was already a nuisance with too much to say for myself, and Tom, like me, could lose his temper. This time he was really angry with me. He picked me up and threw me downstairs. Mum had left the old upright vacuum cleaner at the bottom and I landed on it. I heard a snap. I didn't know if it was my back where the handle had stuck in, or if the handle had broken.

I was out, unconscious. I don't know what the lads did but it seems it was ten minutes or so before Mum found me. By this time I could move my eyes but nothing else. She called an ambulance and I was taken to the Victoria Hospital in Blackpool. On the way the ambulance man kept pinching my skin, tickling my feet, something I hated, and sticking needles in me. I couldn't feel any of it.

I was taken into the emergency treatment room, laid out on the operating table and the doctor, an old man, started to stick more needles in me. When there was no response he decided to inject me, and put me out, before I was taken for an X-Ray. He told Mum I might be paralysed and not be able to walk again. She ran out into the corridor crying and screaming — the doctor started preparing the syringe for an injection. I saw him doing this, heard all the noise from Mum, and just got off the table and walked out to see what was wrong. The doctor was gobsmacked! He just stood there staring, saying, 'I can't believe it, I can't believe it, I've just witnessed a miracle!'

After he calmed down he said, 'It must have been shock that temporarily paralysed her.'

Whatever it was I often think it was amazing how I ever lived long enough to grow up, let alone long enough to become a boxer!

2

SCHOOL

When I was only five years old I was taken to start at Blackison Street Primary School. Mum just left me there — I didn't know that's what mums did, and I didn't like it. I had to remember my house name, my cloakroom colour, my pump bag, and then there were the rules I had to learn. I didn't like it at all, so before the morning break I sneaked off, got my coat and walked the half mile home. Mum took me back again, but I never really settled — in fact, I was a little monkey, naughty but lovable!

I disliked school so much that I would stay home at

every opportunity, faking all sorts of aches and pains. Mum was easy to kid and she let me get away with all sorts. I was away so often, and was so mischievous when I *was* at school, that I would get suspended for weeks at a time, in the hope that I might be better behaved when I came back. In fact I think I just got worse...

It was better when I moved on to Milton Street Junior School, and it wasn't long before I became leader of a gang of about ten girls and boys. The school was right next to Chaucer Junior School, and we would beat up those kids — nothing vicious, we just pulled their hair, kicked them and pinched their sweets. There was a wall between the two playgrounds, probably about eight feet high. I used to scramble up it and scream at the other school's kids, 'Chaucer snobs, shut your gobs!' I would leap off the wall when the playtime supervisors came round, but I regularly got caught, usually by the headmaster, Mr Leadbetter, who always seemed to be watching me from his office window. He would grab me, march me up the narrow stairs into his office, put me over his knee and smack me on the bum with his hand.

Gaylord Leadbetter, as I called him, was a strange person. He was big, about six foot tall, with a solidly built body. His clothes always seemed really weird to me, especially his variety of large check suits, which made him look like a circus clown. He would wear a cravat and carry a great big umbrella in one hand, the other hand held bent at the wrist like a frail woman. He had a posh voice, even though he had come from a working class background. I wasn't the only one to suffer at his hands: he had it in for a couple of the wilder boys, and Suzanne Cartwright got nearly as many punishments as I did. Suzanne got taken away from the school by her policeman father, who was fed up with her being punished. He blamed me for that! I missed her, because she was my best skiving mate. I even taught her to smoke: we used to buy ten No. 6 and sneak to the back of the school or to the Mount. Another bad thing about her leaving was the extra time it gave Gaylord to beat me!

As well as Leadbetter, there was Mr Fishwick. He wore bottle-top glasses, scruffy grey suits and he would often forget to take off his cycle clips. He was all right. If I was cheeky he would, perhaps, throw the board rubber at me or slap me around the head. But he was always sorry and would bring me presents of model toys. His heart was in the right place, though, which is more than I can say for his head on one occasion. Poor old Fishwick, he suffered from epileptic fits, sometimes twice a week. On one of the more serious occasions he was writhing on the floor and I was scared by the way his face was all twisted up, so I covered his head with the waste paper bin. It was a metal bin and it was really noisy as he was throwing his head about banging the bin against the desks and wall. For that little prank I got punished by Mr Leadbetter.

After that I sometimes went to school, but often I skived off. In the end I was expelled for harassing one of the teacher's pets. I would hide and jump out on her. One of my favourite places was under her raincoat, hung on the pegs in the cloakroom. Sometimes I would crawl under the dinner table and bite her legs, push her over in the playground, or tie her up with skipping ropes — it's a wonder they tried to keep me at school as long as they did! Well, that's a laugh really, because they didn't keep me there all that much, as I was skiving off as much as I could. I skived off altogether when I was fourteen, but even when I was about eleven years old, and my brother Tom was fifteen, I used to go off with him and his band as often as I could.

Tom was a drummer, and he was in a few different punk-rock bands before he joined One Way System. I don't suppose when he joined them he could have expected to achieve what he went on to achieve: the band became right famous. I remember girls knocking at the door for him all the time. My mum would say, 'Go away, he's not in.' One year, he got twenty Valentine cards. I was dead jealous, 'cos I didn't get any. He used to say, 'You will when you get older.'

The band used to have a practice room next to The Ship. It was a small room, like an attic, with a three-piece suite, a chair and a cupboard. It looked like someone's front room, and the band played in the middle while me and a few friends sat about watching them. One time they decided to play in an old club that had been recently shut down. I helped Tom carry his drums over to the club but when we got there the band couldn't set up because all the light bulbs had been smashed. They couldn't start without any light so I said I would get them some bulbs. I went back home and took all the bulbs out of my mum's house and brought them back to the club.

We put the bulbs in and the gig began. There were only about fifty people watching, because it was an illegal gig and we shouldn't have even been in there. Everything got under way and was going well until my mum came charging in. 'You little bastards, where's all my fuckin' light bulbs?' Our Tom didn't know I'd taken them from the house so he just thought my mum had gone mental. She ran over while he was playing and leathered him, took all the light bulbs back and went home. I got out of there a bit quick too, because Tom had realised what I had done and he was really embarrassed that Mum had battered him in front of his fans. When he caught up with me, I think that was my first *real* experience of fighting.

Real gigs started coming in more often and after about twelve months, One Way System were called into a recording studio to cut their first record. Then things really began to take off, they had gigs booked all over the country, but mostly in London. It was dead exciting for me: all my friends used to stop me and say, 'Hey, your brother has made a record.' As if I didn't know! They got an offer to support a big well-known punk band called Peter And The Test-Tube Babies. Some of that band came to stay at our house. Fucking hell! There were people gathering outside trying to get a look at the band. I kept walking in and out of the house and the people kept asking me what they were like and all sorts of other stuff. That night they all stayed at our house, there were people in sleeping bags all over the place. I got up to go to the loo and stepped on two of them!

A few weeks later, Tom and the band were playing at the Bierkeller in Blackpool. I remember being stood at the front of the stage with about five hundred punks jumping up and down behind me. When the fight broke out I was in the middle of it, and there were bottles flying everywhere — how the fuck I got out in one piece I'll never know. I'll tell you one thing: it was dead exciting with that lot and it made me grow up a lot quicker than anyone had planned!

One Way System started to make a big name for themselves in the punk world, and they appeared on the front cover of *Sounds* magazine, which really excited them. Tony Mottram, a name in the music and showbiz world, took an interest in the band and put them right in the middle of the 'punk' scene. They didn't look back after that: they cut another four albums and got a big American tour, as well as lots of European tours. So for the next few years it was a case of practice room, touring, back to the practice room, touring. I never went touring abroad with them but they used to take me on the English trips.

Most of my nights were spent either watching the practice, or watching them perform, in some hall or club. With the group's activities came the drink and drugs. I saw it all, what the band members were taking, what the people watching them were taking. For the band it was sex, drugs, and rock 'n' roll. That was a fact, yet Tom seemed to stay level-headed throughout it all. While the others were having different girls every night, or getting stoned, Tom didn't seem to bother. Don't get me wrong, he used to join in the fun but he was always in control of himself. I didn't really see that until later. Because he was joining in the fun, I thought he must be on something. Being around the punks so much I thought it was cool to start smoking. Because most of them did I thought it was OK to smoke and drink, then one thing led to another and I started trying different drugs. It wasn't that I was addicted to them or anything, it was just that if anyone gave them to me I would try them.

It was all exciting, but it didn't last long. When the band were booked to go to America, I was left to go back to school again, and try to lead a normal life. I didn't like it.

My mum had rented the house in Albert Street from a private landlord, but for a long time she had had her name down for a council house. When her name finally made it to the top of the list in 1979, I was just eleven years old. The house was in Lindell Road. It was a bit of a shock to be moving out of the house I was born in, so I was both excited and sad. I'd been born upstairs in the front bedroom, and had never lived anywhere else so I knew all the neighbours well — I bet they breathed a sigh of relief when they knew we were moving. All my friends were there as well, I knew I'd miss them; it was sad really. On the other hand, the house in Lindell Road we were moving into was more modern. We thought it was a bit posh, but I don't suppose it was really. We did have our own bedrooms, though, and the bathroom was nice.

One very good thing was that the Lindell Road house was much nearer the new school I was going to, Fleetwood Hesketh High School, so I didn't have to walk so far. That school was another place I hated. I'd made a new friend, Angela Eastwood, and she hated the school as much as me. We skived off every chance we had, got into trouble for that and all sorts of other stupid things, but we didn't care.

The thing we liked best, and laughed at most, was that when we did something the teachers thought was really bad, we were suspended! That was just what we wanted, not what we thought of as punishment: we would be off enjoying ourselves hanging around Fleetwood Pier, or messing about in the park. Much better than school. Often we would go into school in the morning, get our mark, then wander off until it was time to go back for the afternoon mark. Somehow the school put up with us till we were fifteen years old; then they slung us out. Mum didn't seem bothered — she just said, 'Well, what are you going to do now?'

There was a scrapyard on the dock, not too far from where we lived. I knew a few people who worked there and they said that the money wasn't bad. It was piecework and you got paid for what you did. We went down for an interview and told the boss we were sixteen years old. He knew we weren't, but gave us the job anyway. He said we could start the next Monday. When we arrived on the Monday we were put at a table which had lots of little pieces of metal on it. We had to sort out each different type of metal and throw it into the right bin. We were outside, in a yard, and it was fucking freezing.

After two weeks of learning our metals we got our own table together and we had to start sorting fast because we were getting paid £28 a ton, just £14 a ton each. At first we weren't very fast so we didn't earn that much money, but we got better and really began to enjoy working there. There weren't too many rules as it was piecework, so the atmosphere was relaxed and you could more or less do what you wanted to. The worst thing about the job was how cold it was. We did get really dirty as well.

It was when I was working at the scrapyard that I got the tattoo of Mickey Mouse put on my right upper arm. I did it for a bet with the girls at the yard. When I started boxing, I got Mickey's hands turned into boxing gloves. When I got paid, at weekends, I would pay my mum for my board and spend the rest going out with friends from the scrapyard. After ten months sorting scrap metal I'd had enough, and I started looking for a new job. I got one at Premier Footwear, at Poulton-le-Fylde. The scrapyard had been hard, cold and dirty work and I was looking forward to working indoors. The money and conditions were good but there was a drawback I hadn't foreseen. Rules! As it was a factory they had orders to 'get out on time'. Coffee and lunch breaks were at a certain time, I had to clock on and off so they knew when I was late. I'd been used to having a break when I wanted to in the scrapyard. God, it was almost like being back at school but I soon got used to it. I made some good friends there as well. 'Gesh', Graham Webster and his sister Julie, Jackie Blackmore. They all lived in Fleetwood so we all sort of stuck together at work, and I used to go out with them at weekends, or in Jackie's case, me and her seemed to be out all the time. All of it spent in one pub or other.

3

MY FIRST LOVE

There is love, and there is sexual stimulation. I've experienced both but not always at the same time. In fact, some of the sexual acts were not even stimulating, a bit like the night I thought I had lost my virginity in the Memorial Park. I was just thirteen years old, and love was to come a couple of years later. If I had been sober it probably wouldn't have happened at that time. In fact, it may as well not have happened at all, as it turned out.

I had gone into the park with Angela Eastwood, her boyfriend and some other friends. We sat on a park bench near the tennis courts, and got pissed up on cider and cheap wine before going to the Sea Cadets disco. Gradually the others drifted away and I was left with a lad from school who was a bit older than me. We kissed a little — little baby kisses, really — then he groped around my body a bit before pulling down my pants. I wasn't really bothered, as I thought this was what people did, so I let him get on with it. He pushed me down on the bench and tried to shove his dick into me. I didn't really want him to, but I needn't have worried — he went 'Ugh! Ugh!' and it was all over!

At the time I thought I had really done it and wasn't a virgin any more. We both went to the disco. I must admit I had a bit of a knowing smile on my face when I met up with Angela. I was sort of proud of what had happened. I certainly felt I had grown up a lot. After that night I spent ages thinking I had 'done it'. As I got older, and discovered what real sexual intercourse and love were all about, I realised that the loss of my virginity that night had only been in my mind. Years later, I was telling this story during a very pleasant lunch with some friends in a London restaurant. One of them, an attractive, sophisticated lady, a little older than me, said, with a look of envy or perhaps it was regret, 'Well, at least yours made a noise!'

The park bench feeling and fumbling must have left some impression on me, or maybe it was just my age. I started to be more interested in boys.

One of the boys I started playing out with was Dave Smith, whose parents owned The Kings Arms in Lord Street. Me and Dave really hit it off and our playing out led to us courting. I suppose you could say he was my first love, but more than that we were just very, very best friends. Yes, we did start living together after a couple of years or so — I think I was fifteen then and Dave a year older. His parents had a house in Hatfield Avenue and we moved in there. It didn't seem to bother anyone that we were living together so young, as we had been seen together for so long. We were like two peas in a pod — wild, stupid, wicked, dangerous — certainly all of those. Some of our escapades are best forgotten. We did work though; in fact Dave and I helped out at The Kings Arms at times, even though legally we were too young to drink. Not that that bothered us — we had been drinking for ages — but I would encourage Dave to get money to spend on booze and discos. It didn't occur to me at the time that we were being dishonest, I was only thinking of the benefits, a happy head, music and dancing.

One night Dave took a bottle of Clan Dew whisky before we went to the disco. I was at home when he came to collect me on his bike; we drank the whisky in no time and set off on the bike with me riding backy. We were both pissed out of our heads. Dave was pedalling all right but he wasn't steering too well. I was enjoying myself on the back, and as usual I was fidgeting about and joking. It wasn't a good way to behave.

I don't know when I started to be a permanent hazard, an accident waiting to happen, but this probably wasn't the first time, and it definitely wasn't the last! I was waving my young, and still gangly, legs about, warming up for the disco, rehearsing a dance that ended with my foot stroking the spokes of the back wheel. Why have I always had heavy hands and feet? The stroke stopped the bike, the wheel, and our visit to the disco. Dave escaped, and in a way I suppose I did, but not before a following bus had run over my head! I eventually came round in hospital after being unconscious for two days. Why does everybody laugh with disbelief when I tell them this story? THE BUS RAN OVER MY HEAD! My face was pressed so hard into the ground that the nurses were picking bits of gravel out of my skin, with tweezers, for days. The shape of my head was horrible, as if someone had squeezed a lemon without cutting it in half. God! It makes you wonder however I grew up to be so gorgeous!

My stay in hospital was awful but brightened up each day, if only temporarily, when Dave came in with a bunch of daffodils he had picked in the Memorial Park, and some chocolate he probably nicked on the way. He certainly was a brave Dave. My mum battered him every time she came in saying, 'What have you done to her, you little bastard?' He would complain, 'It wasn't my fault!' When I got home I still had a face like the Elephant Man. Mum wouldn't let me out of the house for days in case I frightened the children.

Me and Dave were around so much together, and into so much mischief, that people used to call us Bonnie and Clyde. We never robbed a bank, but the pub till takings didn't always balance and shop-lifting was seen as an adventure as well as a necessity to get the extra things we thought we had a right to. It never even occurred to us that it was stealing from anyone, we were just taking stuff from businesses that could afford to lose it.

Often when we were living together, me and Dave would have toy fights just as kids do. I usually won, probably because I needed to more than Dave. Looking back I suppose he let me, because as a lad he was bigger and stronger than me and he knew I didn't like losing. Just how much I didn't like losing he awoke to just in time to save his life. Our latest toy fight had got out of hand, each punch harder than the last. It was an indoors street fight, and I was hurt and beaten up. My body hurt but my mind was in agony. We went to bed but there was no way I could sleep. Dave was well away, out of it, in dreamland. I was still seething with rage. I had suffered, he must suffer. How? Hell! I'll just get something heavy and beat him to death. I searched and found a hammer. I stood over him, my only thought was to get revenge. I hit him, full force, in the mouth breaking his teeth. He automatically moved; I swung the hammer again and smashed it into his nose. When he realised he wasn't just having a nightmare he just yelled, 'Get off, you mental bastard.' Eventually we kissed and made up, and he knew he had deserved it for hurting me in our toy fight. I was lucky I hadn't killed Dave, and lucky he forgave me.

Me and Dave finally split up after we had been living together for eighteen months. We were only young and neither of us was really ready to settle down. By this time Tom had finished his tour of America and was living in Clapham, South London, with his partner from Fleetwood, Julie. I went to visit them for a weekend and ended up staying there for a much longer time. I had missed my big brother and it was nice to be around him again. I got to miss Dave as well, but it was time to move on with my life. We had made better friends than lovers and I always knew I could go and talk to him if I needed someone to confide in, because he really understood me. After all, we had been through a lot together.

4

LONDON...

At seventeen years old I could have found many more suitable places to work than the Railway Tavern, Clapham North. Still, I had to work somewhere and working behind a bar was second nature to me. I was staying in my brother Tom's flat, and he was living with Julie McGough at the time. Julie was already working at the Tavern and got the job for me.

On my first night working there she introduced me to some of the regular customers, one of whom was going to play an unforgettable, if reasonably short-lived, part in my young life. I'll call him Luigi — not his real name, but repeating real names of the people who moved in his circles is not a healthy occupation. Julie said, 'Luigi, this is Jane, Jane this is Luigi!' He was wearing a long mac and a Trilby hat, and later I found out that he always carried a gun. He looked to be in his early forties. He just stared at me. I said, 'You're a miserable bastard you, you want to cheer up.' He remained expressionless. He just stared at me then, and for the rest of the evening he didn't speak. If he wanted another drink he just pointed at his glass to be refilled with Benedictine.

Three weeks later, the pub had just opened at midday and Luigi staggered in, dripping with blood — his and someone else's. I heard police sirens and my ingrained anti-police instincts were to protect him. I hid him in the beer cellar, later finding him a T-shirt and track suit to wear. I burned the bloody clothes in an iron bin at the back of the pub.

It was not long after that unexplained things started to happen. On my next visit to a delicatessen I collected up my shopping, took it off to the checkout ready to pay and the cashier just waved me on, 'That's OK, you don't have to pay!' I discovered that Luigi owned the store. My working hours at the Tavern were getting longer and longer and to make my life easier the landlord suggested I lodge in the pub. There was a small flat on the top floor which I moved into. One day I was coming down from the flat into the bar, and as I came in a Spanish-looking woman and two hard men in sunglasses came towards me. The men were carrying a selection of clothes, a leather jacket, and gold chains. 'These are yours, do you need anything else?' I just gaped. They put the stuff down and left.

Another day I was in a shop trying on a really classy white ski-jacket. I put my hand in the pocket and pulled out a piece of paper. Written on it was, 'Meet me outside in ten minutes.' I was scared: how did the note get there? I phoned Julie, but she just put the phone down on me. She wouldn't even let me visit her house. Mafia? Underworld? I don't know, I was naïve. Outside the phone box I saw the biggest man I had ever seen, built like a brick shit-house. He didn't speak, just looked me up and down, gave me an envelope and left. Written on the envelope was 'Treat yourself', and inside was £1500. Someone knew I wanted the coat.

Cars began to call for me after work and took me to a bar down the Old Kent Road. There were a lot of seedy bastards watching women swimming in a pool. Luigi was there, and I ran up to him and told him what was happening. He said, 'No questions, no questions.' He would then take me to his room, we would get stoned on cannabis and play on the bed. There would be little kisses and cuddles but no sex. I thought he must be married. What did he want me for? Then the envelope deliveries started. I would go home for the weekend and he would ask me to put one envelope in a certain number locker on the station. Another envelope would be for me, with two or three grand in it. Didn't I have some good weekends in Fleetwood, treating all my family and friends? They thought I was God!

Then Luigi asked me if I would like to go to Italy. I was really excited and packed my case ready. When I told Julie there was an uproar. 'Whatever are you doing? He only wants you there to carry stuff back for him. What do you say if you get stopped at Customs and you're carrying something you shouldn't be? "Oh it's not mine, it's Luigi's." Luigi, what's his other name? Where does he live? What's his phone number?' I couldn't answer one of the questions. Julie convinced me. I gave the trip a miss.

As well as Luigi's ominous, mostly silent presence, the Railway Tavern had more that its fair share of dubious customers. Villains, definitely; what sort, I didn't know and to be honest I didn't give a fuck, as long as they were all right with me. I suppose it had to happen, that I would become involved in some racket without even knowing what it was, but how could anyone believe that? Certainly not the team of five frighteners who grabbed me outside the Tavern one evening just before I started my shift. They surrounded me, ordinary blokes, or so I thought, dressed in jeans and T-shirts, looking as if they had just finished work on a local building site. They may well have, but now they were going to start work on me! I was grabbed and hustled round the corner next to the pub, up an outside staircase — a fire escape or something similar. I was laughing, because I thought they were playing some prank. 'Fuck off, you stupid bastards,' had no effect, though. I was taken up to a first-floor roof where all was explained.

'Where is he?'

'Who?'

'You know who — Luigi!'

'I know nothing, stop pissing about, fuck off!'

'You'll be the one that's off — off this fucking roof if you don't tell us where he is.'

'I don't know what you're talking about, if you want to throw me off, throw me off, I don't give a fuck!' So that's just what they did!

All I could think of in mid-air was, I hope I don't get hurt too much. I was lucky, I suppose. I had one knee badly banged up — it was really swollen — and scrapes and bruises on my body. The police and ambulance were there almost before I hit the ground. Were they just passing, or did they know I was going to have an unscheduled flying lesson and didn't want Clapham High Street to be cluttered too long? The woman I nearly landed on played her part in the cluttering, dropping her shopping bags, allowing cans to roll in all directions. Whether she was more worried about me or the cans I don't know. She was horrified but managed to gasp, 'Are you all right?'

'Do I look all right?' I heard myself saying. I tried to drag myself back into the pub but I was hurting. Luckily I had been drinking a lot earlier in the afternoon, and the alcohol must have dulled the pain. I was pushed reluctantly into the ambulance. A policeman came with me — he seemed completely uninterested in how I had 'slipped' off the roof, and not at all interested in finding out why I was up there in the first place. Under the circumstances, that was just as well. It took a week until I could walk properly again and get back to work behind the bar in the Tavern. By this time it seemed that the customers and staff had forgotten what had happened to me? Did they really think I had slipped? Did they know that I hadn't?

It was a sharp reminder that this wasn't Fleetwood, and that the games played here had higher stakes. I guess this episode would have had most people running for cover — not me. I was made of sterner stuff, and no one was going to frighten me off. I enjoyed the job, at least until about four weeks later when a loud-mouthed yob walked into the bar and asked for a pint. I took a five-pound note from him and gave him the change. That's when he started. 'I gave you a £20 note.' I knew he hadn't and knew the scam — it was popular at that time in London. I told him to get his pint drunk, shut his big gob, and piss off out of the pub. He got louder and more argumentative. I said, 'Fuck off, now, before you are thrown out.' I too was pissed off.

I only had Julie helping me behind the bar and she was far from strong enough to fight a man. She may have come from Fleetwood but she hadn't lived the life I had. If peace was going to be restored it was up to me. I came from behind the bar, fearless but thoughtless, determined that no gobby prat of a Londoner was going to get the better of me. I started pushing and shoving him towards the door. He didn't want to go, and we cursed and swore at each other as our words turned to blows. I started throwing punches like a windmill in a force nine gale. The fact that he may not have appreciated being battered by a woman hadn't crossed my mind. I certainly hadn't thought that he may use a weapon — but that's just what he did. Something like a small baseball bat was suddenly in his hand and almost immediately smashed into my face.

The pain was awesome, the coloured flashes that went through my brain spectacular, the buzzing like a thousand bees in my head weird. Most normal people would have collapsed but I was high on alcohol and adrenalin. I had only one thought: Get this nobhead out of the pub. I steamed back in. He must have thought I was a mental case as I pushed, shoved and battered him out of the door. The police were in the Indian restaurant just up the road, and they heard the noise, came and dragged the bloke away and comparative calm was restored. The police didn't even bother to come back and ask me if I wanted to press charges! I had to wonder, Is it me, is it them, or is it London that makes such a skirmish a non-event?

Back to the hospital again, this time to have my shattered jaw wired, or plated, maybe both. I was patched up and sent away after a couple of hours. Tom and Julie took me into their care and I shared their lodgings for five weeks. I spent the time reading the 'Situations Vacant' column in the local papers. The Railway Tavern was getting a bit too wild, even for me! I guess there were many similar London pubs who couldn't expect to be responsible for some of their customers...

Looking for a job in London, let alone getting it, is as bad as looking for a needle in the haystack. My patience has always been pretty thin but there was not much else I could do but read the adverts. My jaw certainly wasn't ready for a snogging session, or even a short conversation. Suddenly the words burnt into my wandering mind, as I yet again browsed through the *Evening Standard*: 'Chambermaid wanted at the London Tower Hotel' — that will do. I didn't even know what a chambermaid was — someone who empties pisspots, I supposed. So what, it was a job and I was after it.

The Tower Hotel was a big five-star hotel, right next to Tower Bridge. It was magnificent inside. I was still young, and I suppose still a bit green, so the place seemed like a palace to me. I was really surprised, and a bit frightened, when I got the job as a chambermaid.

It didn't take me long to find out I wasn't very good at it. The whole place was so posh — we had to wear uniforms an all — and the job had to be done really properly. You even had to clean the lampshades! They kept telling me I had to go faster, but I couldn't do all them jobs quicker and *still* do them properly. It was doing my head in. We were supposed to be able to clean twenty rooms each, but I could only manage three. I just wasn't quick enough.

I asked for a transfer to the restaurant, and it wasn't very surprising when I got it. That job was much more me, mixing with people and having a laugh. I'd hated being stuck in a bedroom all day. The restaurant was so much better, and the tips were really good, but that was hard work as well. Sometimes I used to work really long hours! I enjoyed it, though, so I didn't mind. I'd always been a hard worker and my life just revolved around the hotel. I had hardly any time off, and I even lived in. I was making a lot of money, though. I would be earning three or four hundred pounds a week, and that would be without the tips. I was looking after the table of some Labour party lot one night, and they gave me a hundred pounds!

The best individual tip I had was off Barney Eastwood, the Irish boxing manager and promoter. He gave me fifty pounds — that's before I was a boxer, but I knew who he was. Nigel Benn, the famous champion boxer, was with him and I recognised Nigel as well and asked him for his autograph. A few years later, when we were both appearing on the TV show, *They Think It's All Over*, I asked him if he remembered me but he didn't. Not surprising really — when I think of how many autographs I have signed, he must have signed millions.

One set of guests who never gave me a tip were the Japanese, but they were really polite, and quite funny in the way they acted. They would arrive in coachloads, all with cameras around their necks. They were dead regimented and would almost march about in line. When they were sat at their tables, they were very serious about eating their food, and would frequently ask for more iced water. They must have drunk gallons of it.

It was exciting at the Tower Hotel. There would be so many different people coming and going, and they all had to be rich to stay there, so some of them would be quite famous. I'd often get blokes wanting to take me out, and I did go out with a few, but most of them that stayed at the Tower were a bit posh for my liking. I remember one, he was quite a bit older than me, but must have fancied me. He offered to take me out one night, to the Opera. I didn't know what the Opera was, but I said I'd go anyway. By the time he'd collected me, I'd finished work and had a few drinks. I was knackered and a bit pissed. When he saw me, in tights and a top, he said, 'Aren't you going to change?' Cheeky bastard — I had changed!

We went in to this theatre and I think I must have been a bit loud and swearing a lot. I couldn't understand what it was about, all these people jumping around and singing, dressed in white. When I asked, 'What the fuck is it all about?' in a loud voice, I don't think he was very impressed. Anyway, I got bored, and what with the drink and work I dropped off to sleep. When I woke up I knew I must have been snoring with my mouth wide open because I had been slavering all down my chin. When I looked round for him he was gone, and I never saw him again. That was one customer I lost for the Tower.

Mostly, I spent so much of my time working that I seldom seemed to go out and spend money, so every couple of months or so I would go back to Fleetwood, supposedly for a rest but in reality far from it. I would get out and about with my mates, live it up, and blow all my money before going back to the Tower to earn some more. One weekend I came home, and I had been working so many hours I was completely knackered. I meant just to have my usual fling and rest and then go back to work, but this time I couldn't even regain the energy, or enthusiasm, to go back. So I stayed in Fleetwood.

5

...AND BACK

My 'rest' in Fleetwood lasted for nearly six months, and somehow I managed to enjoy myself on what money I had left from my hard-working time at the Tower Hotel. I was partying at night and sleeping most of the day, which was fun at first but, as I always did if I stayed doing the same thing for too long, I got bored. I began to miss London and decided to go back. No up-market hotel this time.

The pub I found a job at in Chiswick was so awful I can't even remember its name, or even how I came to get to know there was a job available there. I should have been warned when the landlord said that he had been advertising in the paper for weeks and no one else had applied for the job. I didn't have much choice — I was back in London with nowhere to stay and no money, and at least there were two tatty rooms above the pub I could live in. So I took the job I could do so well: serving behind another bar. It really was awful, so awful no one else would work there. Even the landlord must have hated it, because as soon as he could see I knew what I was doing he gave me the key, told me to get on with it, and fucked off.

Looking back I wonder what it was about that place that made me hate it so much, what it was that made me so homesick. It was just a pub and I had experienced enough of those to feel at home in most of them. But this one was horrible. It had a strange cold atmosphere, and I couldn't even like the customers — they were all cocky, gobby builders and 'no-hopers'. I stuck it for nearly two weeks before I'd had enough. I rang my mum and said I wanted to come home but I didn't have any money. Mum said she would arrange for some money to be sent to a Chiswick bank for me to collect. She told me that Auntie Hilda had died and left me £500 and her £1,500. I couldn't wait to get the money for the train fare — there wasn't even any money in the pub till. I would have helped myself if there had been.

When I got the money from Mum, and as soon as the pub was empty, I grabbed some of my gear, stuffed it in a bag, and legged it through the pub door. I did stop long enough to lock the door and shove the key through the letter box, but not long enough to pack everything. I wasn't bothered — I'd got £500 waiting for me in Fleetwood and I was always buying new gear anyway.

Leaving that pub was one of the best days of my life. I couldn't wait to get back to Fleetwood, even though Mum had told me that her long-time friend, Bunny Walker, was quite ill. She thought that when he saw me he would cheer up and feel better. I loved Bunny as well. Sometimes I think that he was like a father to me, but then I think, What is a father like? My real father was never around long enough for me to find out, and even if he had been I don't think he would have been an average example. Whereas Bunny, since I was about fourteen years old, had always been close to me and Mum — he would take me with him when he was working at his different jobs. It was Bunny who taught me to gut fish so well. He was originally a fisherman, but then started a business on the docks making boxes for packing fish. It was a good business, but for some reason he handed it over to his brother. I suppose he wanted a change. He started another business, building fences, all sorts of fences, around houses and fields. I would go with him and help.

I had a lot to be grateful for from Bunny. He was always going out of his way to help me out. So it was really sad when I got back to Fleetwood again and went to see him in his flat. I could tell he was really ill: he was lying on his bed in his working clothes, the cap he always wore still on his head. He didn't cheer up when he saw me. He died ten days later. Mum and me tried so hard to talk him into going to the hospital, but he wouldn't go. As he got worse, Mum phoned the emergency doctor. When the Doctor came he was a Pakistani. Bunny took one look at him and said, 'Get out, you black bastard.' He wouldn't let the doctor near him, but he had no need to. It was obvious he was very ill and an ambulance was sent for right away. The ambulance men came in to take him away, and they too were told to fuck off. 'If you pick me up and carry me out and I die, I will come back and haunt you for the rest of your lives.'

Mum said, 'Leave him, leave him, I don't want him coming back to haunt me.' He died an hour later. It was said he had a blockage in a valve to his heart. After the ambulance men had gone he pulled something out of his trouser pocket. It was a large wad of money. I said, 'Don't be stupid, you'll need it.'

'I won't need this where I am going,' he said. I still wouldn't take it. I stuffed it back into the pocket of his grubby trousers. We watched and waited, not quite sure what to do or think, and suddenly he was dead. It seemed a peaceful way to go. Strangely, as he died, the cap he always wore slid forward and covered his eyes. That cap was Bunny's trademark. I had only seen him take it off once, and that was at his best friend's funeral.

It wasn't long after he died that the police came, then his family, then the undertaker. The money wasn't seen or mentioned again. I suppose Mum should have married him — I wanted her to. He asked her once, but after Dad she had had enough of marriage.

It was a bad homecoming. Mum was really upset and she needed my company so I decided to stay with her at her flat in Greenfield Road. I got a job at B & M Bargains in Cleveleys. I caught the tram to work each day, and that's where I met Lisa Clark. She was wearing a B & M overall so I went and sat by her. She was only seventeen years old, four years younger than me, and very nervous. I soon cheered her up and we became great pals. She thought it was hilarious, the things I did to break the boredom of loading a trolley, wheeling it into the store and refilling the shelves. I would grab the cans or cartons off the racks and throw them anywhere, some would go in the trolley, some wouldn't. I enjoyed the ones that missed best.

I got caught pinching chocolate one day when Pauline, the boss, asked me something and I had my mouth so full of chocolates I couldn't speak. Lisa was stood there, almost pissing herself laughing. I had taken this big bag of chocolates and we had both been scoffing them. When Pauline came, there were wrappers everywhere and I couldn't speak. She looked down at the wrappers, and she must have known what was going on — but she didn't say anything.

We got back to work, me trying not to laugh and almost choking on the chocolates. It wasn't long after that I had to pack the job in. Like most things that changed my life I did it on impulse. It was about 10.30 a.m., and I'd been working in the place for over a year. It was hard, boring work and I had

had enough of it. I went up to Lisa and said, 'I'm off!'

'Off where?' asked Lisa.

'I'm leaving, I've had enough. I'm off home.'

When I got home, Mum asked, 'What are you doin' here?' I told her.

'What you gonna do? You'd better go and sign on.'

'I'll find another job.' I went round to see my boyfriend and while I was there his niece Carol came home from work at the scrapyard at the Docks, the place where I had worked when I stopped going to school. I asked her to see if there was a job going for me there.

When I got back to the scrapyard I wondered why I had got to enjoy it when I had worked there before. Just the excitement of getting away from all the rules and regulations at school, I suppose, and of course earning some money. Now here I was again working outdoors, sorting piles of scrap metal. If it rained we got wet, if it was freezing we froze. Back separating the various metals from huge piles, brass, aluminium, cast-iron. Putting each in the right bin before humping the bin and emptying it in the right pile. The bins were heavy and I'd get knackered but I got good at the job. I soon learned to separate the metals just by touch and feeling the weight. Often I didn't even look at the metal as I slung it where it had to go.

It was a really horrible way of earning money, and we were still paid by the ton. Sometimes those tons got sorted quickly when it was clean metal, but when we had to pull wire cables and rubber coating off it took ages to earn a decent amount. My brother Tom came to work with us for a while, but he didn't last long, only about twelve weeks. He was just too slow, too careful, examining everything too carefully before he binned it. One lump he was studying stank, and he handed it to me saying, 'This smells funny, what is it?' It was stuck on part of a steering wheel and didn't just smell funny, it was foul and I couldn't stop myself retching. We often found dead rats, mice, even pieces of human flesh from car accidents, like the eye that one lad found. He stuck it on a stick and ran around shouting, 'Eye, Eye!' and 'I'm watching you!' There were some mental bastards in that scrapyard; one of them ate a big hairy-legged spider for a bet! I didn't hang on to the rotten stuff Tom had handed to me — I gave it to Carol as fast as I could. The stink hit her and she was really badly sick, all over the pile of scrap we were sorting. It turned out to be a rotting human elbow joint. The CID came and took it away.

The work was so hard and so boring that there would often be arguments. Roger, one of the bosses, would say, 'All right, let's get it sorted out.' We would all get round in a ring, maybe as many as sixty of us, and the two people arguing would be stuck in it to fight it out and solve their problem. Bets would be placed on who would win: once I won eleven quid on one fight! It really was brutal. One lad went down and the other grabbed his hair, pulled his head back and booted him in the face. He still got up and carried on fighting. They were a right rough lot there.

After a year, ten months of which Carol and I moaned about the job, we drew our money, about thirty quid for a week's grafting, and that was it. We went home, went out, had a few drinks and decided never to go back to the scrapyard.

6

GEORGE

Everyone is supposed to remember their 21st birthday as one of the highlights of their life. Mine certainly wasn't a highlight; it blurred into the rest of my life with just a normal drinking session at the Sporting Club with Lisa Clark and Mum. Lisa had given me a card and a £5 note, and Mum had taped £21 in the card she gave me. Neither of them could afford to give any money away but it just showed how they cared.

For once it was just the three of us, not men gobbing off and trying to get me to go off with them. God, I'd had enough of them in my time, especially in London — most of them were right tossers and were out of my life almost as soon as they had finished their stupid fucking chat-up lines. George Harrison was different. He wasn't bad looking — a cross between Kenny Dalglish and Michael Barrymore — but it wasn't his looks that attracted me to him when we met at June Clark's party. It was his personality. He was funny: he really made me laugh. It wasn't *what* he said but *how* he said it, and the way he moved.

At 38 years old he'd seen some fish landed, and his short, light brown hair was beginning to go a bit grey. He was taller than me, about 6ft I suppose, green eyes — nice eyes — and very smart in his 'decky' suit. June Clark was George's sister. The Harrisons were one of the largest and most respected fishing families in Fleetwood.

There were four brothers, and three sisters married to fishermen. With so many of them, there was always family coming and going. Piss-ups and parties were regular, all part of a fisherman's life. George and me met a few times at these fishermen's parties. It wasn't long before we began to stay overnight together. He told me he was married, had three children — two girls and a boy — that he and his wife didn't get on together and they were getting divorced. I'd heard it all before; it was the usual sob story, just to get me into bed, but I believed him.

His family were living on the Isle of Man where his boat was docked, and for a few weeks George kept crossing the water to see me. It wasn't enough, we wanted even more time with each other. We found a flat at 35 Bold Street and started living together, at least when he wasn't away fishing. It was then that I really began to feel the pain and anxiety of a fisherman's wife, or woman. I began to understand my mother's sadness, and her attempts to hide it, when her boyfriend Lenny went to sea. The men didn't help. Some of them would get so pissed the night before, they would have difficulty in getting into the taxi that came in the early hours of the morning to take them to the dock. George liked his drink a lot, preferably rum. The night before he sailed he would sit quietly and drink for what seemed hours, rolling a cigarette that he didn't smoke. I could feel and understand the mood of depression, but only imagine his thoughts, thoughts that, I suppose, are shared by every other fisherman before starting a trip. So many lives are lost at sea it must be hard not to think, Will I come back this time? What will the weather be like? Will there be storms that toss the boat about, gigantic waves crashing down on the decks? I remember the *Red Falcon* going down without a trace; could that happen to my boat?

It was horrible for me to know I was going to be at home in a warm bed while George was doing the only job he knew. I would listen to the shipping forecasts on the radio and watch the weather forecasts on Teletext, and my moods would change with the weather, really worrying if there were storms at sea, or if I could hear the wind blowing around the house while I tried to sleep. My mind would go over all my thoughts, that must have been similar to George's, as I had packed his sea-bag in preparation for the trip. I would make sure he had enough clean washing, clean gloves, clean underwear, tobacco and papers to roll, soap, toothpaste, magazines to read when trawling. The washing and ironing had been done days before he left. There was an old superstition that meant no washing would be done the day a fisherman joined his boat, in case it 'washed them away'. Another tradition was no goodbyes. George wouldn't let me say 'Goodbye' or 'Tar-rah', it had to be just 'See you!' Kissing was OK. Often we would have a really good snog, but for only a couple of minutes, not like our record breaker. One time he came home from sea and we went to bed and stayed there for 42 hours! We did get up briefly for an occasional snack, though. It was at times like those George would call me 'chicken'. When he wasn't in such a loving mood he would call me 'lamb chops' because he thought my legs were all bone and no meat.

He knew about meat, and if it couldn't be avoided he

acted as cook when aboard ship. All the Harrison family were known as brilliant cooks. George hated the job, although he was so good at it, and spotless in his preparation. His best meal was curry; even I had a taste of that and I don't like the stuff! Peeling potatoes he hated: he would tell me how hard it was when giant waves were tossing the ship about like a cockle shell. I could sympathise with that — I find it hard enough peeling them in the fucking kitchen! As for doing it being tossed about in a boat, I'd have no chance. Me? I never had sea-legs. I even got sea-sick on the Isle of Man ferry. I was so embarrassed. A fisherman's daughter, what a disgrace!

I loved George and was so sad when I saw him off to sea. I would go down to the beach by the Marine Hall and wave as the boat sailed out. Sometimes there would be other women with me, and we imagined we could see our men waving back, but really they were too busy getting ready to fish.

Sad though I was, I was young and after a short while alone I wanted company, so it was off to the Market Tavern to chat up the lads, or whoever hadn't got a ship. I'd usually meet Carol or one of my other mates, and we would get pissed out of our heads. Often at the end of the evening someone would call a taxi, and I would be pushed into it, half asleep, half in another world. The taxi drivers weren't bothered, they all knew where I lived, and would lever me out of the car and leave me. It was all part of my routine, and what me and my friends did. Somehow I used to get into the flat, stagger upstairs, fall on the bed and be out until the next day.

One night was different. George had come home from sea early, and he was sat quietly in his chair, as he usually did when he had a problem, continuously rolling the same cigarette, over and over. I knew what was coming before he started. 'Where have you been? What have you been up to?' He would go back to rolling his fag, which I knew was a sign of stress. He was angry, but didn't know what to say. I was too drunk to bother what I said.

'OK, so I know a lot of blokes. They don't mean anything

to me. I wasn't shagging them. I've never done that with anyone else while we've been together. It's just that they are young, you are old and I need young people about me.' Then the fighting would start! It wouldn't be much of a fight. George was a real pacifist. I would get into one of my moods, shout, threaten and throw a few half-hearted punches. George would get out of the house as quickly as he could, heading for the first pub he'd come to. I would stomp around feeling sorry for myself and hard done by, eventually calming down, and then I would go and find George and drink with him. George was always very forgiving and after a few drinks, any hard feelings always turned to laughter.

He really was an easy-going bloke, George. If ever there was any trouble, or if I got in a fight, he was off. I could come home all covered in blood and he would be sitting there, rolling up a fag, and he would say, 'Are you all right, luv? There's some chips there, I got them on the way home. They might be a bit cold now but you can warm them up.'

I'd get in fights just to stop people picking on him, because he wouldn't stand up for himself. It was the same when we were drinking in the Kings one night. This big bloke, who thought he was a real hard case, was having a go, shouting at George. George didn't want to get involved, but I didn't mind. I said to George, 'Don't let him speak to you like that.'

The other bloke said, 'Shut up you, what the fuck's it got to do with you?' So I stood up and punched him in the face with my right hand, — it must have hurt, 'cos it knackered my hand. Anyway, just for good measure, I nutted him and knocked him out! He fell over some pub tables, out cold! My friend Rachel was working behind the bar and she said, 'Oh! No! She's off again.'

Gary, the landlord, said, 'Tell her to get out, she's banned.'

Rachel said, 'I'm not telling her, you tell her.'

Gary told Rachel he would go across the road to the phone box and ring back to the pub to tell me I was banned, but it was too late by then — I'd gone. He didn't ban me really;

I went back next day and we all had a good laugh about it.

This all happened when I was still working at the scrapyard, along with a friend of mine called Pinky. It wasn't her real name, but unbeknown to her that's what we called her at school, because in the summer her nose would catch the sun and the skin would peel off, leaving a big pink spot. I've called her Pinky as, like me, she turned to a decent life and there is no way I would spoil that. Sometimes I would meet up with her on the way to work, sometimes I would call for her. Most days we would call in at the Mace shop, on Heathfield Road. We were always short of money and would be lucky to have £1.50 between us. One morning we got some crisps and chocolate for our dinner, and we wanted some fags but we didn't have enough money. When we got to the till there was no one there, so I leant over the counter and nicked some fags. When the man came out, we paid for the crisps and chocolate, went off out of the shop and off to work. I couldn't believe how easy it was to nick the fags, so after that I would make regular visits shoplifting.

When I was skint I used to take a mate with me: he would be drunk and he'd nick all sorts. It would be really funny because he would be so pissed, and he'd stuff all his pockets with tins of steak and chocolate. We used to go in there about five times a week. The shop shut down after a couple of years but I don't think it was because of our shoplifting. I hope not! When the shop was gone we really missed it. That was the beginning of my shoplifting days, but not the end. When I left the scrapyard and was out of work I used to go to Cleveleys and Blackpool, pinching. I used to nick anything, mostly clothes. Then I would take the stuff around the pubs in Fleetwood, selling it. It became a little business and I did all right out of it. I used to sell the stuff cheap to people who couldn't afford it if it was new. It got to the stage where people even placed orders for me to get the stuff. At the time I couldn't see that what I was doing was wrong — I was just making a living and getting by. I got caught a few times, so with what I had to pay out in fines I suppose I wouldn't have been any better off. I didn't look at it like that at the time because usually I just paid the fines off at a few quid a week.

When I was doing the shoplifting, I needed a car to get to Cleveleys and Blackpool, and to drop stuff off at people's houses, or take it round the pubs. So I got a car, an old knackered Mini. I bought it in the street for fifty quid off some lads, but it worked and got me around. It didn't matter to me that I didn't have a licence, tax or insurance. I just thought I had the right to get in and drive. I couldn't afford tax and insurance anyway. I went from one car to another, I used to park where I wanted to, and at one time I had a total of 24 parking tickets and about 12 driving charges against me.

One night, George had just landed from sea and we decided to go for a drink and then a meal, so we had a few drinks then drove on to the local restaurant, The Trafalgar. I pulled up outside and started to reverse into a parking space directly outside the window of the restaurant. My foot slipped on the accelerator and the car ended up smashing through the window. We still decided to go in for a meal, we were that pissed up and laughing. When we got in, Russell, who I had known since he was a small child, and whose parents own the cafe, said, 'Jane, I can't serve you, look at the window. Mum and Dad are going mad.' Then the police walked in and, surprise surprise, I was arrested.

I was charged with drinking and driving, dangerous driving, no tax, no insurance. My criminal record was getting bigger all the time. Anyway, they let me out a few hours later and I went over to a pub called The Jollies to meet George. It was a pub right near to the police station, and I'd arranged to meet him in there when they let me out. So I went in the pub to carry on drinking with George, then we decided to go to the Market Tavern. Now, to get to the Tavern we had to go past the restaurant where the car was. As we came up to it I said to George, 'Fuck it, let's get into the car, save us getting a taxi.' So in we jumped and drove to the Tavern. Being pissed up, I drove down a one-way street, and next thing I knew the police were pulling me over again. Fucking hell! I'd only been caught about four hours ago, and I was even more pissed up this time.

Needless to say I was arrested again, charged with drink driving and all the other offences. This time they kept me in all night, so next morning when I woke up, I had even more charges against me, and I was really in the shit. I just seemed to attract trouble. It was just daft, stupid things, but I felt like I had no control over what was happening. I was out of control, and my life was out of control. I was in a rut and I couldn't get out of it. I was drinking every night, I didn't realise it at the time but I was drinking more than I should have been. I thought I was in control of it, but looking back I wasn't!

Another night, when George was in from sea, we had been out drinking until the pubs shut but still felt in a party mood, so we invited some friends and family back to the flat we lived in. It was above a fruit and veg shop in Paulton Road and there were no close neighbours to complain about noise. Tommy Harrison and June came, along with some of our drinking mates from the Market Tavern.

The music was turned up full blast, and we were all singing and dancing. We opened the windows so we could climb out and dance on the roof. A few of us started dancing on the ledge outside the window shouting at anybody going by, 'Come in and have a drink.' A police car came by and the coppers told us to get back inside, but we just ignored them and carried on dancing, up and down the ledge — we were all pissed up and didn't give a fuck about anything, let alone the police. One of the blokes went down in the street, dancing and reeling about, and somehow managed to fall through the window of the Babyland shop where they sold prams and stuff for babies. The police car was still driving up and down, so we had to go down and drag him back to the flat. We thought we had better carry on the party inside, but we were running out of booze and I thought, What we gonna do? It was a great party and I didn't want it to finish, so I said, 'I'll go and get some!' From where, at 1.30 in the morning, I didn't know — but I *was* going to get some.

There was a shop further down Paulton Road and I knew the person who lived in the flat above the shop. So off I went to wake her up. She wouldn't let me in; still I suppose it was a bit late. I gave up and started walking back to my flat. As I passed the window of a shop I could see all this booze in there, staring me in the face. I thought, Fuck it, got a big stone and threw it through the window, grabbed a bottle of vodka and legged it back to the flat. I would have got away, but someone who knew me saw me do it and grassed me up to the coppers. I knew who it was and I was surprised he grassed because grassing up someone you know isn't the usual practice in Fleetwood. I suppose he was just being an upright citizen doing his duty for the public. Maybe it made him feel important for a few minutes — fucking tosser. Anyway, when I got back everyone was pleased they had more to drink, and I was pleased for them.

I don't think I even realised what I had done. If I make up my mind to get something, I'll get it, no matter what. I wouldn't do that now because I know it's wrong, but then it didn't feel wrong, and I didn't know any different. I soon knew it *was* wrong when the coppers were banging on the door an hour later, telling me I was being arrested. Now I had no choice. I had to leave the party while everyone else carried on enjoying themselves.

I got locked up and was charged the next morning. I also got stuck with another charge. The woman who owned Babyland came to work the next day and discovered the broken window. She rang the police, they put two and two together and asked me if I knew anything about it. I said, 'I think it got broken when we were dancing on the roof,' which was true.

'Did you break it then?'

'Yeah,' I said, which *wasn't* true, but grassing wasn't an

option. I even went into the pram shop next day to apologise to the lady who owned it, and I offered to pay for the damage. Even though I never broke it, it was still my fault for having the party, so I was just trying to make things right. She didn't take the money, she just said the police were dealing with it. Oh! Well! I thought. At least I tried. Next thing I knew I was arrested *again* for 'interfering with witnesses'. I couldn't believe it. I said to the copper, 'Honestly, I went in to apologise and to pay for the window. I didn't realise I was breaking the law. I was just trying to make things right.' Big mistake.

In the end I didn't get charged for that — I think they knew I was only doing what I thought was right. They let me go without a charge for a change. They still had me for the other window; they added that to another sixteen outstanding charges and they heard them all on the same day. I pleaded guilty to all of them and the hearing was all over in an hour.

I got a three-month sentence at Drake Hall Prison — but more of that later. It wasn't very long after that I split up with George. It was a mutual break; we were just growing apart really. I went back to live with me mum in Greenfield Road. I missed George for quite a while, after all we had been together for five years and he was a good laugh to be with. Even when we had broken up and I had left Fleetwood to train, he would ring me up from time to time and I would go back home to see him. As my training got more serious, and I realised I had to become more and more dedicated, I saw him less and less.

George couldn't understand what real boxing training was and that I couldn't just stop and go and see him at any old time. It made him a bit cross, but apart from that he was quite supportive of me boxing.

7

INSIDE

When I eventually got summoned to court on my motoring offences, the list against me was longer than a donkey's dick. Somehow I thought the whole thing was stupid. All these people dressed up in their Sunday clothes, and speaking in posh voices, discussing what I had done, why I did it, and why I shouldn't have done it. I don't think the 'big beak' liked me. He kept peering at me over the top of his glasses as if I was some grubby insect he had found in his salad lunch. I certainly wasn't grubby, I never was, but I couldn't help laughing at them all. I was warned to take the matter seriously. I tried to keep my face straight and for a moment, when I was told I was being fined £600, I succeeded. Then I thought, 'Fuck it, they have got no chance of getting that sort of money off me.' I was told I would have to pay five pounds a week. Yeah, some hope!

I was still feeling a bit cocky as I left the court, but not for long. I'd thought that as I was having to be in the court it didn't matter if I parked on the double yellow lines. It did! There was a traffic warden putting yet another ticket on my car. I'd had enough of authority for one morning, so I backed off and hid until the warden left, hoping, without much luck, that my out-of-date tax disc hadn't been spotted.

Although I knew I wasn't going to pay all the £600 fine, I still needed to get hold of some money. I didn't really give a fuck about how I was going to do it, but entering a wet T-shirt competition was one of my more stupid ideas, with the size of my tits, or rather the lack of size. If I hadn't had nipples and had been looking sideways, people wouldn't know if I was coming or going. I got eliminated in the first round, surprise, surprise, but I did manage to blag £10 off the winner!

Me and my mates had some laughs, though, and we even managed to scrounge enough money to go to Spain on holiday. We went to a place that was called Magaluff, or something like that. None of us had flown in an aircraft before and when the plane took off we were screaming and shouting like maniacs, we were that scared. If it had been a tram they would have thrown us off.

Sunny Spain? It pissed down for days and we were stuck in the hotel. We had been expecting to swim every day and get sun-tanned, but no chance! There was an outdoor pool at the hotel, but it was freezing. 'No matter,' I told the girls. 'We can't go home without a swim.' So we got our towels and changed into our bikinis, then paraded through the hotel to the pool. That woke up all the residents who had been sat about, bored to death not knowing what to do. They came to the windows to watch as we leapt into the pool. It was fucking freezing, but we had decided we were going to swim so we *were* going to swim, that is until a posh old English lady shouted out, 'Come out of there, girls, you'll get hypothermia.' I didn't know what that was but it sounded like something deadly you could catch, and I started screaming: 'Wah! Wah! Get out, get out, we will get hypo..., hypo..., get out, it's dangerous!' Those watching, who could understand big English words, thought it was hilarious as we screamed and ran for our rooms. Luckily, we didn't catch anything and got back to England safely.

Another time, I'd been out with a friend, Jenny, on her motorbike, and we got back to outside her flat and found the bike had a flat tyre. We started to repair it, and were busy working away, when a car passed slowly by, its driver shouting and swearing at the owner of the flats who lived on the ground floor. It seems the driver had been turned out of one of the flats for not paying the rent, so he had decided to drive up and down, cursing and bawling loud enough to irritate the landlord. Instead he irritated me. After a few verbals I grabbed a hammer from the tool kit (what is it with me and hammers?) and hurled it at him as hard as I could. The hammer went through the passenger window, shattering the glass and hitting the loud-mouthed bastard just above the eye. He lost control of the car and hit a wall. He dragged himself out of the car and to the police station to shop me. The next thing I knew a police car turned up, two policemen got out and arrested me for assault. One of them couldn't stop laughing when I told the bastards what I had done.

One night as we sat chatting, we decided life was boring, no money, no one to go out with. We sat wishing we could make something happen. How, without money? Where could we get some? Jenny's mum? My mum? She would have her money saved to repay the loan man and she knew I would pay it back. We got twenty quid each, we were ready to go, but where? 'We need to do something different,' says Jenny. 'How about one drink in each pub in Fleetwood?' What a fucking great idea! Twenty quid each and what we could blag should more than see us round the twenty local pubs. Did it heck, we were legless by number — sixteen, I think! We got a taxi when we couldn't walk, getting more unsteady on our feet after each pub we drank at. We went in laughing and giggling, looking easy meat for any bloke. Every time some daft bastard would fall for it: 'Want a drink, girls?'

'Thank you very much.' We would sling it back and say, 'Gotta go, gotta go, we've important things to do,' and we were off.

The more pubs we went into, the more and more we got pissed. Suddenly it was closing time and only the Market Tavern was still open. One more free drink! Jenny disappeared. She used to sneak off, buy a kebab and go home, fat bastard. Time to go — somehow I got into a taxi. All the drivers knew me and knew where I lived, they also knew I probably didn't have any money but that I would pay them when I did. I would get dumped outside my flat.

God, me and Jenny had some laughs, but that pub-crawl was nothing compared with one bender we went on. As usual we didn't have much money, so we thought we would save a lot by getting a bottle of rum from the shop on the corner. That way we wouldn't need to buy much when we were out, if no one else was buying them that is. We drank half the bottle each so you can imagine we were both well pissed before we got to the first pub The Royal Oak. Downing our first drink there, we listened to a girl blubbing — silly bitch had lost her earrings but she was upset about it. We talked to her for a while, and she seemed nice enough in her own way. Anyway, we thought we would move on, while we could still walk. As we hovered outside the pub thinking about what to do next I saw the jewellery shop on the corner of Lord Street. It suddenly seemed a good idea to get the crying girl some replacement earrings and cheer her up. When I told Jenny what I was going to do she was still just sober enough to say, 'Don't be so fucking daft.' Too late, I was off. Next thing I knew I had kicked the window in, grabbed about thirty pairs of earrings and was back in the pub, handing them out to anyone in sight. Everyone happy, we left and walked down to The Kings. We were both laughing, although Jenny was saying, 'You mental bastard, why did you do that?' I was still laughing. I didn't know why I had done it. It must have been the rum.

I suddenly realised I had a pain in my ankle. I looked at it and found that I had about a five-inch gash from when I had kicked in the window. It was deep and bleeding like fuck. We went into The Kings, where I used to work, and got a drink. Everyone starts looking at my foot. Kath, the landlady and mother of Dave, who had been my best friend and partner, gave me a cloth to try to stop the bleeding. I went and sat down in the bar, put my foot up, and started chatting. A few minutes later two coppers came in, looking around. Someone had reported what had happened at the jeweller's and the coppers were 'making their enquiries'. I tried to blend into the background but with a bloody cloth around my ankle, and drips on the floor, it didn't need Sherlock Holmes to suss out that I might have been involved.

Up comes this cocky little cunt of a copper. 'How did you cut your foot?'

'I dropped a glass on it.' Somehow he didn't believe me and said he was arresting me. By this time I was well pissed. 'Fuck off,' I said. 'I don't know what you're on about.' He was saying, 'Just come outside, Jane, we will sort it out there.' Again I told him to 'Fuck off!' He grabbed my arm and started tugging me towards the door. I had had enough so I headbutted him. We started fighting and two more coppers came to help him and they dragged me outside. The police van was right outside, and they tried to put me in it, but I didn't want to go. By this time a crowd was gathering, and Big John Aka (yes that was his name!) came and asked the police to stop manhandling me. They didn't, and I didn't care, I was giving as good as I was getting.

By this time two more police had arrived and they picked me up and tried to throw me into the van. I still didn't want to go, grabbing the top of the van with both hands and bracing my legs — I must have looked like a Walt Disney cat trying not to go through a door. Eventually one copper gets into the van, grabs my legs, and pulls while the others are pushing. I start kicking in all directions, fall into the van with the one copper, and the others slam the doors and lock them.

All the way to the station I'm having a war with the unlucky copper locked in with me. We're still fighting when the van stops and I'm grabbed, still kicking, and carried bodily to a cell, where I was left for an hour or so until I had quietened down. The police doctor came, looked me over, stitched up my ankle, then they locked me up until the next morning. Next day I felt so ill, and I felt even worse when they charged me with police assault, theft, criminal damage, and breach of the peace!

When I got home I discovered my brother had been watching the police trying to put me in the van from the other side of the road but was too embarrassed to come near me. So I went to court, and for once I tried to appear decent and innocent. But it was no good — with all those previous charges, I ended up with that three-month sentence in Drake Hall Open Prison. I only did six weeks of it, though.

We went to Drake Hall in a minibus, just me, another woman and two female screws. On the way I asked them to stop so that I could buy a Mars bar. They said, 'We can't do that.' I just kept on until they did. When we arrived we didn't know what to expect. It didn't look too frightening, a bit like a little army barracks, and there were about six different blocks called 'Houses'. Once we were checked in with the other new arrivals I was given a room to share with a girl called Maggie. She was a bit rough, but we got on alright. We couldn't believe it, they didn't even lock us up! As soon as we were left alone we started checking the place out, popping in and out of all the other rooms in the House, introducing ourselves to the other prisoners. Most of the women were all right, some were a bit scary, like the one in the kitchen carving something up with a big knife. 'What are you in for?' I asked her.

'I cut my husband's head off.' Fuck that, we were off!

Apart from her, who we thought we would keep well away from, it all seemed more like school camp than prison. The doors were left open, the toilets and showers were at the end of the corridor and you could use them, or visit, any time until bedtime, even then the doors weren't locked.

One of the girls I met on the first day asked me where I came from. When I said Fleetwood, she said, 'There's a girl from Fleetwood in the next House, her name's Jackie Abbott, do you know her?' 'Course I did, there weren't many characters in Fleetwood I didn't know, and even if I didn't they would have known me. I couldn't wait to get back to our room to tell Maggie, running as fast as I could. 'Guess who's in here? Jackie Abbott. I'm off to see her.' There was only one problem — you weren't allowed to go into the other Houses. So what, I was going visiting, whatever. In fact, I didn't even think about it, it was something I wanted to do and I was going to do it. I said to Maggie, 'If anyone is looking around, just cover for me. I won't be that long. I just want to let Jackie know I'm here.'

I sneaked off to the other House and found Jackie, and I was surprised how easy it was. I made a mental note of how to get about the place in future. I hadn't seen Jackie for years, as she was always in and out of prison. She got the shock of her life when she saw me. We sat chatting for ages, her telling me the best way to get by, showing me all the ropes. She was used to being inside and knew how to survive comfortably. Me, in a strange restricted place, I was going to be a quick learner; I wasn't just going to sit and twiddle my thumbs for three months, or whatever part of my sentence I had to serve.

Jackie said, 'There's going to be a drop tonight, it's for a right scrubber, down the corridor.'

'What's a drop?' She told me it was a package of goodies left outside the prison boundaries by a friend or relation of one of the inmates — it could be alcohol, chocolate or drugs — anything a prisoner might need. The only problem was that if you got caught by the staff collecting the parcel you were in real trouble. Most of the girls expecting a drop were too frightened to collect it, so they agreed to give half the contents of the parcel to whoever collected it for them.

My mind started working overtime, this sounded just up my street, a good way to get extra stuff in. I said, 'I'll do it, Jackie, when do I go for it? Where do I find it, how do I get in and out?' Jackie told me to wait for lights out, then go over to the back of the kitchen, and the drop would be outside the gates of the kitchen entrance. I would have to collect the stuff and bring it back to her room. The one thing I must not do, if I got caught, was to say who the drop was for. 'I won't get caught,' I told her.

I couldn't wait to get back and tell Maggie what I was going to do. She said, 'You can't do that! What if you get caught?'

'I won't get caught, and we'll share whatever I get.' It would be nice to have some extras, because we had nothing. So, at lights out, Maggie packed my bed with pillows and I climbed out of the window to go and get the drop.

There were a few screws walking about, but I hid until they had gone. I got to the back kitchen gates and there was this massive dustbin liner full of goodies. I had been expecting a carrier bag or something similar, not a sack. It was dead heavy, and I had to sling it over my shoulder to carry it. I staggered back to Jackie's House. There were still a few screws wandering about and I had to lurk in and out of the dark spots until they passed and then go as fast as I could towards the House. After having to hide about three times, I made it back to Jackie's room. I was knackered!

When I got into her room she was laughing at the state I was in but still a bit concerned about whether anyone had seen me. I assured her everything was OK and she went off to get the girl the drop was for. What a slag, and what a state she was in. She was scruffy, tottering, looked like a druggie, couldn't speak properly and didn't even look at me. She went straight to the bag, rummaged through it, pulled out a bottle of whisky and started swigging it. She looked like she needed it but there was no 'Would you like a drink?' Then she went on to empty the rest of the bag.

I couldn't believe my eyes — there were all sorts in there. Phone cards, booze, chocolates, drugs, cigarettes, food, everything. Then she turned to me, seeing me at last, and said, 'I'll give you a bottle and a phone card.' I looked at Jackie. 'Jackie said I'd get half, that's what the deal was, that's what I want.' I still had to get back to my House without getting caught. I was beginning to get mad thinking of the risks I was taking, Maggie covering for me and expecting some goodies when I got back.

'Half?' she said. 'No way'.

That was it. 'Look, you fuckin' slut,' I said. 'I carried that bastard sack about a quarter of a mile. I could have been caught and I've still got to get back to my House without anyone seeing me.' I was getting even more mad. She could tell by my face that I was really pissed off, but she still tried to bargain with me. I wasn't having it — I wanted half or I was ready to fight her. Jackie said, 'You had better give her what she wants, she can be a mental case if she gets upset and will probably half kill you.'

We all knew that if I started an uproar we would all get caught and be in trouble later, but I didn't care. I wasn't going to be ripped off after what I had done. So the slag, very reluctantly, started to divide the stuff up, then she went back to her room. I gave Jackie a few bits for putting me on to the job, then I was out of her window and back to my House. I banged on our window and Maggie helped me in.

As I was emptying the stuff on to the bed, Maggie was opening the chocolate and eating it, fat cow! I thought to myself, This is a good way to get by. So we got a few of the other girls into the room and had a bit of a party. It was a good way of letting them know I would go for any drops they had coming. They soon spread the word. I got loads of work and I never got caught. All the stuff I got in I would sort out and trade in with the other girls. Drugs were good to get, because I could trade them for phone cards for me and chocolates for Maggie. I did use the drugs a bit myself at times, but they were more valuable for trading.

One drop that didn't work so well was from my mum. She had been to visit us and brought me some cigarettes, but we couldn't have more than our allowance so she couldn't give them to me in the visitors' room. I said, 'Look, Mum, when you get out drop them by the gate.' She knew all about the kitchen gate drops, but it hadn't really registered. Maggie and me went out into the yard to wave Mum goodbye, and watched her as she walked past the screws guarding the gate, turned round and threw the packet of cigarettes back, right in front of them. We couldn't believe our eyes — it was hilarious! We didn't dare pick the cigarettes up, but just walked off and pretended not to know who she was throwing them to. The screw on the gate said to Mum, 'If she had picked up those cigarettes, we would have had to arrest you.' Mum got on her high horse: 'Don't shout at me, young man. Who do you think you are talking to? You can't arrest me, I've got to get back to Fleetwood.' She got a right telling off, but she got away with it. She said to me later, 'Well, I didn't know.'

After a few drops I was starting to settle in. We were getting phone cards and chocolates regularly so it made life in there a bit easier for us. I got given a job in the kitchens. I enjoyed the cooking and was eating well, getting lots of extras — I always enjoyed eating a lot. It was while I was working there that somebody, or something, upset the screws and our milk ration was stopped. That didn't seem fair to me: most of us hadn't done anything wrong, well not at *that* particular time. I decided I was going to do something about it. Working in the kitchen I knew where the milk was kept: it was mostly 'soya' milk, as there were a lot of nutters in there who were veggies or something.

In the early hours of the morning, when practically

everyone else was asleep, I sneaked off to the kitchens, took all these small cartons of milk, and delivered them door to door around the houses. It took me ages, because I had to keep going back for more. I even left some outside the screws' doors. I never got caught for it; even though all the girls knew I'd done it, no one grassed me up. After that they used to call me 'Jane the Milkman'!

I was only in the kitchen about six weeks. Time went pretty quick in there, and if I wasn't too busy I would think a lot about the things I had done to get in prison. Daft, thoughtless things, things I thought you did to have a good time. No matter that I had upset my family by being sent to prison, I was doing what I wanted to do. As I kept thinking, I came to realise that I didn't really want to lead the life that I had been leading. I was just on a downhill slope, and I definitely didn't want to spend any more time in prison. I knew I had to change, and I was going to change, but I had no idea that I would turn my whole life upside-down by becoming a boxer.

PART TWO

I WANT TO BE A BOXER

8

I WANT TO BE A BOXER

When I left prison, I thought I'd be given the first job I applied for. It wasn't to be. Not surprisingly, employers were a bit wary of me, but I eventually got a job in a rock factory in Dock Street. It was mostly helping to produce seaside summer rock, sweets and things. One night I'd just got home from working at the rock factory: it was late, I'd been working overtime and I was knackered. I turned on the TV and crashed into a chair.

It was about 9 p.m. *Cutting Edge* was just starting with a programme about women's boxing. I didn't know women were allowed to box — I was fascinated. I set the video recorder: I needed to see this again. And I did, over and over! The more I watched, the more I thought, I could beat the shit out of those two. It all looked so easy and feeble compared with some of the street fights I had been in. 'That's it, I'm going to be a boxer.' I decided as quickly as that, but no way could I have foreseen how that programme was going to change my life, and just how hard it was going to be to become a boxer.

At work, the next day, the first person I saw was Mark Helsby, the driver for the factory and a good friend of mine. All I could talk about was the documentary I had seen and how it had made me decide to be a boxer. 'Mark, I want to learn to box, I need someone to teach me.' I nagged him for hours, talk about doin' his fuckin' head in! He eventually agreed to come to the local gym with me, an old building in Rhyl Street. I didn't want to go on my own, because I knew I wasn't going to be made welcome. After all, I don't suppose any of them had heard of women boxing.

That evening I met up with Mark and his wife, Michelle, and off we went to the gym. They must have thought I was crazy but they stuck by me. We arrived at the building and I went upstairs to the bar. There was a guy in his late fifties called Tommy Norton sat there. I said, 'My name's Jane and I'm interested in boxing. Can I learn here?'

He had this really big Cheshire cat grin on his face, as if to say, 'You won't last two minutes.' Then he asked me, 'What do your parents think about you learning to box?'

I thought, What kind of a fucking question is that? I'm 25 years old, what the fuck has it got to do with my parents? Somehow I managed to control my thoughts and say what I thought he wanted to hear. 'Yes, they are very supportive.' Lying bastard I was, they didn't even know I was there!

Anyway, he went on to say that Monday, Wednesday and Friday evenings were when the classes were held, and I should bring with me a gumshield, skipping rope and a pair of boxing gloves. Then he introduced me to the coach, Frank Smallbone.

I shook hands with Frank, and told them I would see them all on Monday — I don't think any of them expected me to turn up. I did Michelle and Mark's heads in all the way back home. Then I just couldn't stop thinking about going to the gym on Monday. It was Friday night and the weekend seemed like it was going to go on for ever. I went to the paper shop and bought *Boxing News*, *Boxing Monthly* and a couple of cassettes from Woolworth's on boxing, some old-time fights — well, old for me!

I watched and read for some time, then put my track suit on and went for a run on the beach. It knackered me, as I had never done any sort of fitness training before. I watched the video again and I read some more before going to bed, but I couldn't sleep. I just lay there thinking about boxing and waiting for morning to come so I could go and buy some more books on the sport.

This time I went to Blackpool and bought everything I could lay my hands on to do with boxing. I was possessed that weekend, and determined to get myself on a boxing show as soon as possible. I telephoned everybody I could think of that might be able to help me, and eventually got the number of the WIBF (UK) secretary. She told me that there was a boxing show taking place in Wigan in five weeks' time and that they were looking for female boxers to take part. She asked, 'Have you any experience?'

'I've been training for months just waiting to get a fight.'

My lies were convincing. 'What weight are you? Yes, I can match you at that weight.' I had done what I wanted, I had got myself a fight, and now I had to do some training and learn the rules and techniques of boxing. I could hardly wait to get to the gym on Monday evening.

I turned up early and was waiting outside for someone to open up when a young lad, about eighteen, came along and waited with me. He looked like a boxer and had just finished a run. His name was Mark Bennett and it turned out that he had already had some amateur fights. We got chatting and he was really nice. I didn't know what he was thinking about me, I suppose I was a bit of a surprise for him, but he was OK with me. Then Frank Smallbone turned up with Alan, the assistant coach, and we all went into the boxing bit at the back of the gym. It was just a room with four punch bags and a boxing ring on the floor. I hadn't bothered to get any gloves or a rope, so I borrowed Bennett's rope and used a knackered old pair of the gym's gloves. I'd bought a cheap, mould-yourself, gumshield but I didn't bother wearing it.

Everyone was a bit quiet and Frank kept telling jokes, trying to lighten the atmosphere. Then he asked about when and where I was going to box and how many rounds it would be. 'Oh, it's easy, it's only four two-minute rounds.'

'Easy?' he smiled. 'You just start punching that bag, I'll tell you to stop when you have done two minutes.' So I started punching the bag. It was OK at first, but then, after about twenty seconds (which seemed like five minutes) I started to puff and pant, and halfway through the round I couldn't carry on. I was knackered! Frank laughed and told me to try skipping — I was even worse at that than I was at punching the bag. I was awful. I was thinking to myself, Fucking hell! I've got a fight in five weeks' time, what the fuck am I gonna do?

I went to the gym three times a week for a couple of weeks, and did some running when I wasn't working. I even went to a boxing seminar for women in Bristol one weekend. I'll never forget that. I had been whacking away at a 'maize ball' in the gym there, when along comes this old bloke — the coach — catches the ball and swings it straight at my face. He scored a direct hit, and grinning all over his gob he says, 'You're supposed to move your head, Curly.' Move *my* head? I nearly moved *his* head, right off his fucking shoulders! I just got out of that gym as fast as I could, cursing and swearing until I had cooled down.

As the fight in Wigan got closer, I said to Frank, 'Do you think I'll be OK?'

'Who are you fighting?'

'I'm boxing a London policewoman and she's already had one fight.'

'In that case we'd better start work. We will come to the gym five evenings a week up to the fight, and get Mark Bennett to spar with you as much as possible.'

Frank taught me everything he could in the short time before the fight. Mark was really helpful as well — he would come and sneak into the gym with me when Frank wasn't around. We had what I thought were really good workouts together and became good friends.

When I found out my opponent was a London policewoman, called Kalpna Shah, I couldn't believe it. Fucking hell! I was going to be allowed to clobber a policewoman *and* get paid £150 for doing it, instead of being locked up! All of my mates in Fleetwood thought it was brilliant and I sold a load of tickets for the 'treat'. In fact the show, a mixture of women's boxing and kick-boxing bouts, held in a nightclub, was a sell-out, and I like to think that was because of all the 'Fleeties' who came to watch me.

I weighed in OK and made a beeline for a burger bar, and started stuffing food down me, to make up for what I had missed that day. As I was wolfing it back, I saw this grey-haired old guy at the next table, looking right out of place wearing a blazer with a badge on it, and a collar and tie. He had a silly smirk on his face and he said, 'If you're boxing tonight, I should go easy on that food.' Cheeky bastard, I thought, then I recognised him. He was the coach from the boxing seminar. How could I have forgotten the stupid old cunt? Now here he was again, smirking. The thought went through my head, I can't be doing with him. Why doesn't he mind his own fucking business? One good thing though — he got me in the mood to whack someone, and if it couldn't be him Kalpna Shah was going to get it!

Once back in the hall, things all became a bit of a blur: changing, putting bandages and boxing gloves on my hands, it was almost as if it wasn't real. Just a few weeks earlier I hadn't even dreamt of being a boxer, now here I was about to perform in a noisy packed hall. It got noisier as I entered the ring. I was wearing a black satin dressing gown with white collar and cuffs, and JANE COUCH FLEETWOOD ASSASSIN in large white letters on the back. My boxing shorts and vest were red.

Mike Goodall, the Master of Ceremonies, looking very smart in a suit, bow tie, and a red rose in his buttonhole, came to my corner, checked my name and weight, then chatted to me and Frank while we waited for my opponent to enter the ring. She came, accompanied by Sue Atkins and her partner Mick. Sue, at that time the best known and most experienced female boxer in England, was now trying her hand at training and managing girls. Coming from the London area she was obviously not expecting much of a problem from a Lancashire novice who had only been at the sport for a few weeks.

The MC introduced me first. I stuck my arm in the air to acknowledge the cheers while Frank, arm around my shoulder, whispered last minute advice in my ear.

Kalpna was booed more than cheered, but she didn't seem to mind, after all she was boxing a long way from home.

The referee, Eugene Valerio, who had his hair tied back in an even bigger ponytail than mine, called us to the centre of the ring to touch gloves and be reminded of the basic rules. That was just as well: the last time I had had a battle with the police no one had mentioned rules!

I had a much longer reach than Kalpna, so the first thing I did was stick my right hand in her face. It worked! Her head rocked back. Frank had that worked out! I stuck a lot more long lefts out and followed them with long rights, and the odd flurry of straightish punches. There wasn't much coming back, and towards the end of the round the ref gave her a standing count of eight. The bell rang before either of us could punch again. She started the second round a bit livelier, punching with both hands, but was finding it hard to cope with my extra reach and workrate. She did have a little success knocking me backwards with a right hand to the head, but that only made me want to get my revenge.

So, back on the attack I forced her to take another standing count. Immediately after the count I hit her with a straight left, followed by a right hand to the head, and she fell to the canvas. She got up at eight and the ref allowed me to throw one more straight left to her head, before stopping the fight to give me my first win in a boxing ring. I was ecstatic, and so was everyone who had come to watch me. I was so pleased and grinning all over my face. Kalpna and I were called to the centre of the ring for the result to be announced, and for us to be presented with our trophies. Mike Goodall said over the microphone, 'To present the trophies for this contest we will ask the Women's International Boxing Federation's director, Mr Tex Woodward, to come into the ring...' It was him! — Mr 'Move-your-head Blazer-man'. This time I could smile and mean it. Winning that fight was so exciting. Me and the mob from Fleetwood couldn't get to the bar fast enough, or long enough, to celebrate.

By the time I had sobered up, and remembered I hadn't collected the £150 purse for the fight, it was a couple of days later. Unfortunately I wasn't able to get paid because the promoter had lost so much money. So I lost out for the first time in the boxing world. It wasn't to be the last.

9

MY FIRST FLEETWOOD SHOW

I had never had a lot of interest in my job in the rock factory, but with boxing taking up most of my thoughts, I did so much 'skiving off', and so little work, that I should have been sacked. Instead they sent me over to the 'Wibecs Units' in Copse Road. My job was to look after the stockroom where the rock, sweets, and fudge were stored. I had to weigh the stuff up and put it in bags.

It didn't take me long to get to know people in the other 'units'. 'Celia's Cakes' was my favourite. It was a right scruffy old building but her place was spotless. She was about forty years old and a bit fat, probably because of all the sweets I used to pinch and swap with her for cakes. It was in 'Wibec' that I met Steve Presnail: he was a printer there and would come and take away all the cardboard boxes I had unpacked and just thrown out in the corridor. I think he must have used them for packing his printing stuff. It saved me having to get rid of them, anyway. The first time I really spoke to Steve was when I was trying to sell some tickets for the Wigan show. He had a BMW car with some boxing gloves in the back window, and it turned out that he was a mad keen Chris Eubank fan. When I saw the gloves I thought he must be a good possibility to buy a ticket. When I asked him, he said, 'What? Kick-boxing?'

'No!' I said. 'Real boxing.' So he bought a ticket!

After that first fight, Steve was hooked, as well as me. He was a massive boxing fan and really fancied the idea of being a promoter. This gave him the idea that if he promoted a show in Fleetwood, with me fighting on the bill, he could raise some money for the town's football club, which was having a bit of a money problem. Steve had been involved with Fleetwood Football Club for some time. He had been a goalkeeper when he was younger. He wasn't very old when I met him, just a bit older than me, but he had started to wear glasses — that must have stopped him playing in goal.

Steve started the ball rolling by arranging for me and him to meet the football club chairman, Stuart Kay, after one of the home matches. That was a mistake, meeting him on a Saturday evening after I had been on the piss all day. I'd been in town and bumped into Tommy Harrison, and we went for a drink. Tommy was one of the town's top Skippers on the Isle of Man boat, a fun boat that sails out of Fleetwood and Heysham, on trips to the Isle of Man. Tommy Harrison was supposed to be a sensible guy when he was ashore but when he bumped into me all that went out of the window, and so did my training. We went into The Kings for a drink, and three hours later I had forgotten about going to the football club. 'Fucking hell, Tommy, I'd better go, I was supposed to be in the football club three hours ago.'

He said, 'I'll come with you, we can get a drink there.' I agreed and off we went.

I wasn't really drunk but I'd had enough. When we arrived, Steve was stood by the door with Stuart Kay. Stuart was small and scruffy. When Steve introduced us Stuart shook my hand and said, 'Pleased to meet you.' 'Fucking hell,' I said, 'you've got dandruff.' I started brushing his shoulders because his jacket was covered in it. I never could stand scruffy people. I didn't listen to much he was saying — I was so naïve at the time I didn't realise they were looking at me as a money maker. I just wanted to fight in Fleetwood and, more importantly at the time, to get back to the bar and my drinking binge with Tommy.

That was our first meeting — our second was hilarious. The boxing show was in its middle stages of being put together, and Steve had started trying to find a ring. He didn't really know how you got a ring, whether you had to buy one or what. Anyway, Stuart Kay rang Steve and said that Blackpool Tower used to do wrestling shows and they had a ring for sale, would we be interested? So off we went to meet Stuart and see the ring. When we got to the Tower we were expecting to see a boxing ring, not a new one or anything like that, but just something that *looked* like a boxing ring. When we saw it, we nearly pissed ourselves laughing. Even street fighters or gypsies wouldn't have got into it. All the ropes were dangling down like they hadn't been tightened. I asked the man who was showing it to us to tighten the ropes so we could see what it looked like. He said, 'They are tight.' It was a really old ring, only three ropes and they were that worn and frayed they looked as if they would snap if you leant on them. There was no padding in the corners, just iron posts. The moth-eaten canvas had no felt or any other underlay, the whole thing was a shambles.

Stuart said it was a good price, and would be all right with a bit of doing up. Steve and I tried to tell him that boxing rings just weren't like that any more, and just because it was cheap didn't mean it could be used. Anyway, the new boxing rules stated that there must be four ropes. Steve had also found out that you could rent a ring quite cheaply. That got us out of that mess.

Steve and I did most of the rest of organising the show ourselves. It was great and made some money for the football club, but the money wasn't enough to solve the club's financial problems. Sometime later Stuart Kay left Fleetwood FC and its massive debts and from then on the football club went downhill. We had once had a great side, even making it to Wembley for the final of the FA Vase. The team got weaker but at least it existed, and the ground wasn't sold for building houses or to build a supermarket on it.

So it was that on the 29th of January 1995, in only my second boxing match, I topped the bill in a WIBF licensed show at the Marine Hall, Fleetwood. In my home town it was going to have to be something special, and it was! Looking back, I'm sure those Londoners were at it again. My opponent, Fosteres Joseph, a black woman who was a social worker from the East End of London, was said to be the European Kick-boxing Champion!

After my fairly easy win at Wigan I thought I was a female version of a cross between Rocky Marciano and Muhammad Ali, and I didn't think I had to bother to make serious preparations for a fight if boxing was that easy. So, when the chance of partying the night away before the fight came, I took it and enjoyed myself. I arrived at the weigh-in an hour late, with a hangover and completely knackered. I must have looked a right mess, but at least I was there. Fosteres had weighed in, on time, eight pounds overweight. Frank said that she must take the weight off — but there was no chance of that. It looked more like a stone to me, anyway, but I didn't give a fuck, I just wanted to get rid of my hangover. Then it was suggested that the fight be called off because of the weight difference. No way! It seemed like everyone in Fleetwood was packing into the hall to see me fight and there was no way I was going to let them down. 'I'm going to fight her.' That's what I said and that's what I did.

Once in the dressing room, and changed ready for my first fight in Fleetwood, with boxing gloves on, my hangover took second place to my nerves and my nerves didn't get any better when, for the first time, I had a TV camera stuck in my face. I didn't know what to say or do. I got all my words mixed up because I was so excited — and embarrassed — but I don't think anyone could tell as I had had a lot of experience talking my way out of situations in the past, so I was never short of words.

Lots of my family and friends came to see me box and a lot more saw clips of me later on TV. Everyone seemed so excited about what I was doing, and people stopped me in the street to talk about my boxing. I didn't realise at the time that I had started a whole new lifestyle. Frank was in the dressing room with me, and was possibly even more nervous than I was, something he tried to control with frequent disappearances to the bar. That was more than I could do at this stage — I had had enough in the hours leading up to the fight, anyway. Unfortunately for me and Frank, he couldn't come in the corner with me this time, as he had been warned by the Amateur Boxing Association that he would lose his amateur status if he was seen working with me — what a load of bullshit! So I had no other choice than to have Pauline Dickson, a WIBF official, and her helper, Dave Shirley, in my corner.

Pauline led me to the ring at a snail's pace, which at least gave me time to enjoy the excitement and encouragement of the crowd. I was soon lost in the enthusiasm, my nerves fading away as I danced, smiled, waved and shouted at everyone I knew, and there were a lot of them. In complete contrast Fosteres Joseph, her yellow shorts and vest enhancing her black skin, massive pony-tailed dreadlocks hanging down to the small of her back, was met with a chorus of boos, and then almost complete silence as she climbed into the ring.

Steve Presnail, now adding the job of Master of Ceremonies to his position of promoter, introduced the fight to the crowd as a 'Six, two-minute round, final eliminator for the welterweight championship of Great Britain'. At least, I *think* that's what he said. It was hard to hear or concentrate, the crowd were going that mad, and as I walked to the centre of the ring the cheering changed to the stamping of feet and the chant of 'Jane! Jane! Jane!' I got the feeling that there may be a riot if I didn't win.

The bell went for the first round. I walked towards Fosteres and poked her head back with the left lead Frank had been teaching me. It was one of the few straight punches either of us used throughout the fight. When the battle started we began flailing at each other, any thoughts of technique long gone. In fact, if we had been doing impressions of windmills whirling in a force eight gale, we would both have won an Oscar.

The pattern for the contest was set: the one who lasted the distance better and slung in the most punches was going to win. Between rounds I collapsed, rather than sat, on my stool, dreading the sound of the bell that meant that I had to get up and wade into war again. We would meet in the middle of the ring and the hailstorm of punches would start. I can only remember thinking, However many times she hits me, I've got to hit her more. Occasionally I would push Fosteres back, despite her extra weight; occasionally she would switch to 'southpaw', but it made no difference: we kept on hitting each other, and what I lacked in skill I made up for with an energy that could only have come from adrenalin rather than training.

In the interval before the sixth and final round, Frank couldn't keep away from the corner: he rushed over, tapped my arm for attention and said, 'Keep boxing and jab your left.' It was good advice but it was too late. By this time I couldn't have changed what I was doing, I was on 'automatic pilot' — set for the night. It wasn't boxing, it was a brawl, an almost non-stop brawl that thrilled the crowd. When the final bell rang we were still slugging it out. We gave each other a hug before returning to our corners.

I thought I had won the fight, but there is always a doubt until the referee raises your arm. When Eugene Valerio raised mine, I bounced up and down on the spot like a Jack-in-the-Box, before dashing round the ring waving to my fans on every side. Now, really excited by the battle they had just seen, they were clapping me and cheering me even louder than before the fight. Out of the ring I was grabbed, hoisted on the shoulders of my friend Steve Clark, and carried back to the dressing room.

The celebrations continued later at the Fleetwood Football Club's bar and clubroom. It seemed that all the boxers, officials and a lot of the spectators had transferred themselves from the hall to the club. Steve Presnail had done a good job with his boxing show and now, I thought, an even better one with the celebrating. Food, music, booze, dancing — this was my idea of heaven.

With the adrenalin still flowing from my triumph over Fosteres Joseph, and all the congratulations that kept coming, I really was on a high. I was buzzing around that club, from person to person, like a bee in a flower patch. Then I was stopped in full flight: it was the grey-haired old bastard of the WIBF, Tex Woodward. 'Would you care to dance?' he says, in his poncy voice. The band was playing 'Rock Around The Clock', and I thought, Fuck me, he's a bit ambitious, he'll probably have a heart attack. It was me who nearly had the heart attack, though — he was twisting me left and right, and round and around. When the music stopped he said, 'Thank you very much, I think you might have more chance of making a career out of boxing rather than dancing.' Cheeky bastard! I was off, back to the bar with people who didn't take the piss out of me.

It was a good night, and going on and on, the crowd gradually dwindling away as it got later and later until finally there was only Steve Presnail, Tex Woodward and me left drinking. We had all had a right skinful, Tex slinging back the vodka with the same enthusiasm he showed with his rock and rolling. Steve was beginning to look out of it but still nodding his head in agreement of almost everything I said. I was getting to be higher in the clouds all the time, but somehow I was still standing, talking and smiling.

We talked about how I beat Fosteres for the umpteenth time, and then the words came out that were going to affect a lot of people's lives. Tex said, 'I thought you put up a terrific fight. What a shame you can't box, come to my gym and I will teach you how to box.' I looked at him, my head surprisingly clear, and saw that he meant what he said. Then I heard the words come out of my mouth: 'Yes, we'll go to America, and I will win the World Title.'

That was my last memory of that night. I think we got a taxi and dropped Tex off where he was staying. I do remember going to see him next morning, or rather later that same morning, but he had already left to go back to Bristol.

10

MY LAST TWO FLEETWOOD FIGHTS

If I had to give a prize to someone for being the most optimistic, enthusiastic and unrewarded female boxer I ever met, it would have to go to Jane Johnson of Tunbridge Wells.

Jane was one of the small group of women boxers who had actually boxed competitively before the WIBF had tried to bring organisation and legislation to female boxing in the UK. Like me, she was a Rocky Marciano fan, so much so that some of her friends nicknamed her 'Rocky'. Like the real Rocky she was a tough fighter in the ring, but she didn't have his ability to win — a fact not completely of her own making, although she always admitted that her preparations for a fight were never as thorough as they should have been.

Her enthusiasm to box drew her into contests she should have never agreed to, the first mismatch being against a German girl, just announced as 'Diane', in 1987 at the Half Moon pub, Herne Hill. Jane Johnson weighed in at eight-and-a-half stone, her opponent at thirteen stone! Even with the weight difference Rocky was there at the end of eight rounds, losing on points. She got paid little more than her travelling expenses.

Then there were fights in France and against Irish Champion, Deirdre Gogarty, at the Foresters Arms, Tooting, and the Park Tavern, Streatham. She was beaten on points each time but was still trying at the end, a quality that brought her to Fleetwood to box me on April 18th 1995. By this time it was getting hard to find opponents to box me, and Steve Presnail's second show looked like it would have to be cancelled, because if I didn't box, no one would buy tickets just to watch outsiders. Jane Johnson, willing, as always, to box anyone, stepped in as my opponent and saved the show.

For three rounds she tried hard, but my extra reach and energy were too much for her. It was probably a good thing that when I knocked her down in the fourth round, she twisted her ankle and couldn't continue the fight.

The last chance my local fans had to see me box, without travelling, was against Julia Shirley, another southerner, with a right cocky London attitude, on July 1st 1995, at the Marine Hall. It was the last of the brief run of 'Presnail Promotions', and it was a promotion that wasn't as easy to organise as the earlier ones. Suddenly all the travelling expenses were getting more costly, the boxers wanting over-the-top purses, and more officials, trainers, and the like were wanting paid accommodation. Steve was being ripped off, any chance of making money out of the shows gone.

Both he and I were beginning to have misgivings about the whole women's boxing scene. I told him, 'Steve, this is a load of crap, all these boxing people think they know everything better than everybody else, all slagging each other off. I can't be doing with it. I think I will have to pack it all in, or go to America and box there.'

As well as seeing the organisational problems, I was beginning to hear stories from some of the more experienced female fighters of how they had already been exploited, boxing topless on seedy shows, being overmatched, never being paid as much as they deserved. Then there were the other female boxers, some of them with more tattoos than the punches they threw. OK, so I had Mickey Mouse with boxing gloves on tattooed on my upper arm, but that was all. At least I had my long ringletted hair, not cropped to my scalp like some of the other girls, which made them look more butch than they really were. Even Julia Shirley, a mother of two children, had really short hair. When she came into the boxing ring wearing combat-style khaki shorts, vest, and sunglasses, I thought, For fuck's sake, what are you wearing? She looked just like a bloke — in fact people in the hall were asking, 'Why is Jane fighting a man?' Even years later people would say to me, 'Yes, I know you. I saw you boxing that "man" on TV.'

Now, I wasn't expecting all the girls to come into the ring wearing frilly shorts and buttons and bows. But I was expecting them to be wearing boxing shorts and vest like me. Even if some of them were crap boxers, at least they could have tried to look the part. I could see myself getting involved in an environment which, as far as I was concerned, was creating the wrong image for its participants. Somehow I had to change the image of women's boxing in the UK, or get out of it and maybe just box abroad where it was being taken more seriously. First, though, I had to fight the 'man'.

How Julia Shirley ever agreed to box me in a serious contest, I could never understand. Some weeks before I fought her, I was invited to London by Pauline Dickson, the WIBF secretary at that time. Pauline was also training a group of female boxers at Casey's Gym, Streatham, and Julia was being touted as a future champion. So much so, in fact, that a TV company was filming a documentary on women's boxing with Julia the main star. Unbeknown to me, I had been invited along as a sparring partner, who would make Julia shine on the film. Jane Johnson was one of the group in the gym, and she and I got on well with each other — there was no jealousy in J. J. She told me, 'You have just been training hard for six rounds, Julia has only warmed up. Just watch yourself when you get in the ring!' I was that green I didn't understand what was going on. I was already knackered when I got in the ring to spar — I didn't do much training in those days and six rounds was like a marathon for me. I started sparring with Julia Shirley, throwing light punches as I had been told, and suddenly she was all over me trying to make a name for herself in front of the cameras. I thought, Fuck this, you bastards aren't going to get away with that game. So I just whacked back, as hard as I could with both hands.

I couldn't believe it, but before we were halfway through the first round Julia had collapsed on the ring ropes crying her eyes out with, I imagine, pain and embarrassment. I was a bit embarrassed as well, especially when the TV cameraman came up to me and said, 'I think we are filming the wrong person.' Then, just a few weeks later, they all came to Fleetwood saying that Julia had been specially coached and trained, was really fit, and was going to beat me. I thought they must be off their heads.

The crowd in the Marine Hall, who had nearly all come just to see me, gave Julia a hard time with boos and jeers as she tried, without much success, to dance her way to the ring in her combat gear. Pauline Dickson, this time in my opposition's corner, lead the way into the ring, and then stood on the ring apron 'firing' an imaginary pistol at the crowd! That wasn't very clever — some of them tried to drag her off the ring.

After that crap entrance the fight wasn't really that much better. After clobbering Julia such a short while ago I didn't train very hard for the fight. I'd done some sparring with Mark

Bennett and Eddie Pinder, who were doing an exhibition bout on the bill, and that was about it. Still, I was too lively for Julia, although she did last until the end of the fight this time, which was more than she had managed when we sparred in Streatham. The crowd enjoyed the scrap, but that's all it was, with me hitting her about six times to every punch she landed on me. In the last round I was close to knocking her out, but she made it to the last bell. When the decision was announced, the crowd, who had been noisy all through the fight, really let rip, shouting and singing, 'You'll Never Walk Alone' as I was carried back slowly to the dressing room. None of the southerners stayed for an after-fight party, even though rooms had been booked for them overnight. It didn't bother us Fleeties — we got around to the Market Tavern and did some serious celebrating!

All thoughts of packing in boxing had gone from my head. If there was one way of getting on a legitimate high it was winning, and I was becoming addicted!

11

FRANK, FRANK AND BRENT

After the third Presnail promotion in Fleetwood, my publicity began to grow. I was seen on TV a few times, and often had write-ups in the local press. My first really memorable TV appearance was on *The Frank Skinner Show*. Luckily I got my mum to record it for me, as I would never have remembered it all. I was a bit pissed up before I went on stage, but afterwards I was really gone. It was my first experience of free drinks in the Green Room, and I made the most of it! Steve Presnail had come with me to the studio, and it was just as well he did. I was pretending I didn't drink, sending Steve for glasses of wine. I started on red wine, and when that ran out I finished off the white.

Brian London, the ex-British Heavyweight Champion, was there as well; he came from Blackpool. We had a right laugh, him telling me about his fight with Ali, and a lot of other big names. We got on really, really well. I had been told that some people didn't like Brian, but I did!

Marvin Hagler was there as well. He was something else, an ex-World Champion, and so famous — I was really nervous to talk to him. I couldn't believe it when he said he had actually already heard of me! He could see I was nervous and when I went on he took me to the edge of the stage and said, 'Go, get 'em, kid!' He waited there until I came off, and was full of praise and said I had done very well. Then he asked me if I would like to go to Planet Hollywood with him. I was so star-struck at the time I could hardly believe he was asking me. It seemed Marvin had something he wanted to deliver there, and he said we would have time for a quick drink and still get back before the TV filming was finished.

There was a car waiting for him and I was suddenly alone with one of the world's greatest ever boxers. I was in such a state of excitement, what with being with him and the drink I'd had, I just didn't know what to talk about, but Marvin kept chatting about boxing. He told me about his fight with Sugar Ray Leonard, how he thought he had won, and how disillusioned not getting the decision made him feel about boxing. He went on to tell me that there had been a women's fight on that bill but he couldn't remember who it was. We only had one drink in Planet Hollywood, because so many people recognised him that it was more peaceful to go back to the TV studio. I carried on where I had left off in the Green Room, where they had found some more wine. I think I finished that off as well — I don't really remember.

While I was waiting to hear when I would be boxing again I took a rest from training. I couldn't see the point of working out with nothing definite to aim at. Anyway, training ate into my going-out time, and I wasn't going to lose any more of *that* than I had to!

After a few weeks, though, I was beginning to feel that I should be doing some training, just in case a fight did come along suddenly. I went around to Frank's house, which was directly opposite the Fleetwood boxing gym. I knocked on the door, and when he answered and saw that it was me he looked a bit taken aback. I said, 'Are we training tonight, Frank, or what?' He didn't seem to know quite what to say.

'Jane, we can't train there any more. It's that Tommy Norton, you know, him that's the Chairman of Fleetwood gym. He said that as you are being paid to box, that makes you a professional, so you can't train in an amateur gym. What's more, if I continue training you, I'll be suspended by the ABA and not allowed to train any more amateurs.'

I couldn't believe it! Frank had been training boxers there for thirty years and brought on some good lads, the Pinders, Dave White and others, that had done well for the club. Now, just because of me, he was being barred from the gym. I was getting my first taste of the stupid, old-fashioned rift between amateurs and professionals. Stupid or not, we were out of there!

The next day I was wandering around Fleetwood, and going down Dock Street I came to a building where I knew there was a gym called Body Quest. I hadn't taken much notice of it previously, but now, as I had nowhere to train, I thought I would check it out. I went in, and saw the owner Brent Latham sat behind the reception counter. I started to introduce myself but Brent said he knew who I was. He turned out to be a mad keen boxing fan, attending as many fights as he could: Benn, Tyson, Eubank, all of them. I couldn't believe my luck. It was brilliant talking to him about boxing and we immediately struck up a good friendship.

I told him about Frank and me being chucked out of the boxing gym, and straight away he said, 'Well, this isn't a boxing gym but you are welcome to train here, whenever you want.' I couldn't believe it. It was a lovely gym and within days I had moved my punchbags in. Brent was brilliant helping me with my fitness and he introduced me to a friend of his called Ray Jackson. Ray was a keen runner, in fact a very good one, and he had already run a few marathons. It wasn't long before he had me running with him on Fleetwood beach, and he gave me lots of fitness advice. I needed it! Running was never my strong point, and after just a few minutes running with Ray I was fucking knackered! He was patient with me, though. He could have run at his own pace and lost me, but he didn't; he would wait for me and say, 'Don't worry. You'll be OK, you'll get better.' That's where he was wrong — I did get fitter, but I never did get better at running.

In the evenings I used to meet Frank at Body Quest, after he had finished work, and he would take me through some boxing training. Brent started to encourage me to take boxing more seriously. To do that I was going to have to find another gym that specialised in boxing, and had good boxers to spar with. I didn't know of a gym like that, but I knew if I could find one, Frank could go back to Fleetwood amateur club, and get no more hassle from the Amateur Boxing Association.

Then something struck a memory chord! Tex Woodward's gym...

Fuck me! I was drunk at the time I said I would go down to Tex's gym and learn to box. I didn't really expect Steve Presnail to start dragging me off and taking me down to Spaniorum Farm in Somerset every other weekend. It was even worse when he started leaving me there and just coming down to take me away for a weekend break. Don't get me wrong, it's what I wanted really, but after the carefree, reckless life I had been leading, to get stuck in a farmhouse in comparative isolation, with a couple of what I thought were a bit posh old-age pensioners, was almost as bad as staying in Drake Hall Prison. In fact, with Tex it was worse — I think he thought he was still a PT Instructor in the RAF and expected me, and everyone else, to do *what* he said, *when* he said it. He would stick out his bottom lip, study his watch, and say, 'Training starts at half past six, and when I say half past six I mean half past six, not twenty past six or even twenty-five to seven, I mean half past six!' I thought, You can fuck off, I'll train at what time I want. It wasn't to be: Tex was a hard old bastard and he was used to having things done just as he wanted them. We both knew there were going to be battles ahead, and didn't we have them!

The most regular rows happened each morning when Tex called me at ten o'clock. Yes! I know boxers are supposed to get up early and run their tits off before breakfast, but not me. I'm not a morning person and I thought ten o'clock was a bit early. Tex would shout at me, shake the bed, and make as much noise as he could. 11.30 a.m. was the time for my morning training and I thought 11 a.m. was plenty early enough to get up. Not Tex — he had almost had a fit when I insisted on staying in bed until 10 a.m. So each morning we would have this battle: 'Good morning, Jane, time to get up.' I could hear him but couldn't be bothered to answer, so he'd start to shout. 'Come on, get up, it's time for breakfast.' What's so important about a few minutes? I'd tell him, 'Fuck off, you stupid old bastard!'

He'd try again, this time even louder, 'Get up. It's time for breakfast.'

So to hell with breakfast. 'Fuck off, you grey-haired old cunt or I'll shove your fucking head in.' It was no use — he wouldn't give up, shouts, threats, buckets of water. I would stick it out as long as I could, trying to prove I couldn't be told what to do but he wouldn't let me rest so I'd reluctantly get up. I was going to have the last word, though, so I moaned and groaned right up till I started training at 11.30 *exactly*!

When the training started my attitude would change. I had come to learn, and Tex had made his mind up I was going to learn properly. We worked well together most of the time — I was inexperienced but really enthusiastic, even if my attention span, as Tex called it, wasn't as long as he would have liked. He said I was no ordinary pupil, but I never did make my mind up if that was a compliment or a criticism. One thing was sure: when the timer bell rang I started training, skipping, punching the bag, shadow-boxing or whatever, and I didn't stop until the next bell signalled the end of the three-minute round. After a minute's rest the bell would ring again to signal the start of the next session.

We both worked hard, me mostly physically, Tex sometimes physically when we sparred lightly together; but most of his work was mental, trying to coach me, coax me, urging me to greater thought and effort. It was hard for my body, but even harder for my mind. I'd never realised you had to think while you were boxing. I can't remember thinking about anything when I was having a punch-up in a pub. Discipline was a word Tex kept using. I sort of knew what it meant but it wasn't something I bothered much about. He did, though, and he nagged and nagged on about it until I thought it was easier to save all the arguments and just get on with my training at the time he said, unless I was in one of my stroppy moods and decided I wanted to prove a point by being late. I soon learnt that wasn't a very good idea as we would then be at each other's throats and it would ruin the training session. I really, really did want to learn how to be a good boxer, but Tex had a hard time convincing me that the idea was not to let my opponent hit me if I could possibly avoid it. I didn't really give a fuck if they hit me or not — if a bloke couldn't knock me out with a head-butt or a baseball bat, no woman was going to bother me wearing 10oz boxing gloves. Little did I know!

It wasn't just the skills of boxing I was finding hard. One of Tex's favourite torture sessions was a thing he called circuit training. He said he'd learnt all about it in the RAF, but I think he had made it up just to watch me suffer physical exhaustion and not be able to gob off for a while. Whatever the reasons, he made me do it three times a week and it didn't half get me fit. The circuit was made up of ten exercises on which I was tested for maximum repetitions over one minute, with a minute's rest between each test. Then when I did the circuit it would be three laps of half my maximum reps, non-stop against the clock. Each time Tex would expect me to be a bit faster, and shout and urge me on, when all I wanted to do was just collapse and lie on the floor. Mostly I would get a bit faster, and Tex would smile and say, 'I enjoyed that.' I would think, If you enjoyed it so much, why didn't you fucking do it?

Steve Presnail was doing everything he could to help me get on in the boxing world. He would drive me wherever I needed to go, or collect me from the farm if needs be. He was also managing my boxing business, handling publicity and trying to arrange fights for me. This started to be difficult for Steve. As media interest grew and I spent more and more time at the farm, telephone messages had to be transferred and eventually the farm number became much simpler to use.

Not long after I had begun to settle into my training routine, a TV crew came to the farm filming a documentary about women's boxing. They followed us about for days. By this time I was working really hard and getting very fit. The crew were more than impressed and I hogged most of the time on the film. They even followed me to Denmark where Steve had arranged with Jimmy Finn, the vice-president of the WIBF, for me to box the reigning champion, a French woman called Sandra Geiger, for her title in Copenhagen. The date that I will never forget: May 31st 1996.

I was so excited, but Tex was his usual sceptical self. 'Don't believe it till it happens,' was one of his favourite sayings. He had a certain justification in being cynical: he had worked with Jimmy Finn for some while and had been let down before, so he found it difficult to take as gospel some of Mr Finn's announcements. One such fight was supposed to be against Diana Dutra of Canada for the World Welterweight title. As the fight date approaches, Jimmy's on the phone: 'I'm sorry, the fight's off. Diana has had a car accident and is permanently paralysed.' Another call, another name, another date but this time a more interesting excuse for there being no fight. 'Terrorists have blown up the hall.' A fight in Hungary sounded a lot more definite, though. We even had a strangely worded fax from Hungary stating that a fight had been arranged against Iona

Papp who, it was said, was the granddaughter of Lazlo Papp, Eastern Europe's most famous ex-boxing champion. The thought of Jane Couch, Fleetwood's wild child, putting a foot on the stage of world-class boxing inspired Brent Latham, owner of the Body Quest Gym in Fleetwood, to travel to Budapest with three of his friends to watch her fight. The fight was 'postponed' for a week, but with the travel arrangements made and paid for, the Fleetwood four decided to take a short holiday. In Brent's words, 'It was a mistake to go to Hungary but at the same time it was very exciting.

'We landed in a snowstorm and as the plane touched down we watched disbelievingly, through the windows, as a pack of wolves ran beside the plane. It was even more discomforting as we walked down the steps from the aircraft on to the snow-covered tarmac, to see snipers in Russian Army-style winter wear shooting at the wolves. Going through Customs, travelling the streets of Budapest looking at the walls of the buildings, which appeared to have countless bullet holes in them, I felt I had stepped back in time to the 1940s. It was a strange feeling, almost as if I was an actor in a black and white movie.

'We walked around Budapest trying to get information on Jane's proposed fight the coming week. There was no information: everyone knew of Lazlo Papp, no one had heard of Iona. We had the name of the hall and checked it out — it was tiny and used as a Cultural Centre. Enquiries about a boxing show were meaningless. None of us will forget Budapest. It was cold! We crossed the bridge over the Danube, the large temperature gauge measured minus 12°c. On the way back, our inadequate English winter clothes now frozen to our bodies, the gauge was reading minus 20°c. Of all the places I have travelled in the world Budapest will be remembered most clearly, but for all the wrong reasons!'

With less than a week to go before the proposed Hungarian expedition, the fight, unlike the snow, melted away and we were at least saved the discomfort of following in the frozen footsteps of Brent and his friends. It was not surprising that we began to think that Irishman Jimmy Finn's fight predictions were bouncing off the Blarney Stone.

As May 31st got closer it seemed as if, at long last, I was going to get a fight. Tex was still muttering about Jimmy and his promises, saying, 'I'll believe it when we get the tickets and we are on that plane to Copenhagen.' Nevertheless, he made me train as if the fight was a certainty: he was determined that what I lacked in boxing skills and ring experience was going to be made up for with first-class fitness. Let's face it, my experience amounted to just four previous bouts in a boxing ring, none of which had been totally demanding, even taking into account my previously low-key fight preparations.

My fitness was achieved by intense traditional boxing workouts and, on alternate days, the dreaded pressurised circuit training. The main theme of every workout was maximum effort in a specific amount of time. The fight for Sandra Geiger's title was over ten two-minute rounds. I was going to be fit enough to punch non-stop for those ten rounds! As the fight neared and this target looked feasible, we began to think no woman of equal weight could match my physical condition.

Tex, like I expect every other caring boxing coach, had his moments of apprehension, though, pondering my ability and that of my opponent. He had just such a moment before the battle of Copenhagen. On one of the rare occasions when we sat quietly chatting in the farmhouse living room, he was looking for reassurance in his mind that he wasn't over-matching me. 'You tell me that you've had loads of street and pub fights, Jane. How many do you think you have had?'

There was a moment of pause and I stared at him, thinking, Why is he asking me that? Am I going to get a lecture on the errors of my ways? When I decided to answer, my voice was challenging. 'About two hundred.'

The serious face staring back at me relaxed. 'Great, if you can survive that amount of fights, and still want to be a boxer, I can't see you coming to much harm in a boxing ring against an opponent wearing gloves, and with rules to adhere to under a referee's supervision.'

Collecting the travel tickets at Manchester Airport finally convinced us we were all off to Denmark. Steve Presnail had been good enough to collect us from the farm and get us into the Departure Lounge in good time. We were there when Wally Swift, ex-British Welterweight Champion, now a well-known boxing manager, came in with Mark Dawson, one of his fighters. Excellent, the show must be on! Tex, with a rare fit of conscience, said, 'I should have been more trusting. I've dealt with Mogens Palle [the Danish promoter] before, and I've had no reason to doubt his credibility. It's just that Jimmy Finn's track record as a matchmaker has left a lot to be desired!'

The flight to Copenhagen scared me a bit. I'd only flown to Spain and back before, and that was some while ago. Good old 'I've- Done-It-Before' Tex was saying, 'Look, there's Old Trafford.' I didn't *want* to look, I just wanted to be left alone to feel ill. I did shout a bit on take off, but I shouted a lot more when Tex nicked my meal and said, 'Just have these lettuce leaves and a rice cake, that will keep you going till the weigh-in.'

The weigh-in was at 6 p.m., over four hours away. I told him, 'I want some food, I'll make ten stone OK. I need some food to keep my strength up.' I was wasting my time: food and drink were barred except for the offer of another rice cake. From that moment onwards I made myself a promise. 'Never again will I eat a rice cake!' They were foul. I couldn't even have a drink of water, I was watched that closely.

When we landed, I dashed into the ladies toilet, but couldn't bring myself to drink foreign water. I couldn't work the tap anyway, and I had no idea how the flush worked. I asked this woman for help but she didn't seem to know what I was talking about, and when she answered I was lost. I went out and shouted at Tex and asked him why she couldn't understand me. He laughed and said, 'You're going to meet a lot like that, Jane. As we are in Denmark the majority of people will speak Danish!'

God! I was glad to get to that weigh-in and closer to food and drink. That was when I first saw Sandra Geiger, and she seemed very calm and relaxed — quite a strong-looking girl too. She had boxed in Copenhagen before, winning the WIBF welterweight title with a stoppage victory over American-based Norwegian Helga Risoy, who, although she had the famous American trainer Emmanuel Steward working in her corner, was stopped in the 7th round. That win had turned Sandra Geiger into a star boxer, and it quickly became obvious that I had been brought to Denmark in the role of opponent, as I was to discover that most other visiting boxers were.

It seemed that Geiger was expected to win comfortably: after all, I had only had four fights in a boxing ring. I know I won them all and didn't expect any other woman to be able to beat me anyway, but that record did look a bit feeble up against her twenty wins and four losses, and that didn't count all the fights she had had to become a karate champion.

It was the first big, important weigh-in I had been to. Sandra Geiger stood on the scales looking very relaxed and ladylike while photos were being taken of her. I thought, I'll change all that, mate! She made the weight, OK. So did I — fucking rice cakes!

After the weigh-in, a lot of the boxers hung around chatting with each other, the reporters, trainers and the usual gathering of hangers-on. The Danish boxers went somewhere, probably home, but the overseas boxers were happy to chat and pass the time away before going back to the hotel. I chatted a lot to Wally Swift: he was old and grey like Tex, and he was tut-tutting away about women being allowed to 'fait' (I think he meant *fight*!), but he liked me and I thought he was great, especially as he had been a champion boxer in his time.

Peter Harris was on the bill. He was a very good Welsh boxer earlier in his career but I was told he is just a good opponent now. He had his brother, Michael, with him, and I could tell he fancied me! The boxer I spent most time with, when I could sneak away from Steve and Tex, was American Heavyweight, Mike 'The Bounty' Hunter: he had just come to pad up Danish Brian Nielson's unbeaten record. I was going to learn a lot about the boxing world and its goings on from Mike.

He was fascinated with cricket, and he kept pretending to bowl at me. Little did he know I was one Lancashire girl who had never seen a cricket match. It didn't matter, every time we saw each other we would bowl some imaginary balls, even at the breakfast table next day. Sandra Geiger and her French team were there. They must have thought I was out of my mind — or practising a 'bolo' punch in reverse.

From the weigh-in until fight time, the American, English and Welsh boxers all made small talk with me and offered false encouragement. They had all been opponents many times and knew the boxing business, whereas I was about to start my education. Tex reappeared, I don't know where he had been — last time I had seen him at the weigh-in he had been complaining that the only hot drink he could find was raspberry tea, which he tried but was totally unimpressed. Now he had that look on his face that says, 'I know something you don't know.' He was like a big kid at times. This time he says, 'Do you know where the fights are being held?' How the hell should I know? I'm in a foreign country and can't understand a word of what the locals say. 'It's the K.B. Halle!'

'What is the K.B. Halle?'

'It's where I boxed for the RAF against Denmark with Dick McTaggart, Bruce Wells, Brian London and the rest of the team in the fifties.'

'Did you win?'

'Yes and no. I fought the same bloke twice, Holger Robert Peterson, won one, lost one. If someone had told me then I would be back forty years later, seconding a woman in a world title fight, I would never have believed it.'

Travelling by coach from the hotel to the arena was a bit nerve-racking. I hadn't slept much the night before (I'd had a couple of whiskies but that didn't help). I spent a lot of time sat on the stairs chatting to Mike 'The Bounty' Hunter. I couldn't believe it when I saw him smoking so much; still, he said he couldn't sleep either. All I could think about was, Oh! Let's get the fight on, I want to knock her out and get in the bar.

Sandra Rouse had flown over from England earlier in the day to help Tex and Steve with the cornerwork. The three of us walked around the hall taking in the atmosphere. Tex checked out the colourful advertisement-covered ring and the corner steps before we found where our smallish dressing room was. The 'Bounty Hunter' was sharing the room, but luckily there was a washroom where I could undress privately so as to avoid embarrassment — not that I would have bothered, him being a big heavyweight. Mike watched, with great interest, as Tex bandaged and taped my hands: it seems he does them differently from most trainers. Mike studied the whole process, and when Tex had finished he felt my hands, got me to close my knuckles, and seemed to approve, which is more than Jimmy Finn did!

Mr Finn, now acting as WIBF Official in Charge of the women's title fight, bustled into the dressing room just as Tex was about to ease one of my hands into the boxing glove ready for the fight. He glanced at my hands and said, 'They won't do. Get them off!' I was taped up, warmed up and almost gloved up, and there was no way Tex was going to let me go through all that again when it was time to head for the ring. 'Jimmy, I have been bandaging boxers' hands for years and no one has ever complained about the way I did it before. Now you, who have only been involved in boxing for five minutes, are telling me my job.' The French trainer André Panza was called, he took a quick look at my hands, winked at us and said, 'OK!' Then Tex had to look at Sandra Geiger's hands. He wasn't bothered as long as she wasn't wearing knuckle-dusters. He just wanted to get me into the ring as quickly as possible before all the aggravation spoilt my focus. He needn't have worried: I was enjoying it. I always did when Granddad got on his high horse and started getting stroppy — as long as it wasn't with me. It got no better when Jimmy Finn came back, his face red, saying, 'You have still got to get them off.'

The normally calm, polite Tex had had enough — like me, he can't stand pompous officialdom. He grabbed Jimmy Finn by the shoulders and shoved him towards the door saying, 'Get out of this blasted dressing room. Out! Out! Out!' Those words were recorded for ever by the documentary camera crew who were following me about. They must have thought it was Christmas getting a shot like that! Just to add to the excitement, the 'Bounty Hunter' loomed up from his chair to help Tex, almost filling the room. I was glad he was on our side!

Peace was restored when the Danish supervisor, Dr Jurgen Huuson, suggested that Tex should just trim back the bit of bandage that was offending Mr Finn. A couple of snips with his surgical scissors and the problem was solved. Gloves on and it was time for the short walk to the ring; this was delayed as we waited for the entrance music. I occupied the time with some vigorous shadow-boxing, much to the concern of Wally Swift, who had come to wish good luck to this first woman boxer he had met. He was a bit worried about the energy I was using: 'Take it easy, girl, you'll be worn out before you start!' Loss of energy was one thing we weren't worried about: my warm-ups were the equivalent to some male boxers' training sessions!

The music started and Steve Presnail, now acting as standard-bearer carrying a large Union Jack, led us into the ring. The music seemed to get louder. I was dancing and waving to the crowd, a lot of whom didn't seem to appreciate my lively smiling entrance. Perhaps they felt sorry for me. They had seen Geiger before, toying with and then stopping Helga Risoy. What did this laughing, hyperactive woman think she was going to do against someone of that ability?

I was the first to enter the ring, wearing my black and white boxing strip, and started to entertain the crowd with some brisk shadow-boxing as I waited for my opponent to appear. Once again this wasn't overly appreciated by the Danish fans. Hadn't somebody told this English girl, with so little experience, that she wasn't here to entertain, but to give the French World Champion a gentle public workout? Public it may have been, gentle was a word no one could have considered after the first bell sounded...

Classical music was played when the French girl came into the ring, and at first sight she looked to have dressed more for an audition for the musical *Cats* than for a world title professional boxing match. She wore a leopard-skin patterned, knee-length cape with a high-winged collar, giving the impression of being more like an aloof queen than a fighter. When she removed her cape it revealed matching leopard-skin shorts and crop top. If it had been a fashion show, although I was smart, I would have been out-pointed before we started!

The preliminaries seemed to take for ever, the national flags waved, the anthems played, and at long last my chance to prove myself had arrived. The bell went and we met, head to head in the middle of the ring, trading blows with both hands. She was the one to take the first backward step, but she was never far away and was counter-punching solidly, with an accurate right cross and uppercut. She was even more dangerous with her head and got cautioned by the Danish referee. When we watched the video tape later, it showed I had thrown over a hundred punches in that round, a lot of them missed and a lot of them scored. Geiger only threw fifty but they were accurate and I felt them. Still, I won that round.

The second round just carried on from the first, at the start anyway. I was going forward again, throwing a load of punches, and she was counter-punching but getting a lot more accurate. She seemed to have found her rhythm. The round was nearly over when she hit me with such a hard right hand to the head that bells started ringing. It didn't matter, three more rights to the head cleared all the noise. There was one more right landed, but by now I was feeling nothing. When I watch that part of the video tape I can't believe I stayed on my feet: it would have felled an ox. As it was, I went into the equivalent of a drunk doing a breakdance. The crowd were roaring, as they always do when someone is getting clobbered. The referee jumped between us and led me back to my corner. Tex thought the fight was over. He told me, 'I was sat on the ring steps thinking, "Oh, my God! After all the hard work we have done." ' He was even phrasing words of comfort in his mind to try and soothe the disappointment he knew I would feel in losing a fight I was so sure I was going to win. Then I heard someone shout, 'The bell's gone, it's the end of the round.'

The crowd had been making so much noise that the sound of the bell had been drowned. I didn't know where I was at first when I sat on the stool in the corner — I thought I was at home with my mum making a cup of tea! I reckon it was all the experience I had of being drunk that saved me. It was hard to stay upright but I knew I mustn't fall over. I wonder how many boxers can say drinking alcohol saved their careers? When he realised the fight wasn't over, Tex was quickly into the ring, sponging water all over me, trying to revive his vacant boxer. As I began to show signs of being awake he asked me a question, to see if my mind was clear, 'What's the name of the girl you are fighting?'

I didn't know — she had a strange surname — but I knew she was French so I said, 'Frog.' That was enough for Tex, he knew my brain was in its near normal state!

From round three onwards I won every round. Although I say it myself, my recovery and fitness was brilliant! Sandra Geiger never stopped trying to get me with her big right-hand counter-punch, but she was always on the retreat as I plodded after her throwing loads of punches, some of them with more hope than success. I eventually caught up with her in the fifth round, forcing the referee to give her a standing count in a mutual corner. She was tired and bleeding a lot, but the referee counted to eight and then let her carry on. I think he was enjoying it. The crowd certainly were; they were all yelling and clapping.

By this time Tex knew that I was going to win if I didn't walk into something too hard. He said to me in the corner before the sixth round, 'The only danger you have got is her right hand, so keep your left hand up.' He was wrong — the biggest danger I had was her head! She had smashed it into me so many times my left cheekbone and eye were beginning to swell.

For the rest of the fight the pattern was set. I was wading in throwing almost non-stop punches with both hands to the head and body, and the French girl was still trying to find that one big punch to turn the fight around. The crowd were loving the battle, showing their appreciation of us two fantastically fit females, who had provided what proved to be the fight of the night, by almost non-stop clapping throughout the last two rounds.

In the interval before the last round my confident trainer said to me, 'One more round and you will be the World Champion.' If any words could have kept me going, those were the ones! Those last two minutes were a long time, my opponent had by no means given up and had now brought a stinging left hook into her counter-punching, and that kept me active. At long last the final bell rang, and I was back in a very happy corner waving triumphantly to a noisy but appreciative crowd. They had forgiven me for what they had thought was a bit of an over-confident entrance. They didn't know, did they? Now they did. We all waited impatiently for the MC to announce the result.

The announcement was made in Danish. I'd had enough of listening to a foreign fucking language. Now here was this MC waffling on about probably the most important decision in my life and I couldn't understand a bastard word! Me, Midge, Granddad and Steve were all sure I had won the fight, but in the past we had all seen some very clear victories turned into losses by judges and referees — and this lot were all foreign!

Then the words came, in English, 'Jane Couch — and we have a *New World Champion.*' The scores: 98-91 100-90 99-91. It was a one-sided score and I must admit it felt a lot closer. How the judge that gave me every round thought I had won the second I'll never know. He must have enjoyed my breakdance, or gave me extra marks for recovery! I certainly didn't look like a winner. I was covered in blood — fortunately all French blood — and I had a very swollen *English* bruised eye and cheekbone.

I was presented with the coveted title belt by none other

than Mr Jimmy Finn. Poor Jimmy, he looked as if it was the last thing on earth he wanted to do. Still, it was him who made the match! Perhaps he'd lost a bet, or just some good French friends? The presentation ceremony over, the kisses and cuddles started. I even kissed Jimmy Finn! I must have been on a high... The crowd appreciation and excitement cooled down and it was back to a triumphant dressing room.

I just collapsed on a settee, physically drained. I lay back, still with my bandages on, ice bag pressed to my rapidly closing eye with one hand, water bottle in the other. The longed-for belt was around my waist, the boxing gloves that had been quickly taken off were now placed upon my knees, ready to be nicked as souvenirs.

Then the thought hit me, almost as hard as Sandra Geiger's head had. 'Look! I'm not joking, she was head-butting every fucking round, bam, bam, the referee kept telling her but didn't do nowt!' I was really pissed off. I stamped my feet, slapped mid-air a bit, spat in Tex's bag and went for a shower. So did Granddad, he had that much blood on him. He looked as if he had been working overtime in a butcher's shop.

When we were both clean and changed I headed for the bar, but Tex was worried about Sandra Geiger and went to see how she was. He was horrified to find that after such a gruelling fight, and all the hard thumps I had given her, she was alone in her dressing room, no lights on, lying under a blanket on a massage couch. There is an old saying in the boxing world, 'There is nothing as lonely as a loser's dressing room.' It was certainly true on this occasion! Tex felt for her hand and asked if she was OK. All he got for an answer was a mumble, in French, so that didn't help much. He tried to find the doctor, her trainer André Panza, Jimmy Finn, anybody. Nobody seemed bothered. I know if it had been me he would have had me on my way to hospital.

As it happened, maybe I should have been on my way to a *mental* hospital. No, I hadn't drunk myself stupid, yet! It was something else, a thought maybe, I don't know. I was happily supping away when I just had to get out of that bar and away from people. I ran through every door I could see and ended up outdoors on a patio. I slumped on a wooden garden seat and sobbed and sobbed. Midge had followed me, saw the state I was in and ran off to get Tex. He came, sat down and for once didn't lecture; he just put his arm around my shoulders to comfort me, and let me cry myself better. He had seen it all before with other sports people. So it was no great surprise to him that even a hardened, loud-mouthed street fighter like me could suffer anti-climax symptoms when all my physical energy had been drained, and my supply of adrenalin used up. There were very few words exchanged, but the temporary calm and quiet restored my excitement at what I had achieved just a short while ago. The smiles returned and we headed for the bar, this time with serious intent.

When we left the K.B. Halle to board the bus taking us back to the hotel, we saw Sandra Geiger being taken away by car. We hoped she was going to hospital for a check-up. It may have been to the pre-arranged celebratory dinner we were told that the promoter had organised, and that she and Jimmy Finn would be attending. We'd had little contact with the promoter, the only memorable moment being when he had seen me eating a large ice-cream cornet on the afternoon of the fight day. 'Where do you think you are, on holiday?' I think if he'd had any doubts about Geiger winning, they would have been forgotten when he saw me stuffing myself! He'd have had even fewer worries if he'd seen the whisky going down the night before!

Back in the hotel, strangely without a bar, a group of boxers, managers and trainers gathered in the foyer and were served drinks from the reception counter. We didn't care where they came from, we were ready to drink the night away. Wally Swift didn't stay long, he was off to bed, but not before he had said a hundred times, 'Caw! That girl can fait!'

There was a Russian trainer called Igor, drinking neat vodka with us, or perhaps to be more exact, with Tex. They seemed to be having a great time together, laughing and toasting everyone. How they were communicating, God knows. Neither of them spoke the other's language, although Igor was one up on Tex, as he kept saying, 'Sean Connery 007 KGB,' at the same time opening his jacket and revealing a row of pencils and pens in his inside pocket!!

By the time Jimmy Finn arrived back from his dinner, we had all drunk enough to forgive the devil, but not quite enough to let Jimmy get away without a fair bit of ribbing for his earlier performance.

Party over in Denmark and it was back to party time in Fleetwood. Now I was on my home territory and I made the most of it. I'd been well known in some areas before I had left, now I felt I was famous. It seemed everybody wanted to stop me for a chat or to get my autograph. The hard work in the gym, the green fields of the farm, with all its horses, faded from my mind, as the more familiar sounds of trams and seagulls took their place. The acute muscle soreness from extreme effort, the black eye and badly bruised cheekbone, all eased away with each day's intake of alcohol, smoke and clubbing.

Suddenly, though, the party had to stop. A title defence was arranged to take place in New Orleans USA against long-time 'tough woman' fighter, Andrea DeShong.

It was a sobering thought, in more ways than one. I would have to go back to the farm and slave away again. I knew it had to be worth it: I had come from nowhere and had been a no-hoper. Now I was getting to be famous!

12

THE GIRLIE SHOW

When I was offered the chance to appear on *The Girlie Show*, I thought, This is more like my kind of show. Young women in flash gear using my kind of four-letter words and slagging off men. That was my idea of a fun night — TV cameras or no TV cameras. As it happened it was a long day and I got bored. Tex was beginning to understand my wandering instincts and left me to my own devices. He had great fun when the researchers and presenters were trying to find me: 'Oh, she's probably gone out to the shops,' or 'Might have gone home, she gets bored easily,' or 'She went off with some bloke.' He was even more difficult about the script. 'I must see the script before I let her on the set.' They tried hard not to show him but he was like a dog with a bone and he wouldn't let go. 'I want to see the script.' I think he was worried about 'uncouth' (his favourite word when he was describing me) questions. He eventually got his own, bossy, interfering way and OK'd the script. It was really quite mild compared to the rest of the show.

The few minutes I was on camera were OK. I made quite a spectacular entrance down the stairs between the audience, dressed in my boxing kit and dressing gown. I was only the British Champion at the time, and what I think of now as a crap boxer, but the crowd loved me — they always do. They cheered and clapped almost everything I said. After the show I was asked a lot for my autograph. It felt a bit funny really, mostly young girls getting me to write on scraps of paper and cards. Every one of the TV crew thought I was brilliant, the producer even asked me if I would like to become a presenter. I said I would think about it. I did, for a minute. What a fucking life, stuck in a studio all day, dealing with all sorts of weirdos.

The best part of *The Girlie Show* was the Green Room. The food was bloody marvellous. The quantity and quality was amazing. It seems a new company had been given the entertainment contract and they must have been trying to create an impression. They certainly did on me. The chef was yet another person who loved me. He couldn't do enough for me. Whatever I wanted — food and drink — he got it. Tex wasn't doing too bad either, he was sat quietly scoffing and supping back the white wine. Sneaky old bastard, filling his boots, he could sink a drop when he wanted to.

Leon Perkins, a welterweight amateur boxer from the gym, had come to the show with us, and we were supposed to do a bit of 'sparring' together in front of the cameras but nothing much happened. It was a bit disorganised really. One of the presenters was going to spar, but she had hurt her wrist.

Tex bandaged it for her but the way she was yelling and jumping I think he made it worse. Show over, we got back into the Green Room. Leon thought it was his birthday and Christmas rolled into one. He was trying to out-drink Tex, which was a mistake. He didn't last the course. Eventually we had to leave, and a car took us to a posh hotel not too far from the studio.

We booked in at reception and I legged it for the bar. It was closing but I used my charm, or *smarm* as Tex calls it, on the barman and got some drinks in. The two chaps had sat at a table, and Leon was just about out of it — one drink later he was. Tex, smartly dressed, grey hair groomed, had *that* look on his face that was supposed to say, 'I'm jolly well enjoying myself and feel amiable towards the world at large', but really means he's pissed out of his mind. He would never admit it though, the lying old bastard. It was a big hotel, big bar and big keys for the bedrooms. They had long brass rods on them to stop people pinching them!

They were also too big to put in your pocket, handbag, suitcase, or whatever massive piece of luggage you had. So they were thrown on the table which was, luckily, strong enough to take their weight, plus the weight of our glasses and Leon's head resting on his hands. His bedtime long past, he managed to lift a key and staggered away muttering something about a late night and bedtime being overdue. The two remaining keys lay on the table like crossed swords. Symbolic? A forecast for things to come, undoubtedly, as Tex and I were to cross swords and punches on many occasions in the future. We had another round of drinks, or was it two, maybe three. I never did see the bill and Tex wouldn't have paid it. We each took a key and bundled into the lift. Tex got out somewhere and I continued upwards. I don't remember going to bed, so I suppose I must have just fallen down and gone to sleep. Ah, well! It saved time getting dressed next morning, which was just as well as when the taxi driver came to collect us I was nowhere to be found.

That driver was a tosser but more about him later. 'It was

JANE COUCH / 114

all because of the keys,' Tex said. What he meant was, he was too pissed to read the numbers when he picked one up to go to bed. He had gone to bed, woken up, washed, shaved, had breakfast and started trying to find me. How did he do it? I'm the young, fit, experienced drinker.

The pantomime started when Tex asked at reception what room Jane Couch was in. The receptionist checked the computer, gave him the number, and as Tex walked away he realised it was the number of the room he had slept in. Slightly embarrassed, but with no other option, he returned to reception and asked what room Tex Woodward was in, guessing quite correctly that he had picked up the wrong key. Enduring the strange look he was given, Tex watched the computer tapping and was politely given the number he wanted, mentally praying that it wasn't Leon's and that he would have to go back again.

Worse happened: he got into the lift, started chatting to an old lady and forgot the room number. Back to reception, the straight-faced receptionist and the humming computer. 'I've forgotten the room number.' He had had more to drink the night before than he would admit. He had a hangover. Ha! Ha! He thinks he can drink but he suffers as well, even though he denies it.

The receptionist, capable of handling all situations, said to an assistant, 'Take this gentleman to room number...' Tex told me later, when I could think again, how stupid he felt. Serve him right, he was too old to drink so much. He felt even more stupid when he was guided to my room to find the door wide open and me fast asleep, fully dressed on the bed.

The hotel man tried to hide his bemused (or was it amused) expression, and politely wandered off. Tex shouted and shook me, 'Taxi's here, got to go,' and off he went. At that time Tex didn't know that just shouting and shaking wouldn't get me up straight away, even if I did open my eyes and say, 'All right, all right, I'm coming.' The fiasco wasn't over. Tex went downstairs, I went back to sleep and a really bedraggled, hungover Leon met up with Tex and the taxi driver in reception. Tex had had enough. 'You go and get her, Leon.' Leon went up in the lift at the same time as I was coming down the back stairs. Now we had lost Leon, and he was hunting for me.

Tex had got his stern face on. 'Where have you been? Where's Leon got to? Taxi's been waiting for ages — we're going to miss the train.' Luckily, before the crazy game of hide and seek started again Leon reappeared, looking completely mystified. When he saw we had all finally managed to get to the same place at the same time his relief was obvious, but he needed to get home and back to reality.

Tex said that I am not a nice person before 11 a.m., and I think he had his doubts about me at other times, as well. This time he was right: I *felt* horrible, and I *was* horrible, especially to the taxi driver. I said he was a tosser but I think that was flattering. He couldn't keep his fucking gob shut. I made the mistake of sitting next to him in the front seat. He gobbed off with stupid questions and boring information from the time we left the hotel, wherever that was, until we reached Paddington Station. Why ever did he think that I wanted to know that the Arabs own that block, the Jews own that block, Lord and Lady so and so used to live there? If I had wanted a guided tour, I would have got an open-top bus.

For once I was glad to get back to the farm. Peace and quiet for a moment was welcome. Even the horses were a pleasant sight in my condition, except for that grey bastard who hated me and had kept trying to bite me ever since I stuffed the extra-strong Fisherman's Friends down his throat. I wonder if some horses have a sense of humour? This one didn't.

Soon the thought hit me, Fuck it, I've got to start training. Well, bollocks to that, I'm not going to, this boxing is a load of crap, I'm going home. I didn't, of course, and I was soon back into the routine I was beginning to learn was compulsory. God, I'd got away with more in Drake Hall

Prison. Tex would say 'Once the training programme is written down, that's what you must do, exactly at the times stated.' He had a clipboard he would refer to at each session, on which he'd make notes about what I did, especially my circuit times. I began to hate that fucking clipboard. Many's the times I threatened to stick it up his arse, only to be told in his poncy posh voice, 'Don't be uncouth, Jane. You know it's a physical impossibility.'

13

NEW ORLEANS

'And we have a *New World Champion*.' I must have shouted that to myself fifty times a day, and wherever I went people that I didn't know must have thought I was crazy — and those that *did* know me must have had their doubts. I had had a month at home in Fleetwood, and me and my friends partied and partied for the whole time, it was ACE! Half the time I didn't know where I was or what I was doing, but it was good — until the time I had to go back to Spaniorum Farm Gymnasium, and start training again.

Tex met me at Bristol Parkway Railway Station. He didn't comment on the state I was in but it wasn't hard to read his mind.

'Oh, my God! What on earth has she been doing to herself? Can this be the same person as the fit, vibrant athlete I let go home just a few weeks ago? I knew it was going to be hard work getting back into my training routine, but I couldn't have imagined how much I was going to suffer. The muscular pain and stiffness was agony at first, but it gradually became easier. The detoxification, the gradual weaning from large amounts of alcohol, the initial regular visits to the local Fox Inn gradually being phased out and replaced by all-in wrestling with Tex, often taking place on the normally peaceful living room floor, with Tex's wife Pat saying, 'Stop it, you are like two big kids!'

Gradually, as Tex refocused my mind on to training and living a more civilised life, the Fleetwood flings faded into the past, and the desire to get fit was rediscovered. Regular daily sessions in the gym, and the dreaded fitness circuit navigated, and the previous first-class fighting fitness was restored. I was going to be ready for my first title defence against a tough-woman fighter, Andrea DeShong, in New Orleans.

New Orleans was a long way to travel, in miles and in hours, but our journey took twice as long as it should have done. The various airlines excelled themselves at discovering reasons why we shouldn't be flying. Steve Presnail, Tex and I arrived in the very early hours of whatever morning it was, however long after what day it should have been. At that time we didn't know or care, we just wanted to get to our hotel and sleep.

We were met at the airport by Bobby Walshak, the promoter, who apart from offending Tex when he commented on the Old Grey One's almost equally old and battered suitcase as he loaded it, apparently reluctantly, into the back of his expensive car, seemed like a nice guy. Bobby took us to the Landmark Hotel, and landmark it was, really big and high.

Next day we had our first taste of Southern hospitality, with the staff in the hotel trying to feed us as if we were Americans. They were completely baffled when I tried to explain why I couldn't eat too much before the weigh-in. Maybe the information lost something in translation, my broad Lancashire accent probably sounding like a foreign language in New Orleans. Chad Nutter, a good-looking and very black guy, went out of his way to make sure we had everything we needed to enjoy our food. Good service, pleasant informative conversation, and even an invitation to visit his family home — something I would really have enjoyed doing but there just wasn't time. We all liked Chad so much that I resisted telling him what his surname implied in the UK!

We were all in our rooms resting when my telephone rings. A voice says, 'Angelo Dundee wants to meet you, he's in the restaurant.' I thought I was hearing things — Angelo Dundee wanted to meet me? A living legend in the boxing world wanting to meet *me*. I was off to the restaurant, heart beating at a hundred miles an hour to meet this most famous of all boxing trainers. Angelo was staying in the hotel, with his wife Helen. He had a boxer, Terry Ray, boxing on the same bill as me, or maybe I should say it was me boxing on the same bill as him! Angelo and Helen liked me, and I was on my best behaviour, smiling a lot and chatting away, trying not to be too foul-mouthed. I don't think they had ever met anyone like me, certainly not a boxer! I think they would have liked to adopt me, or maybe just take me home for a while to show the neighbours: 'Look what we found when we went to New Orleans.'

I couldn't wait to get back to my room and ring Tex to say, 'You'll never guess who I've been speaking to!'

'No, Jane, I can't guess. Just calm down and tell me.'

I was too excited to play my usual games of, 'No, you guess,' so I just burst out, 'Angelo Dundee!'

'Have you? How very interesting. Was he a nice chap?'

'Yes, come on, I'll take you up and introduce you to him.' By the time we got back Angelo was gone, but we were to meet up with him again.

I was all over that hotel, floor to floor, chatting to anyone who would talk to me, or stand still long enough to listen to me. 'Hey! What are you doing here?'

'I'm boxing here tomorrow night.'

'Hey! You're not a boxer, you're too girlie to be a boxer.'

Another well-known boxing name, Beau Williford, was also staying at the Landmark. He had, some years before, managed Glenn McCory, and now, amongst others, he was managing Deirdre Gogarty, an Irish woman based with Beau and boxing in New Orleans for the WIBF Lightweight title. As most people do, Beau took to me and gave us a lift to the gym. As we passed a cemetery, he pointed out that all the bodies were buried in tombs above the ground, as otherwise regular flooding in the area would have disturbed them. 'Do you know how many dead people are in there?' he asks me.

I did. 'Yeah, all of 'em.' It was the same in Fleetwood!

The gym we went to was great — the building must have been as old as Spaniorum Farm Gym. It had a similar atmosphere, but whereas the farm gym sprawled in all directions, this one went up three floors, with a ring and equipment on each floor. The idea was that various camps could train in private at the same time, the Australian owner told us. After his initial, 'have you all paaaaayed at reception', he was a good and interesting host.

The building itself was something like an old 1930s dockside warehouse (but I didn't see any water). It would have made an ideal setting for an old-time boxing film. The floors were bare wood, the walls covered, like most boxing gyms, with old posters, pictures and notices. It was a workplace, nothing flash but everything functional. I got into my loosening-up routine, I skipped a bit, shadow-boxed and stretched. Tex didn't have much to say, and the workout was relaxed and light as all the hard work had been done in England. I wasn't going to get any fitter by using all my energy at this late stage. The most important reason for the visit was to check my weight on reliable scales. I was a couple of ounces over 140lb. Ideal, as long as I did nothing stupid.

The official weigh-in was held the evening before the show in Bally's casino, a converted, old-time Mississippi paddle steamer, permanently docked — or so we thought until the engines started rumbling halfway through the evening. We thought we might be away on an unscheduled trip, but we didn't move. Maybe the noise was to create a realistic atmosphere, we never did find out. The first deck down was massive. It was full of countless numbers of slot machines, with almost as many fat black ladies sat playing them, some of the women playing two machines at a time, all of them holding plastic tubs, filled to a lesser or greater degree with coins. They had dressed for their night out, hair carefully and often uniquely styled, smart attractive clothes. It was an exciting, fascinating scene against a background of constantly clinking coins and droning machines, almost an hypnotic atmosphere.

There were men there using the machines, but they were outnumbered by women of all ages. I suppose there must have been a minimum age to get on-board, but there was certainly no maximum. Some of them looked like they were a hundred years old, but they were all still smart and enjoying their night out. I wondered where they all came from and where they got their money to use the machines for so long. Tex and Steve were off that deck in a flash, thirty dollars gone between them — talk about the last of the big spenders!

As weigh-in time drew near, Tex was back on more familiar ground arranging a check weigh-in for me, on the official scales. We had no worries about my weight but Tex would take no chances. I was a pound overweight and Tex blamed the scales, as all experienced boxing trainers do, and he was probably right as several of the boxers were overweight. The last thing he wanted me to do was to have to skip off a pound — that would have been a blow to his pride and organisation. 'Go to the toilet, Jane, and if you can't go, splash your wrists with cold water and see if that helps.' I went in to the loo and tried the water trick. No response — nothing! I was trying again with the tap when Angelo's wife came in and saw me looking worried. She asked what the problem was. I told her and she said, 'Don't worry, Angelo will fix that.'

I went back to tell Tex but before I could speak he asked, 'Did you go?'

'No,' I told him.

'Go back and try again.'

I shook my head. 'No, it's all right.'

'It's not all right, go and try again.'

'No, it's all right, Angelo Dundee is going to fix it.'

Tex stared at me. 'How is he going to fix it?'

'I don't know, but his wife Helen was in the loo, saw me looking worried and asked what was wrong. When I told her she said, "Don't worry, Angelo will fix it!" Then she went off to find him.'

Tex and several others were fussing around the scales. The floor, the deck, was sloping, perhaps that was why the scales were weighing heavy. 'Try the other way.' 'Put a board under them.' Then Angelo Dundee turned up with a different idea and a two-pound tin of peas! Where did he get a two-pound tin of peas? Perhaps it's part of a top trainer's equipment! He put the tin on the scales, adjusted the balance arm and said, 'These scales are weighing a pound heavy.' As the official in charge of the scales took a closer look, Angelo kicked the tin off before any further examination could be made. Problem solved! Who was going to argue with Angelo Dundee? All the boxers made the weight.

It wasn't just Angelo and Helen that took to me so much, so did Bobby Walshak, the promoter, and his brother and sister-in-law. Bobby particularly liked me and discussed with Steve and me how I could become a superstar, be ultra-famous, and be a millionaire within a year. Could this be what I had been dreaming about? A wealthy backer to ease the endless battle of expenditure over income during long periods of training? It certainly sounded promising and was a pleasant thought to occupy my mind until fight time.

That didn't happen. As evening drew near I started to feel ill. On the coach to the steamer ship casino I began to lose my voice. Tex told me not to talk but I had to keep answering people's questions politely, even if I could only manage it with a croak. In the dressing room I felt worse. I told Tex, 'My fucking head is spinning and the floor is coming up to hit me.'

'If that's how you feel,' he said, 'I *must* pull you out of the fight. You can't take any chances with Andrea, she has a lot of experience and has even beaten Christie Martin. Remember what she said when you said you were an unbeaten fighter on TV yesterday: " 'Til tomorrow night, baby." I watched her train, she's a rough character and you need to be well to beat her. You can't fight feeling poorly. I'm going to pull you out.'

'*No*, I'm going to fight.'

'You are *not* going to fight.'

'I'm going to fight, even if I have to go out on my own.'

'I'm going to get the doctor to examine you.'

'I don't want to see the doctor.'

Tex wouldn't listen. He got the doctor, who got his stethoscope out and listened to my chest, he looked in my eyes, and said, quite unconcerned, 'She seems OK. It's probably only jet-lag.' The heartless bastard! The fight was on.

The warm-up started, the sickness disappeared. I suddenly felt a surge of energy in my listless body, and started hitting the pads as sharply as ever. I followed Steve and Tex to my corner, firing on all cylinders, dancing, beaming and waving to a crowd that seemed very small in such a large venue. The dancing and shadow-boxing continued in the ring as we waited for Andrea DeShong to make her entrance. She stepped into the ring, wearing a pink(!) satin hooded robe that somehow failed to match her rowdy nature and sturdy build.

The first two rounds were a war. I had been told to box and I was trying to, albeit a bit on the aggressive side, and Andrea, who looked as if she had been training by chopping down trees, was now trying to chop *me* down with swinging blows. Gradually my better technique, and surprisingly my fitness, began to subdue Andrea. I was enjoying it, and playing to the crowd a bit, smiling and talking over DeShong's shoulder. Tex wasn't in the least impressed. I got a good talking to in the corner, and a light slap on my cheek when I was looking at the crowd and not paying attention to what he was saying.

Luckily Andrea's fitness faded faster than my enthusiasm. I kept going forward, throwing the straighter punches, and she kept leaning back trying to counter-punch with swings from all angles.

Tex often said, 'A good straight puncher will usually beat a swinger.' It was working on this occasion. I was getting on top. Round seven and DeShong's defence was weakening. I was ripping her open with combination punches. I forced her to take a standing eight count, in my corner. Tex called to her, 'I should pack it in, love, you're going to get hurt.' He was right. She came at me again but now I knew I had her. A good combination of punches made the referee start a standing count before deciding she had taken enough punishment and stopping the fight in my favour.

I was still the WIBF World Champion. I celebrated with what I thought was going to be a classy forward roll on the canvas, but to be honest, away from boxing I am one of the most awkward, clumsy people around. I almost succeeded in flattening the referee, Andrea and her trainer, Sam Jones. On the way back to the dressing room we passed the doctor, who looked straight at Tex and said, 'It's a good job she wasn't fit!' Saucy sod!

Willie Pastrano came up to me to get an interview. I had been talking to him earlier and it had struck me how sad it was to see a great World Champion boxer right down on his luck and experiencing hard times. He had been asking me to get him some passes to get his mates in to watch the boxing, which of course I did. He'd enjoyed my fight and told me he thought I was a good boxer. It was hard to believe somebody who had been so good could be so complimentary to me.

It was late when we got back to the hotel, so the usual celebratory drink was sacrificed for an early night, as we had a lot of hours travelling to endure the next day. Before we left the hotel, Steve Presnail went to collect my wages for fighting from Bobby Walshak. He came back from Walshak's room saying, 'There is no money. No one's getting paid!' Terry Ray, Angelo Dundee's light heavyweight boxer, said, 'We'll see about that; there is no way I am leaving here without my money!' We had no option — we had a flight to catch and we had return tickets. I had lost out again, but this time for a lot more than the £150 at Wigan.

14

COUCH VS. BARRYMORE

How I got on the Barrymore show I don't know. We went for an audition in some big, bleak rehearsal rooms, in South London I think. Steve Presnail drove us there — he was always willing to help but as usual he got lost. Tex wasn't much use either. I'm sure the last time he had been to London the cabs were drawn by horses.

Anyway, we got there. It wasn't much of an audition, as far as I was concerned. I skipped for a while, Tex held the pads for me to thump, I had a chat with a couple of people and came away. It was a bit boring really, and seemed like a waste of time after all that hassle with the traffic and trying to find our way, so it was quite a surprise when I was asked to appear on the show, but it was a good job they picked me. My bit was the only part worth watching — well that's what I thought, anyway!

The show wasn't filmed live, which was just as well, as some of the acts were cut, and I thought they needed to be. Michael Barrymore didn't even take part in the rehearsal, which was just as well, I suppose, as if I had hit him then like I did when it was being filmed I probably wouldn't have made it to the TV screens.

Lynn Perrie, Ivy in *Coronation Street,* didn't make it, I don't know why. When Lynn came back to the refreshment room, where the hangers-on had been watching the rehearsal on a TV monitor, Tex must have had his grumpy face on, so she said to him, 'Why are you sat there looking so miserable?'

Back comes the answer, loud and clear: 'I've been watching you for the last twenty minutes.' The other people sitting around tried to hide looks of shock, horror and amusement. Ms Perrie, apparently oblivious to his remarks, and not realising that Tex was a very different person from the average fan or luvvie duvvie from the entertainment world, tried to cheer him up with a kiss on the forehead! Tex jumped away and said, 'Push off, you silly old devil.' Poor Lynn was a bit taken aback — people didn't usually talk to her like that. I was killing myself laughing inside, but I had to control myself and tell Tex off. He didn't want to listen and kept muttering, 'Silly old fool!' I didn't mind Lynn Perrie, though, she was all right.

I wasn't very keen on the Kelly Family, though. They were like they were from a different world. I suppose they were, really. They were a band and singing group made up of young, and very young, males and females, some kind of travelling family. I think they were based in Germany at the time. Their music, which I'm afraid I really couldn't appreciate, had made their fame and fortune in Europe. We were told they had flown to England in their own private jet. They even had their own German bodyguards, God knows why — no one was hunting them down for autographs or anything. I thought their act was crap. As for clean, their costumes looked like a bunch of Morris dancers had discarded them because they weren't worth washing or ironing. Then there was an old woman, dressed all in white, pale, and with too much make-up on. She looked like, and wailed like, a ghost. She was supposed to be a singer but I'm sure she was only there for Barrymore to take the piss out of to make people laugh. It was a shame.

So it wasn't very surprising that I was the star of the show! When I went on stage to do my bit with Barrymore, I had to walk down some steps wearing a long purple dress, so long it was dragging on the floor. The dress was intended to disguise the fact that I was a boxer and I suppose it did. It undid down the front and came off like a dressing gown when it was time for me to strip down to my boxing kit and do some skipping and punching.

I got on all right with Michael when we chatted. He asked me what sort of protection I wore under my kit. I told him that I should wear a groin guard but I couldn't remember what it was called. He thought it might be called a cod-piece. I told him, 'It's not a cod-piece, it's got nowt to do with fish.' The crowd thought that was really funny. I don't know why.

We did some skipping — I was good and fast but Michael was a bit like a beginner. Then he held the pads while I hit them. It surprised him when he felt how hard and fast I punched. Then we sparred — well, almost. I did warn him it would be hard, but when I threw a few punches he fell over on the sofa. I whacked him on the head and in the ribs as he lay there, and he said, 'Hold on, hold on,' and went down on his knees on the floor. I tried to pull him up, and said, 'Get up, stop muckin' about!'

'I'm not muckin' about, love, any chance of pulling me head back out?'

'Try and hit me back,' I said.

'What do you mean, try and hit you back?'

Then he hit me without warning, so I clobbered him down on the settee again, and punched until he tried kicking me off. I told him, 'It's not kick-boxing, it's boxing, you don't have to kick as well, you div.' The crowd were loving it. Michael was grimacing and saying, 'Whose idea was this?' He then got a giant of a man out of the audience, who was nearly a foot taller than him and twice as wide! We got involved in a rough house wrestle and I got him down on the sofa and started hitting him, until Michael pulled me off, so I pushed him away. He got up, panting, told the big guy to go and sit down, and said, 'Ladies and gentlemen, Jane Couch!' Then he gave me a cuddle before I went off stage.

The audience had really enjoyed our bit of fun. At least *I* thought it was a bit of fun — poor Michael had a few sore bits!

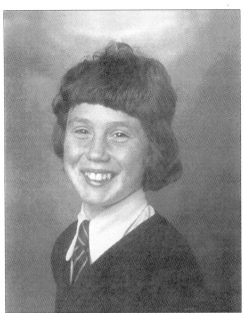

Top left: Me aged 5: I'm the one in the checked dress!

Top right: My school picture.

Bottom: With Tex, my coach and mentor, at Hartford airport in the USA, eating the pretzels that we never finished!

With two others that know how to throw a punch: Nosher Powell (*top*) and Roy 'Pretty Boy' Shaw (*bottom*).

Inset: My friend and 'night watchdog', Nipper

Training hard to retain my title.

Top: Tex and I take a well-earned break from my heavy training schedule.

Bottom: Outside Spaniorum Farm Gymnasium, where I do my training.

Inset: The farmhouse – an idyllic place to live.

Top: With Marvin Hagler before appearing on *The Frank Skinner Show*.

Bottom: Talking to Dick McTaggart, ex-Olympic Gold Medal winner. Dick was one of the UK's best-ever amateur boxers and fought in over 600 contests.

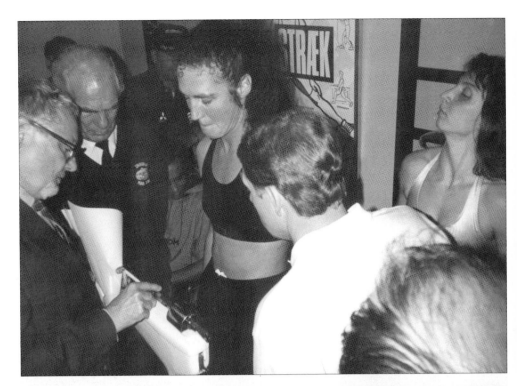

The WIBF World Title in Copenhagen. Weighing in before fighting Sandra Geiger (*top*) and bruised but victorious, accepting the WIBF belt with Tex.

Fighting Simone Lukic in November 1998. In the heat of the match (*top*) and celebrating my victory after the fight was stopped in the second round (*bottom*).

15

SIGNING MY LIFE AWAY

God! I don't know how I managed it, but I didn't half attract some tossers into my life when I started to become a bit famous. They came from all walks of life and they all wanted part of me, my fame, the money I didn't have, or my body. I don't know which was worse, those drooling over me or those after the non-existent cash. I think those with the randy thoughts were the easiest to handle — at least I knew where they were coming from and what they had in mind. It was those who thought they might be on to a good earner that were the more devious.

Through fame comes fortune, or so the saying goes. In my case it was more a case of *mis*fortune. One of the local papers was left lying about in an office in Bristol and was picked up and read by a London business man called Morris Rosen, who was there to attend a meeting. Considering how often there was a story and picture of me in the papers at that time it was far from an unusual occurrence. Right from the start the media liked me. They knew I was going to say something different from the other up-and-coming stars, and anyway I took a better picture than most of them. Morris Rosen must have thought so — either that or he could see my financial potential as a new type of boxing star and media celebrity. He rang Tex from the office and made an appointment to meet us at the farm.

When he arrived, he brought with him a boxing promoter called Roy Cameron, and the very well-known professional boxing matchmaker Frank Turner. They had a look at the gym, watched me work out a bit, and had a chat with me and Tex. I don't think they really understood my strong Lancashire accent, they were smoothy southerners with suits on.

They must all have been well impressed with me and the gym, anyway. Morris was back again within a few days with his solicitor, Andrew Brecher, plus a managerial contract for me to sign. Morris Rosen's entry into my life hadn't seemed in any way unnatural. Tex was satisfied that he was an honest, straightforward business man, and that was a rare achievement. Tex was quite happy for me to sign a three-year contract with Morris as my business manager, at first. At the time there was no other real option if I wanted to stay in full-time training. As usual I had no money — Steve Presnail had been helping me out, but his contributions were getting rarer, and apparently given with more reluctance.

Tex was optimistic about Morris's involvement in my career, but was a bit nervous about the 30% commission Mr Rosen wanted on all my boxing and associated earnings. If

Morris took 30%, and Tex was to take a trainer's commission and expenses for my keep, I would be fighting for nothing for the next three years! Before I signed it, though, Morris gave me the rosy picture. 'I'll give you a weekly allowance to cover your expenses and keep. You will get lots of PR work, TV shows, new clothes. You must sign off from Social Security, Jane, it's bad for the image we need to create. I will make sure you are OK for money.' To be honest, he did give me some money, but he could have never realised how much a trendy young woman like me needed to live comfortably and keep up with fashion. What he gave me was gone before I'd got it. Then he made his biggest mistake — he tried to re-create my image! 'Good idea,' said Tex, but he would, the grey-haired old bastard.

So, I get introduced to Rosemary Livingstone. 'This is my Personal Assistant,' says Morris. Rosemary was quite a bit older than me but not as old as Morris, I would say. I suppose some people would have said she was attractive, for her age. Quite smart, I suppose, but a bit toffee-nosed as far as I was concerned. She was married to a really old guy called Percy who I met later on — he was especially nice and we got on together like a house on fire. He was a bit posh too, so I expect it was a bit refreshing for him to have someone down to earth like me to talk to. He laughed when I cursed a bit! Not Rosemary, though: her job was to try to stop me using four-letter words and dressing in trendy teenage gear.

Her and Morris Rosen would have liked me to become an elegant, sophisticated young woman, with a southern accent, dressed in up-market clothes and styled hair. In fact, one time they took me to a photographic studio in London, got me dressed up in all this flash gear, messed about with my hair and put me through a photo shoot. I hated having to admit it, but the photographs that came out were brilliant. They would have excited any aspiring model, but they just weren't me! I hadn't enjoyed the shoot at all — I wasn't feeling very well. I had pneumonia — Tex said it was a cold, but he never believed anything I told him. I couldn't wait to get out of that studio. I was through that door in no time, rubbing the make-up off as I went — I hated the stuff. 'Fuck that, those bastards aren't putting me through that again!'

I had been promised the clothes I had worn for the shoot, just to get me to do it, I suppose. I didn't get any, though — they were soon stuck back on the rails. Just as well, really, as I'd probably just have slung them in the first dustbin I came to — along with the brand new costume and shoes I wore for a newspaper shoot!

They took me to a NatWest Bank to open a joint business account in the name of 'Fleetwood Promotions Ltd'. I met some other wanker there, he was introduced as my 'financial director', or some such name. Was I going to have to pay all these people out of my earnings?

A form was produced and I was asked to sign it. I wouldn't. No way — what Morris and the others didn't know was that I owed NatWest a lot of money and I didn't want them knowing where I was, or what I was up to. I asked Morris to let me use his mobile phone. I rang Tex and I told him what was going on. 'Don't sign anything.' I didn't.

I was really ill at ease because I didn't fully understand what was going on — they were talking about the company being 'floated on the stock market'. It was all too much for me to take in.

I was glad to get out of that bank but one scare followed another. Rosemary took me to a hairdresser, a black guy who was used to working with Afro-style hair, and who would know how to handle ringlets like mine. He was told, by her, to comb my hair out straight so that I would have 'soft feminine curls'. I was out of that chair. I'm perfectly feminine, thank you very much. I don't need straight hair to prove that. I hadn't had an Image Consultant very long, but it was long enough to know I didn't like it. I was quite happy with me the way I was.

Morris and Rosemary kept trying to give me this new 'persona', as somebody called it. They got a PR firm called

Public Image to try and get me TV work and things. I did get some work from them — they were good at their job and a lovely bunch of girls. All this meant that Tex was left to organise my boxing training and management without interference and in many ways he was much happier just teaching me to box and getting me to peak fitness. He didn't want, or need, any other jobs to do. And as time went by I spent more and more time living in the farm with Pat and Tex. Morris would telephone most days and check on my progress; sometimes he would talk to me, sometimes to Tex. I found it difficult conversing with him and would often make Tex take the call and pretend I wasn't there. Tex wouldn't be impressed — he would get that look of disapproval on his face that I came to know only too well. It wasn't that he didn't *like* speaking to Morris, he just didn't like giving me messages that I would forget, either accidentally or on purpose. Some people never gel, and me and Morris were a good example of that. We really had nothing in common. He was an educated, successful business man, living in a fine home with all the trappings of success, and accustomed to having his own way in life. Me, the product of a single-parent family in the fishing community of Fleetwood, my father having spent most of my childhood years in jail. I was born to be a rebel, under the star sign of Leo. I hated school and only went if I couldn't avoid it. I started drinking, fighting and learning the skills of surviving the hazards of the streets at an early age. What could this business manager and me have in common? No wonder it was hard for us to communicate with each other.

How much Mr Rosen had originally intended investing in my career I never knew. What I *felt* was that there was a reluctance to part with too much up front. I'd heard that you had to speculate to accumulate, but Morris's speculation wasn't adding up to my expectations. I was getting fed up with having to wait what seemed like ages to get a cheque through the post or some notes passed my way. Tex would try to disappear when I started on about money. He said, 'I can understand his reluctance to part with too much money before there is a return in sight. Anyway, Jane, your constant need for money reminds me of a fledgling bird in a nest with its mouth wide open, waiting to be fed.'

Pat and Tex looked after me, providing accommodation, and food if I didn't have any money to go out and buy my own. They weren't rich enough to invest much cash in me — in fact when Tex offered to lend me money I was too proud to take it at first. I didn't mind taking it off Morris, though, as he told me he was a property millionaire and that seemed fair game to me. As I spent money faster than it came, I became more and more depressed and insecure. It wasn't like being at home where I could go out and get a few bob one way or another, work, borrow off me mates, and there was always the loan man as a last resort. Now I was depending on other people for the first time and I didn't like it. I was so frustrated and felt so helpless at times that I couldn't stop the tears from flowing.

Morris would occasionally come to the farm and take me to my favourite chippy, Harry Ramsdens. Once, we were quietly eating and chatting and he suggested I move to London and train there. 'I don't want to move to London. I've lived there, it's crap.' Morris never mentioned that to Tex. Just as well — I can just imagine old Granddad's face and what he would have come out with! As it was, I carried on training at the farm, but became more and more depressed as the expected living allowance was spasmodic and less than I had been promised. Tex didn't know just what was going on, and said because of this he couldn't make any judgements; but he decided to make Morris aware of how I was feeling and sent him the following fax:

Morris,

As you will have realised from recent telephone conversations with Jane and myself, I have got a very unsettled young woman on my hands. Something has to be done and the problems, whether they are real or in Jane's mind, have to be resolved. I am a good coach and people, of all levels, who work closely with me improve their ability, but there is nothing I can do with someone who has lost the enthusiasm and will to work. Jane's will-power, even more than her boxing technique, is what makes her, possibly, unbeatable. So what has taken away this spark? There are several reasons.

Money

Jane comes from a culture that believes that money, wherever or however it comes, is meant to be spent. She is generous to a fault and finds it totally embarrassing if she cannot buy people (anyone) a drink, give away her boxing gloves, clothes, whatever. Old-fashioned 'home truths' and advice from me are not met with the kindest response.

Length of time between fights

'What am I doing all this training for if the fights keep getting cancelled? Even when I do fight, I don't get paid.' This I can relate to, it's equally disappointing for me as I too have to give a lot of myself, mentally and physically, to Jane's training.

'Whispering'

Whenever a manager has a potential star the 'whispering' starts — 'You would be better off in London', 'Why aren't you fighting more often?', 'So and so would get you more fights', 'Is that all you're getting? You should be getting more than that!' And so it goes — I lost unbeaten fighters when I was a manager, even though they were signed to me on a BBB of C contract. I could not compete financially with the big names and decided it was a bit pointless working hard for months or years to produce quality boxers for someone else to poach. I have always been aware that this could happen to Jane but until recently she has been fun and Pat and I both enjoy having her here.

Somehow we have got to get that 'fun' back.

Tex

To reinforce the message sent by fax, Tex knew he would have to speak to Morris face to face about the problems that concerned us all. We met him at a London hotel. We dined together, enjoyed the meal and then chatted over a drink until I thought I had better push off and leave them alone for a while.

Earlier in the evening Tex had given Morris a piece of paper, outlining in capital letters the things that were bothering us: JANE NOT SLEEPING, WORRYING, APPOINTMENT WITH DOCTOR, NO MONEY, NO SOCIAL SECURITY, NO INDEPENDENCE — the list went on, but it didn't seem to have been taken in. Tex tried to explain it all, with little success. The rich business man could never understand, or have experienced the trauma his newly signed boxer — and previously independent, carefree, free spirit — was enduring. Jane Couch, the Fleetwood Assassin, was nearing the end of her patience. I even went so far as to say to Tex, 'I'm packing in boxing, I'm going to get a job, I've had enough of living out of a suitcase, being stuck on a fucking farm, no family or friends to talk to. I'm going back to Fleetwood.' What my business manager thought of Tex's plea on my behalf I shall probably never know. What I *do* know is that it made no difference to the fact that I was still having to ask for money — and I didn't like that.

I decided to go home, get a job and train part-time. Tex wasn't at all impressed. 'You're crazy, you can't train part-time and box at your level. If you want to keep your World Champion's title you have to train even harder and learn more skills.' In the end he convinced me, and it was back to the farm for my workouts, at 10.30 and 6.30 — *exactly*!

16

FOXWOODS CASINO

The best thing about having Morris Rosen as my business manager was that he had one extremely good connection in the professional boxing world, Panos Eliades, a London accountant who was the financial backer of Panix Promotions, Lennox Lewis, and a host of other boxers. How close the friendship of Panos and Morris was never became completely clear. Morris said that they played tennis together. Panos said that he had once advised Morris on a possible company liquidation. However close their relationship, the important fact was that it produced a fight for me, my second world title defence. The opponent: Leah Mellinger, from Lancaster, USA who, according to her profile, was a black belt in karate, an undefeated FFKA World Champion kick-boxer with a 100% amateur record, and a professional record of three wins, a loss and a draw. The venue: Foxwoods Casino, Ledyard, USA. The date: August 7th 1997. It was a high-profile televised show, chosen to launch me as a personality as well as a boxer.

The other fights on the bill were all between male boxers. The star attraction for the evening was a return match between Roy Jones and Montel Griffin for the World Light Heavyweight Championship. It was expected to be one of the major fights of the year.

The journey to Connecticut started from the farm, as scheduled. Sandra, 'the Midget', arrived right on time, and Pat, in her role of caring wife and taxi driver, drove us to the coach station in the early hours of the morning. The coach left Bristol with more than adequate time to reach Heathrow for a midday flight to Newark, USA. That is, until a vehicle crash on the M4 brought everything to a standstill.

Nothing was moving. The driver turned off the engine and we were marooned on the motorway. Most of the passengers patiently waited, dozed, read or chatted. Not me! Patience may be a virtue but there are limits to mine — about five minutes on a good day, less on others. This was one of the others. I wanted to get moving, and moving right away. It didn't happen. I started yelling at Tex, 'It's your fault, I told you we should have gone by train, the fucking coaches always let you down. We'll never make it in time. You didn't listen. I told you.'

'Yes, Jane, I know you did, but accidents do happen. I was going on a train to Gatwick once and the train broke down. I was travelling to Germany and only just made the flight with literally seconds to spare.'

'No, it didn't!'

'Yes, it did.'

'Trains don't break down.'

'Yes, they do, that one did.' That was the end of the argument. Tex was off — he grabbed his bag and newspaper, moved to a seat in the back of the coach and started doing a crossword. He wasn't getting away that easily; I followed him and kept nagging him only to be met with, 'Jane, shut up, there is nothing we can do, just give me some peace.' God knows how long we were stuck. Then, at long last, the driver started the engine and we began to crawl forward. He finally made it into top gear, but it was going to be close. All we could do was wait and wonder.

We weren't the only ones waiting, wondering and worrying. Morris Rosen had been doing his share at the check-in desk. Who could blame him? With two minutes to go before they closed the boarding gate, Sandra, Tex and I strolled into view as if we didn't have a care in the world. It was Tex who had calmed us down — well me, anyway — saying, 'Look, there is no point in getting too excited or worried, we are either going to catch the plane or miss it, there's nothing we can do about it.' Oooh! I did hate him at times!

We were acting cool, but I know we were all glad to get into the departure lounge just before they locked the door. Then, just to add to our frustrations there was a problem with the plane and it was delayed for what seemed like hours. The plane wasn't the only thing delayed. Morris had mentioned £500 spending money to buy clothes and things, while we were in America. I assumed he would give me the money when we met at Heathrow Airport. He didn't. OK! We were late and he was cross but it wasn't our fault there was a traffic problem. Ah, well, I thought, I'll get it when we get to Connecticut. I never got £500. Morris did spend some money on me here and there, but I had to keep asking and I didn't like that — it was getting me moody and bad tempered. Even the Midge had a go at him about giving me some more money but he didn't seem to pay close attention to her either.

When we finally took off from Heathrow, me, the Midge and Tex sat together. Morris was alone four rows in front of us, and it wasn't long before Tex left to join him. I think he'd had enough of me for one day — I was getting restless and we hadn't even crossed the coast yet. Still, he wasn't going to escape me that easily. 'Granddad! Granddad! Granddad! I'm hungry!' I often said he was deaf and now he was trying to prove it. I kept on, and gradually each row of passengers joined in, 'Your granddaughter wants you.' I'd got him! He had to come back with his travel bag and organise some food!

We landed at Newark and then flew on to Hartford, where Morris hired a car to drive us to Mystic, where he had booked three excellent suites in the Residence Inn. I used to think all American cars were massive — this one wasn't, it was only just big enough to take the four of us and our luggage.

The hotel was great — smashing big rooms, swimming pool, all-weather tennis/basketball court, beautiful weather. It was like being on holiday, but training had to be done and the tennis court was ideal, before it got too hot. We were just finishing a light workout there one morning when the car Morris had hired pulled up in the adjoining car park. He had collected his PA, Rosemary Livingstone, from the airport. Much to our surprise she had travelled alone from England to join us. It was a bright sunny morning and Rosemary had dressed for the weather. She could well have been dressed for a part in an old-time Jamaican plantation film, and as any good actress would, she made an entrance. She was wearing a large-brim straw sun-hat and dark glasses, almost hiding her travel-worn features. As she floated towards us we were acknowledged with a limp-wristed wave and an almost enthusiastic 'Hi!' The long journey had obviously taken its toll, as there was no energy left for conversation. Rosemary disappeared into the hotel, not to be seen again until recuperation had restored her ravaged features.

Another late arrival to our small but multiplying team was Chris Webb. Chris had been following me for some while, making a 'fly-on-the-wall' documentary about me for his company, Outlaw Films. Chris was made of sterner stuff than

Rosemary, and he quickly overcame his late-night travelling, with a soothing amount of alcohol and an early morning to film a training session. Chris, like me, was from Lancashire, and like me he had also made the most of ruining his schooling, although at a much higher level. He had attended the world-famous Millfield School in Somerset. Chris was a good-looking chap in his early thirties. I could probably have fancied him a bit if he hadn't been such a nutcase. Like me, he believed pleasure should be mixed with business and that life should be enjoyed. On that super, sunny, American morning, Chris's idea of enjoyment was to try and imitate my skipping technique. I've seen lots of people skip — and *try* to skip — since I started boxing, and I must admit Chris wasn't bad: it was just the gear he was wearing that made us all laugh. Large brown boots, Doc Martens or something similar. I suppose they *could* have come out of the Army and Navy stores, but the socks *must* have — big woolly things, sagging over the boots. The khaki shorts he was wearing hung below his knees, and he had an off-white T-shirt, a baseball cap on back to front, and a cigarette dangling from the corner of his mouth. The picture of an aspiring athlete? No way, more the product of living too well, and working and playing too hard. Granddad thought the sight was too valuable to be left to fading memory, so he grabbed Chris's discarded video camera and recorded it for posterity. The 'fly-on-the-wall' got caught by the 'fly-on-the-wall'. It must have caused some amusement in the editing room.

In the brochure for Foxwoods Casino, it is described as the 'Wonder of the Connecticut Woods'. It would be hard to disagree with that description — it was a wonder we ever got out of those fucking woods! We went along, mile after mile of straight road, laid through the middle of a dense forest that could have stretched for ever, as far as I knew.

We would pass scarce, scattered houses, mostly individual buildings, all set back from the boring road in man-made clearings. They were dotted about haphazardly here and there, some with colourful flags flying. It looked as if people had thought, I'll build a house there, gone into the forest, felled some trees and just built it. I couldn't believe it. Who the fuck would want to live in the middle of a forest? What would they do? Where would they go? How would they get anywhere? It would take them a year the way they drive.

I had only glanced at the brochure, and I thought the picture of the casino was amazing — I couldn't wait to get inside it. Not Tex. He had studied the booklet and he started waffling. 'All this land is an Indian Reservation owned by the Mashantucket Pequot Tribal Nation. Years ago English and Dutch settlers came here, and with the help of the rival Mohegan tribe, almost completely annihilated the Pequots. In one attack alone the Pequot Fort at Mystic was burnt, and over seven hundred Pequots burnt. Just imagine all those Indians in warpaint with tomahawks and bows and arrows, lurking through those trees.' Poor old Granddad, there are times I think he never grew up.

Now the Indians, or 'Native Americans' as we were told is the politically correct name for them now, own the casino and all the land around it, and that's a lot! They don't scalp 'pale-faces' any more — they take their money legitimately at the gaming tables. In fact, from what we saw of it, the colour of your skin didn't matter: they took your money anyway.

When we finally got out of the trees, we came over the brow of a hill, and there lying below us was Foxwoods, the largest casino in the world. It was big! I don't know anything about architecture but this place almost took my breath away. It was a weird mixture, something between what I had imagined a large old cathedral would look like, and one of those cities from space you see in films. The car park alone seemed to go on for ever. It needed to, as Tex informed us from his boring brochure: 'This place has over 11,000 employees and receives 55,000 visitors a day.' Despite all those people coming and going, parking was no problem. A valet removed the car, almost before we got out of it, at the massive hotel entrance.

Me and Sandra legged it for the loo. Tex found the gym, and the scales, of course! We had a light workout before the sight-seeing tour started. The gym was high-tech, large but with only just enough space, free of machines, to skip, shadow-box and punch pads. Work over, and it was into the palatial shower room, which had everything from shoe-shining, free razors, bowls of fruit, the vitally important scales, and even Panos Eliades coming out of the sauna with just a towel draped round him.

My weight was no problem, so we gathered up some free fruit and the grand tour began. Up the escalators from the ground floor, the gym, the health shop, the foyer and God knows what else. Off the escalator into a shopping arcade with lots of good quality shops, market stalls, cinemas, restaurants, casinos. We found the hall where the boxing show was to be held. We couldn't go in to familiarise ourselves with the surroundings, as a bingo session was being held, so we peered through the windows of the doors.

The hall was big and filled with a mass of people concentrating on their bingo cards. 'My God,' says Tex, 'I haven't seen so many people with eyes down since I accidentally walked in on a Jehovah's Witnesses Convention in the Olympia Hall in Munich.' All I could manage to gasp was, 'Fuckin' hell!'

Inside the casino complex it was like being in another world, so many people saying, 'You're welcome' and 'Have a good day now', but somehow they didn't have the more relaxed friendliness we felt we were given in New Orleans. I liked the Native American staff, they were really nice, especially Running Bear — I quite fancied him. As for the young women in their short skirts, wearing headbands with feathers in them, I don't think they had ever seen a wigwam. Most of them were the wrong colour anyway.

One guy who did look as if he'd seen a wigwam, or perhaps more accurately a tent in a jungle, was Arthur Mercante, who looked like he had just come back from safari.

Or perhaps he'd been for an audition for the part of 'the great white hunter' in a Tarzan film. He was dressed in a khaki drill outfit, long shorts, just below his knees, thick woolly socks up to the knees, a tunic with large patch pockets for whatever great white hunters carry about with them and, of course, the silk scarf knotted loosely around his neck, to keep the mosquitoes off.

I'd seen him refereeing so many times on TV, in some big fights with famous names. I was really excited when we met and after a while I said, 'I must take you to meet my coach, he will be really impressed to meet you.' Tex was waiting to meet someone in the shopping street of the casino. I almost dragged Arthur towards him. I said, 'I'll bet you don't know who this is?'

I couldn't believe his answer. 'No, I don't know who this is.'

'It's Arthur Mercante!'

'Who is Arthur Mercante?' I looked at Tex — had he suddenly gone senile in the half hour or so since I had last seen him? Perhaps it was jet-lag. Everybody in boxing knew Arthur Mercante! I tried again. 'He's the famous referee.'

Tex had another look at Arthur. 'Oh! Is he? Well, I don't like boxing. I think it should be banned. I'm only here under protest. If it wasn't for her needing someone to look after her, I wouldn't be here.'

Mr Mercante just didn't know what to say, and then that look came on Tex's face, and I knew it was a wind-up. I tried to explain to Arthur that Tex was only teasing, and it was his English sense of humour, but I don't think the great white hunter saw the funny side of it — he said, 'Goodbye' and pushed off. I wasn't all that impressed either, so when we joined Cedric Kushner, the large South African promoter, at the bar, I told Tex to keep his sense of humour to himself and not upset anyone else.

So he left me alone and let me give Cedric the Couch chat-up treatment without interfering. Cedric Kushner was sat at the bar, more casually dressed than I would have expected him to be. He looked surprised when I asked for a whisky. I told him, 'Yeah! I like a drop of whisky before a fight!' It wasn't what a promoter expects to hear from a boxer, and he certainly didn't expect my next suggestion that I become the next Mrs Kushner. He was obviously very flattered, but he didn't jump at the offer — just as well, because he was well down my list of proposals that night!

My first sight of Leah Mellinger at the weigh-in, held in a large cinema inside the casino complex, prompted me to say, 'She looks like a fuckin' tart.' Needless to say, Granddad wasn't impressed. 'She looks quite smart.' Smart! She looked as if she was dressed for something very different than a weigh-in for boxers, perhaps an audition at a model agency, or even a low-budget film. She was wearing high heels, a short tight black dress, and her face was painted up with a heavy make-up.

Me and Leah both made the weight OK. Too OK for me, I was 2lb under. I told Tex, 'I'm always giving away weight, they are always bigger than me. I could have eaten a lot more than you let me.'

'Jane,' he replied, 'what you have eaten in the last few days would have kept a navvy and his family satisfied for a week. Anyway I checked Leah's weight as she weighed, it was only ounces more than you.'

'I know that, but she has dried down more than me.'

I was hungry and I was pissed off. I got more and more pissed off — and hungrier and hungrier — before I got to see the doctor for my medical check-up. Tex found some fruit and sandwiches to stop me moaning. They were a bit stale, but a little Mexican flyweight, who looked like he had been drying out for days, nearly snatched Granddad's hand off with delight when he was offered the leftovers.

The thorough medical examination was not without its drama. The BUPA examination result papers, that had cost around £1,000 in England, were apparently worth nothing in the USA. The eagerly awaited fight looked doomed. It was a good job it was a male doctor! I forgot my moans and hunger pangs, turned on the charm and charisma, and captivated the doctor with my plaintive pleas to be allowed to box. He was hooked. 'Well, I'll just give you one or two co-ordination tests to check your brain's reaction...Yes, very good, you will be fine.'

Launching my career under the Rosen banner was an expensive exercise for Morris. As well as paying out for four, possibly five, air fares to Connecticut, three excellent en-suite hotel rooms, car hire, plus a lot of extras, he had committed himself to paying Leah Mellinger's fight purse of ten thousand dollars. The payment was designed to ensure that I, his new star signing, would be seen on an ample stage. I, in turn, was to forfeit my own purse for the privilege of exposure. It was a forfeit of which the State Boxing Commissioner totally disapproved. He ruled, 'No boxer can box in this State for nothing!' Morris's reasoning was rejected. We later heard that a minor controversy took place, and a suggested fee of five thousand dollars was reduced to two thousand dollars before agreement could be reached that that was what I should be paid for fighting.

This extra contribution from Morris Rosen may well have been the reason for his increased reluctance to give me more money. I've never liked having to ask for things and thought it would automatically be given to me — it was embarrassing and really pissed me off with Morris. I mean, he could have afforded it, being a millionaire and dealing in all that property and stuff. Me, I had fuck all. Being without money is the worst thing that could ever happen to me. I would keep seeing something I wanted to buy, and have to borrow off the Midge or Tex, and he was even more reluctant to part with his money than Morris Rosen! 'What do you want it for? You don't need that, you can buy it cheaper at home!'

I didn't even want to go into a bar because I couldn't buy a round of drinks. Tex was trying to keep my mind focused on the fight, which was the reason we were there in the first place, but I was unhappy and felt hard done by. An atmosphere developed that you could have cut with a knife. It became Us and Them: 'Us' being Tex, Sandra and me, all being caught in Chris's 'fly-on-the-wall' video camera. 'Them' being the business manager and his PA.

The day before the fight we'd had a good laugh. Tex and I were wandering about, not particularly worrying if we got lost or not, in the massive casino buildings, when the Midge ran up and said, 'Roy Jones is loosening up in the gym, let's go and get his autograph.' We dashed off leaving Tex. In the gym there were two black guys having a gentle sparring session — we watched but weren't over-impressed with what we thought was the world's top pound-for-pound boxer, but we still wanted his autograph. When the boxers had finished and taken their gloves off, we handed them paper and pen for their signatures. We had a few pleasant words with them and left. As we looked at what they had written, we couldn't read their names, but one thing was certain — neither of them was Roy Jones! I could have swatted that Midge. Unfortunately, we had to let Tex in on the secret — he thought it was hilarious. He would...

It had seemed a long wait before the first bell rang for my battle with Leah Mellinger, but it finally happened and it was hard. Despite her over-the-top, cover-girl look, Leah was a strong, fit, tough fighter. As always, I had had a good long warm-up, but not surprisingly I wasn't really mentally prepared for what was in store for me. I was a bit tentative as I tried to focus on what I was doing and why I was there in the first round. There nearly wasn't a second round — Mellinger hit me with a right that staggered me, shocked the Midge and made Tex's hair go a shade greyer all in a few seconds.

That punch did two things: it nearly put me to sleep, but it actually woke me up to the job in hand. After the first round, a quick revival in the corner, and a lecture from Granddad about keeping my hands up, I went out for the second with more care and determination. I began to get the upper hand — I was fit and I was working. We had been hearing, before the fight, what a marvellous training regime Leah had been through in preparation for this fight, but she wasn't as fit as me. I was grinding her down slowly.

Once, as she tried to lean on me and use her strength, I stepped neatly outside her left hand and hit her with a sharp right to the head. I was amazed to hear the referee, Steve Smoger, say, 'Nice move, champ!'

After that, though, Steve's words were not so full of praise. I had Leah in trouble: I'd hit her with a good right hand, over her left, and it looked as if I was going to stop her. I got a bit too enthusiastic and went after her, my head down, chin tucked in. Mr Smoger stopped the contest and gave me a long lecture about careless use of my head. By the time he had stopped talking, Leah Mellinger had recovered enough to finish the ten rounds.

Michael Buffer, the renowned Master of Ceremonies, announced the result, a unanimous points victory for me! As Mr Buffer finished his announcement, and the crowd showed their appreciation for what turned out to be the best fight of the night, I cornered him and said, 'My mum fancies you.' The quick reply — 'You're not so bad yourself!'

My mind buzzes more than usual after a fight, so many different thoughts varying from excited elation, pride and just satisfaction for a job well done. At least I didn't cry this time, but I did do some pretty colourful cursing at the American telephone system as I tried to phone my mum and tell her how I had got on. Tex had the same trouble phoning Pat, so it wasn't just my hyperactive mind — I'll bet that woman telephone operator thought I was a nutcase. We both got our calls through in the end, though.

Back in the sheeted-off section of the big dressing room that gave each boxer some privacy, things were quiet. The security was so strict that no one could get in, but Steve

Smoger paid us a visit. He said, 'That was the first time I have refereed a women's fight, and it's the first time I have never had to say "Break" throughout a contest.' He gave me a kiss and congratulated me. I bet that was the first time he ever kissed a boxer!

Two other comments passed about my efforts are worth mentioning. George Foreman, the ex-World Heavyweight Champion, who was doing inter-round summaries for TV at ringside, said to Tex as we passed him, 'You've got a good girl there.'

17

THE HIJACKING OF JIMMY FINN

I've met a lot of taxi drivers in my life. Most of them let me get out of the car on my own, some have had to drag me out and leave me on my doorstep. None of them were ever more willing to help than the giant, laid-back character who first drove us from Mystic to Foxwoods Casino. His size, looks and manner would have made him a perfect understudy for the butler in the Addams family.

To us he was 'Lurch' on first sight. When he found out who I was, he really took a fancy to me and couldn't do enough for us, especially when I conned him in to the sell-out show to watch me fight.

Often after a boxing show there is a party, and Chris, Sandra, Tex and I tried to find it. Morris and his PA had long since disappeared, but Lurch was right at heel. We traipsed around for a long while before discovering that the party spirit seemed to have faded away with the fight fans. So it was time for the trip back to Mystic and the pre-arranged party in our suite at the Residence Hotel.

As we waited outside the foyer of the casino, while a valet retrieved Lurch's car from the dark depths of the massive car park, we were joined by Jimmy Finn, vice-president of the WIBF, and the official in charge of the female title bout that evening. He was staying in the hotel next to us. 'Do you think you could give me a lift back to the hotel?'

'Of course, Jimmy.' It had been a good evening, we had all had a drink or two, and would have felt kindly disposed to our worst enemy. Jimmy Finn didn't *quite* fit that category.

With Lurch back in the seat of his car, we all piled in, Chris in the front, Jimmy and Tex crammed in the back with us girls. It was a fairly long ride back to Mystic, and often the devil finds work for idle hands or in this case 'minds'. Tex's mind, to be precise...

We had been driving along the long tree-lined roads at what seemed to be about ten miles an hour, us girls cackling away, with Chris occasionally joining in. Tex was quiet, but his mind active, thinking, Jimmy Finn? Why am I so pleasant and understanding towards him? This man has probably caused me more problems, and irritations, than many people I have worked with. He has let Jane down before. It's time he was taught a lesson. 'Lurch, stop the car. We have an impostor in the back. He's not really a WIBF official, he has got to get out.'

Lurch hit the brakes — it didn't make much difference, we weren't going that fast anyway — and came round to the back door, opened it and started to drag Jimmy out saying, 'Get out of my car, they don't want you here, get out!' Tex was pushing Jimmy with great enthusiasm and enjoyment. Jimmy was resisting with equal vigour — it was dark and lonely outside the car.

'No, Tex, no, Tex, be-jaysus, I can't get out here.'

Lurch was insistent. 'Get out, they don't want you.'

Tex was helpless with laughter, but had to rescue Jimmy. 'It's all right, Lurch, let him stay, we will take him back to the hotel with us.' Like a dog with a bone, Lurch wasn't pleased to let go, but the joke had gone far enough — well almost.

We arrived back at Mystic still in high spirits — well, the Couch team was, if not our now subdued passenger. Suddenly he came alive: 'Stop, stop, that's my hotel.'

'It's OK, Lurch, keep going, Jimmy's coming back to the party with us.'

'I don't want to go to the party,' he wailed. 'I've got to ring Barbara [Barbara Buttrick, President of the WIBF].'

Jimmy became keener to join the party when Lurch 'helped' him up the stairs. 'Have a drink, Jimmy.'

'I don't want a drink.'

'Have a drink!'

He had a lager. 'Can I go now?'

'No, have another drink.' Another can of lager and Jimmy Finn was beginning to get into the spirit of the occasion. Well enough, at least, to argue with Tex about various aspects of women's boxing. Tex was thoroughly enjoying the 'discussion', as he called it, when Jimmy's voice, raised in defensive tones, captured Lurch's attention. For some while Lurch had been totally preoccupied with chasing me around, trying to get me to stand still long enough to kiss me. Keeping me still for any length of time is like trying to trap a sunbeam in a jam-jar, and Lurch was having just about as much success.

The Irish brogue distracted our driver from his hunt, and he decided to beat Jimmy Finn up. 'I don't like the Irish and I don't like you!'

Jimmy, now looking for a saviour, reverted to his 'Oh be-jaysus!'

Help came from an unlikely source. Chris Webb,

unfortunately camera-less for the moment said, 'Oh, go on, Jane, give him a kiss to calm him down.' Lurch's dream was almost fulfilled, and I offered him my lips. But as the giant closed in on me, my sympathy for the WIBF vice-president disappeared — I would rather have seen Jimmy beaten up than kiss Lurch. 'Ugh! I can't!'

During the distraction, Mr Finn had made a Houdini-like escape.

Lurch was the next to go, in the early hours of the morning. We never saw him again, which was a shame as he had been a good sport, especially the way he had terrorised Jimmy Finn.

In his absence, Chris Webb resumed his rightful role as clown prince, keen to add trampoline skills to his previous skipping prowess. Fortunately neither the bed nor Chris broke as one of his upward bounces was a little off-centre, and he landed flat on his back, head against the wall, grinning the inane grin of one who had had too much to drink, knew it, but was enjoying the feeling anyway. Tex, too, had been drinking, but not enough to stop him grabbing the ever-present video camera and filming the whole gymnastic exhibition. Another fun moment for the editing room.

Then he made a mistake that has haunted him ever since. 'Taste the Tequila,' I said. It was an order, not a suggestion.

'No, I don't like Tequila.'

'Taste it.'

'*No.*' It was a typical Tex versus Jane power struggle over nothing, so, on this occasion, he thought he would humour me. He tasted it. 'God, it's awful, I told you I didn't like it!' The damage was done — that sip registered as half a bottle in my mind, and he was never allowed to forget it, or deny it!

Shortly after the drink from the Tequila bottle, he made his way, possibly a little more carefully than normal, back to his room.

Midge and me were still dancing about the room, laughing, music blasting and I was singing. There was a nice young man on reception, he kept ringing the room saying, 'Miss Couch, can you *please* turn the music down, people are complaining in the room next door.' So I thought I would give them something to complain about and went and banged on their door, but there was no answer to my knock. I went down to reception and said to the man, 'Look you, I told you we were having a party and you said it would be OK, now you're telling us to stop. What's up with you?'

'It's not me,' he said, 'it's your neighbours, and it *is* half past three in the morning.' I agreed to turn the music down, but without any music and everyone else gone it was suddenly a bit boring. And when you've just defended your title in a hard fight in front of a big crowd, you feel like partying!

Using the telephone was one of my favourite ways of passing the time, but who could we call? We didn't even know what time it was anywhere else. I decided upon Japan — not one of my regular calls, but my brother, Tom, had gone there on tour with his band. He couldn't have known what time it was in America either, because he had phoned up *before* the fight to find out the result!

I knew what hotel he was staying in, and where it was, so I got the Midge to make the call — she was more used to long-distance calls than me, her working in an office and stuff. It didn't take her long to get through to the hotel, but the woman who answered was talking in Japanese and didn't speak English. Midge started shouting down the phone, 'I want to talk to Tommy Couch.' The woman didn't have a clue what the Midget was on about. 'Tommy Couch, put him on the phone now.' After a few minutes Midge got pissed off with asking for Tom and she banged the phone down.

Then she decided she was going to telephone her office — we reckoned it must be morning in England and she could tell the other office staff the result of the fight. Somehow she got straight through to the manager of the branch of General Accident, where she worked. We took it in turns to tell him all about the fight and what a great time we were having. He said to me, 'Have you had a drink?'

'Yeah! We're pissed out of our minds,' I said. He took it very well and didn't sack Midget when she got back!

We were still bored and wanted to go to a disco or something, but that part of America seemed to have gone to sleep before we'd even started partying. We started wandering around the corridors of the hotel, and we banged on a few doors but nobody answered. Then I had the bright idea of waking up Morris. I thought this would be a good time to discuss a few things. Midge said, 'You had better phone him first, see if he is awake.' I think I must have woke him up, because he *did* sound sleepy. I said, 'It's me, Jane. We're coming down for a drink with you.'

'You're not,' he said. 'Whatever time do you think it is?'

Then I went into one. 'You miserable bastard, I've just won a really hard and important fight. You haven't even had a celebratory drink with us.' I was gobbing off — Morris had got on my nerves for a while and I had felt like saying a lot more.

Morris wasn't impressed. 'I'll see you in the morning, Jane,' he said, and put the phone down.

Midge and me gave up on getting any more excitement that night, but there was still some drink left, so we sat drinking and chatting for another hour or so. We laughed some more about our phone calls and then started on about Morris, the way he was as a business manager, and how he was with us. We thought he didn't fit in. He didn't seem at home in the boxing world and he certainly didn't understand me, which I suppose wasn't really surprising. I don't expect he had ever met a street-fighting, boozing, boxing fisherman's daughter before — not a lot of them about in Kensington. We waffled on a bit, decided it was going to be impossible to work with Morris again, and eventually dropped off to sleep.

Bang, bang, thump, thump. 'Come on, wake up, we're going in five minutes, lovely day, wakey, wakey.' Oh, God. It was Tex again, kicking and banging on the door to wake up. I never could understand how he could get up so early after a piss-up and be so cheerful — as if he had a full night's sleep. He wasn't normal!

Midge and me felt like hell, but we would have felt worse if we had known about the nightmare journey in front of us.

We grabbed some fruit from the breakfast room, and met Rosemary and Morris outside by the car. If the atmosphere around us had been a bit cool before, today it was *icy*. It was going to be a long journey home. It turned out to be longer than we expected! The car had been just about OK, travelling from Hartford Airport to Mystic, if not exactly spacious or comfortable. Now, for the return trip, it was going to have to carry one more person with some big luggage, Mrs Rosemary Livingstone!

She was going to have to share the back seat with Tex, with a large suitcase stuck between them. Morris, at least, had a seat to himself as the driver. Me, I had the Midget on my knees. She might have only weighed just over eight stone, but she felt like a fucking ton on my fight-sore body.

Before we could start the journey to the airport, I had to get my fight payment cheque cashed. We had hoped a local bank would do it for me, but no, we would have to go via Foxwoods. I should have cashed the cheque the night before, but Morris had been looking after it for safe-keeping. He was probably very sensible — if I had cashed it, half of it would have been spent on the spot.

So, we all crammed into the car. Somehow the casino seemed a lot farther away than it had the night before. We arrived, extricated ourselves with considerable relief, and stretched our legs. That's when the pantomime began. 'Who has got the cheque?' Morris? No. Rosemary? No. Tex? Not interested. Me? Don't be daft! Pockets were searched, Morris's case, the glove compartment in the car. No cheque!

A phone call to the Residence Inn solved the mystery — a

cleaner had found the cheque, left in Morris's room. We were paying a return visit to Mystic far sooner than we could have expected. We all packed back into the car, the Midget bouncing on my knee, and Tex craning his neck away from the suitcase. When we got back to the hotel, Tex, who had had enough of lop-sided travelling, said 'I'll wait here while you go and cash the cheque.' But there was no escape. He was told, 'Get back in, we'll be going straight on to the airport.' And so back to Foxwoods!

Worse was to come. Prior to this day, we had travelled to and from Foxwoods several times, on each occasion with no problem. Not this time! Morris took the wrong turning, and we were hopelessly lost. Foxwoods Casino, the largest casino in the world, couldn't be found. I was going mad. 'Where the fuck is it? All these bastard trees! I'm sick of it, let me out of this fucking car!' What I thought I was going to do, out in the wilds, I don't know, but I was really pissed off — and sore! With all the straight roads and seemingly never-ending forest on each side, the likelihood of ever seeing the casino again — or the aircraft we were booked on — was looking pretty slim.

Then our saviour appeared in the form of an old man, who seemed to have ambled out of nowhere. He pointed us in the right direction. What a relief when we found Foxwoods — straight out of the car and stretch, stretch, stretch!

The cheque finally cashed, we were back into the car like the Keystone Cops. Homeward bound! Now, on the main highway we couldn't get lost, especially as Rosemary had taken over as back-seat navigator: 'Move over, Morris. Turn now, Morris. That driver's let you in, Morris, acknowledge him.' I was getting more and more pissed off. I started moaning and groaning more than ever. I'd fought ten hard rounds the night before, and it was beginning to tell. The Midget was perched on my knee and trying to massage some life into my aching arms.

We arrived at Hartford Airport and, finally, the departure lounge. If the earlier atmosphere had been tense, it was now electric. Not unexpectedly, our flight had long gone, but we were lucky enough to be booked on a later flight that had just three seats vacant. Morris and Rosemary appeared happy to wait for the next flight to New York.

It had been a while since we had eaten, and Morris went to the refreshment bar to buy us all a snack. He came back with a large pretzel for each of us. Neither Sandra, Tex or me had tasted pretzels before, but it didn't matter — we were hungry enough to eat anything, or so we thought. We all took a bite, and it was like chewing salty cardboard! I caught Tex looking at me, and said, 'It's a bit salty, isn't it?' For some reason we both felt the comment was hilarious. We burst out laughing. The Midget was also having a hard time with her 'treat' and couldn't help joining in with our laughter.

After the frustrating and irritating hours we had spent driving around and hanging about, it was a great relief to be able to laugh again, and the more I laughed, the more Tex laughed, both of us with tears streaming down our cheeks. Not one to miss a good picture, Sandra quickly focused her camera and the moment was captured forever.

Sitting to one side of us, Rosemary and Morris both seemed quite happy with their snack, and must have wondered what the semi-stifled hilarity was all about. We couldn't eat the pretzels, but we had no idea what to do with them. It would have been too rude, even for me, just to throw them away. Tex was first to solve his problem. He stood up, put the pretzel to his mouth, and walked away as if he was chewing it. Sneaky old bastard, he got out of sight, found a waste bin and dumped the thing. When he came back, me and Sandra were still pretending to nibble at ours. 'Where's yours?' I was always suspicious of what Tex was up to, especially when I couldn't see him.

'I've eaten it.'

'You lying bastard, what have you done with it?' Being closely watched by the two of our group who had presumably enjoyed their snack, it was a bit difficult for Tex to own up to what he had done, but the Midget guessed. She suddenly decided to go walkabout and I wasn't far behind her.

Our flight was announced, brief goodbyes were said, and finally, hours later than scheduled, we were homeward bound. Once on the flight we were in a much better frame of mind, and if I had known that I was never going to speak to Morris Rosen again I would have been even happier. I had had enough of promises to make me rich and famous.

Tex, as usual, tried to see both sides of the problem. He knew what was annoying me, but he also knew, probably better than anyone, what an extreme problem people had working closely with me, especially if they didn't live up to my expectations — and as far as I was concerned, Morris hadn't. There was a clause in our contract I believed he'd broken. In fact, when he didn't even telephone me when we got back to England, I thought he had probably had enough of my company anyway. So I faxed him a letter telling him I believed he had broken his contract with me and therefore was no longer my business manager.

I still didn't get a call from him, but I did get a letter from his solicitor, Andrew Brecher, saying that Morris had not breached the contract and would be expecting repayment of all the money he had 'expended on your behalf' and '30% of the further net receipts generated by you from, and incidental to, your boxing career during the term of the agreement'.

When I spoke to Andrew on the phone about the situation I intended to be polite, but he didn't seem to want to listen to my side of the story. He said they would take me to court, sue me, and my career would be over. That did it. 'Right, you bastards. Take me to fucking court. I've got fuck all to sue.' I carried on, a bit strong, for a while and I think Andrew got the message. Poor chap, I don't expect anyone had ever spoken to him like that before. They didn't bother me again. What I had told Andrew was true — I still had no money, and most of what I hoped would be coming I owed.

Not for the first time, and certainly not the last, I

wondered if being a boxer was worth all the hassle and hard work when the possible monetary reward seemed as remote as the pot of gold at the end of the rainbow. Yet that strange hold boxing has over people that get deeply involved in the sport had got me, and I knew I wasn't ready to leave it for a while.

18

REPORTERS, OLD FOGIES AND WOMEN'S BOXING

In all walks of life, you meet people you get on with, those you can tolerate, and those you can't. Reporters were no different. Just occasionally, the odd one came along who fancied his chances with me in the ring, rather than just trying to chat me up outside of it.

One of these was a scrawny little bloke called Gavin Evans, the boxing correspondent from *Esquire* magazine. He even brought his kit along to spar with me! As always I was happy to play along and move about gently for a while. Not him! He tried to take my head off. I had to give him a couple of light taps to quieten him down. Then he writes in his article, 'I open my account with a double jab and a hook to her face and one to her ribs...' In his dreams! He was honest enough to continue, 'But my fifteen minutes of fame passes, the gas runs low and the opposition changes gear...' Changes gear? I didn't even get *into* gear. At least I didn't drop him which I did to one or two others. Tex would say, 'When you interview Jane, keep out of her reach.'

I was more gentle with Colin Hart of the *Sun* newspaper. He was old and grey like Granddad. We got on really well together, so I didn't hit him — well, if I did it wasn't very hard. He was a right old smoothie, full of charm, and I thought, At last, I am going to get a good write-up by possibly the most famous boxing journalist in the country. I did, but it was more about me and my past than my boxing.

Colin took us out to lunch, and we had a really good chat about boxing and boxers, old-timers and the modern fighters. Colin, a real Muhammad Ali fan, told us about him, what a nice chap he was and how he was the best heavyweight of all times. Tex disagreed. 'Ali wasn't my favourite, he had too much to say for himself, couldn't fight inside, and should have been disqualified for holding. Give me a fighter like Rocky Marciano. I know he was a bit of an "odd lot", but he must have trained so hard, got so fit and gave everything he'd got in the ring. I know he wasn't the cleverest of boxers, he was quite small, but...'

'Shut up, Grandad! Rocky was one of my first heroes too, but Ali was special.' I think Colin was surprised that I knew something about boxing, and boxing history. After all, I was a woman and he didn't approve of women's boxing. He approved of me as a woman though!

He wasn't the only one to disapprove of women's boxing. I had been through it all countless times before, and I suppose, not surprisingly, most of the bad comments came from middle-aged and older men. What was surprising was how many of these older blokes thought, because they had done a bit of boxing when they were younger, they could cope with me in the boxing ring. Every now and again some unsuspecting veteran training in the gym would say, 'I'll spar with you!' Tex would say, 'I wouldn't if I were you.' When they insisted, he would give in saying, 'Be it on your own head!' If they were all right and didn't take liberties, I would pull my punches and let them feel they were boxing OK; but as always there were the cocky bastards — I could read their minds: 'She is only a woman, I'll show her what a *man* can do.' When he saw a bloke had a bad attitude, Tex would shrug his shoulders and let me get on with it. In fact, I know he enjoyed it when I put them in their place.

One guy in particular, who had been arguing with Tex about how high the left hand should be held, really made our day when he came at me with his left at waist level. As he lunged towards me, intent on battering me, I hit him with a right cross, flush on the chin, and he went out like a light before he hit the canvas. I looked at my normally critical trainer, who did not approve of me hurting anyone of lesser ability, and he was grinning his face off! 'That was the best right hand you have ever thrown.' When my over-confident sparring partner dragged himself back to the corner, Tex couldn't help adding to the guy's hurt pride by saying, 'I told you you should keep your left hand up.'

It wasn't long before I earned respect in the gym. Boxers and keep-fit enthusiasts alike all admired me for the serious effort I put into my training. The fitness training was hard, but in a way it was easier for me to cope with that than learn boxing skills. I was going to be fit, strong, and had been in enough brawls to stand toe to toe with any woman and win a slugging match. What did I want to dance about poking out poncy left-hand leads for?

It was something Tex and I disagreed about for a long time. I wanted to be a tough, crowd-pleasing fighter; he wanted me to be a clever boxer. 'The worst thing you can be in professional boxing,' he would say, 'is a crowd pleaser. You will end up with a smashed-in face and a lot fewer brain cells.' To remind me of this fact he made me pin up in my room the photograph of a boxer whose nose had been flattened all over his face. 'If you don't keep your hands up and learn to box, that's how you will look before long!'

Whether it was the photograph, or Tex's constant nagging which, like water on a stone, finally made its mark, my boxing skills gradually became recognised. With this recognition I began to be accepted more as a successful boxer, and less as a freak show. Even Claude Abrams, the editor of *Boxing News*, did a complete about-turn in his thoughts on women's boxing, and recently praised me for my efforts in beating Sharon Anyos on points at Raynes Park in October 1999. 'If this had been a man's fight,' he said on TV, 'people would have been talking about it for months, and I don't see that because they are women, they should be treated differently.'

That really was a breakthrough, but more for me, rather than women's boxing in general. A couple of years or so earlier, that wouldn't have bothered me. I was boxing because I wanted to box, and to be honest I couldn't have given a fuck about any other women boxers taking up the sport. I wasn't interested in opening up the floodgates for a load of women to apply for boxing licences. I wasn't interested in being a flag-bearer for feminism or women's rights. I just wanted to be left alone to train hard, win all my fights, and be known as the woman who had held the world title unbeaten for a record amount of time.

It wasn't to be. I began to realise that, whether I liked it or not, I was becoming a role model and figurehead for women's boxing in the UK, and to a lesser degree for boxing in general. Lads and girls would come to the gym asking me to help them learn the sport, and give them advice. I would get letters, E-mail and phone calls from far and wide, and after the initial irritation and impatience I began to get some pleasure from helping people.

Tex said I was a natural coach, but though I wouldn't

admit it, I did enjoy working with youngsters and watching them box. Twelve-year-old Harry Bartlett and his brother Tommy were great little lads. I would have liked to work closely with them and make them into champions. Claire Cooper, a twenty-year-old country girl, showed talent and had a sense of humour — in fact, I think she was off her head, her! I travelled hundreds of miles to see her win her first amateur fight.

Much as I liked helping and advising the female boxers, it *was* frustrating. The ABA had passed rules saying that girls could box, but as far as I was concerned that was window dressing or, as people say now, just being 'politically correct'. There certainly wasn't much co-operation from clubs and amateur coaches. So many girls said, 'The coaches won't let us in the clubs, and if they do they won't coach us.' I would tell them, 'Go back again, they have to let you in, it's the ABA rules.'

If Tex had half a chance, he would grab an ABA coach and say, 'Why don't you coach girls?' The answer would vary: the older guys just not wanting to see girls in the gyms, and certainly not boxing, the not-so-old coaches just not knowing how to go about coaching girls — some even worrying about being in a situation where they could be accused of sexual harassment.

The governing body of professional boxing in the UK, the British Boxing Board of Control, made a token gesture towards being seen to condone women's boxing by licensing a few women boxers, even though many of the members of the board could not give their full approval. As far as I was concerned, some of these women should never have been given licences — maybe some of the old die-hards of the BBB of C thought boxing for females would self-destruct if the women boxing were of such a poor standard that no one would want to watch them. That wouldn't happen while I was boxing!

When my copy of the revised rules of the BBB of C for

the year 2000 came through the post, I read it, with great interest, looking for the inclusion of rules for women. There were none! Not even using the words 'she or he' or 'her or him' when referring to boxers.

It doesn't do for me to think too much about these doddering old bastards' opinion of women boxing. The more they waffle on about 'Oh! You might get your nose broken,' or more frequently, 'If you get hit on the chest too much you might get cancer', the more I get pissed off with them. What about the blokes? God, I've seen a few broken noses in the dressing rooms and if, as no one has proved, cancer could be caused through a blow to the chest, why haven't some of the blokes got it? After all, some of the heavyweights have got bigger tits than me! Perhaps *they* should be made to wear chest protectors!

Really, I think chest protectors are a fucking nuisance and in my early fights I didn't wear them. I always thought they did more harm than good. Let's face it, it's far better to block a punch to the body with your elbows, than be hit on an open target because you are being restricted by the chest protector and can't tuck your arms in. Anyhow, a hard blow is still hard even if you have some padding on your chest, and with some of the junkie plastic guards it hurts even more.

The only doubts I ever had about getting seriously damaged, and believe me every boxer has doubts at times, was the fact that every time I got hit to the head I might be losing a few more brain cells. I don't know how many I had when I started boxing, probably not as many as I should have when I think back to the alcoholic punishment, the head–nutting, and the beating with a baseball bat I had endured in the past. Each time I had the compulsory annual brain scan I would worry until I got the results. The year I got the letter from the boxing board saying that the latest scan showed 'a slight alteration' I was really worried. Tex didn't help — he said, 'Don't worry, any change must be an improvement.'

When I went into one of my worrying modes, which

could last for days, I would think, Why am I boxing, why am I taking a risk with my brain? Always the same answer: I was obsessed with boxing. I've heard people saying that the fight game gets into your blood. I don't know about that, but it was in my mind that I wanted to box more than anything else in life, and that I was sure the risks were no greater than those involved in everyday living. Crossing the road, riding my mountain bike, travelling by car, plane or railway — they all have more fatalities and serious injuries each year than boxing does!

The article Colin wrote about me wasn't as bad as some. One that really pissed me off was by Robert Phillips in the *Daily Telegraph*. He was going on about how much publicity I had received, and how male boxers had to go away from their families and friends to prepare for fights. How did he think I got fit, staying home and going out on the piss? I gave up years of my life, only going home occasionally from my training camp at Spaniorum Farm. I'll bet he never trained until he could hardly stand, or be doubled up with agony each time he tried to move the day after a fight. And all this, just like a lot of male boxers, for very little money — in fact, when I didn't get paid in New Orleans I had to borrow £200 off the loan man in Fleetwood just to live. That's the sort of story Robert Phillips should have been writing, showing more understanding and sympathy, not knocking what a person does for a living. His article made me feel upset.

I suppose the reporters were only doing their job and trying to make their stories interesting, but they should have got their facts right. Some of them just came in the gym, read bits out of the cuttings about me on the walls, and made up their own stories. Didn't bother checking the facts with me — I was just a temporary news object, until something, or somebody, else came along. No consideration about me as a person, or how my family and friends would react to things that weren't true. 'Fancy Jane doing that.' 'There's a thing for Jane to say.' 'All that money she got for that fight.' When in reality, I didn't do that, didn't say anything like they wrote, and rather than getting paid all that money got ripped off by two promoters, and never received a penny for fighting — and one of those fights was a world title fight in New Orleans!

That really did piss me off. I would let it eat away at me until I wanted to explode. At times I would frighten myself at the extremes of my anger. When I had been open and fair to people I expected them to be the same to me. Oh no! When I was taking legal action to get my boxing licence, the press were just going completely over- the-top. I was on the front page of the *Times*, in every other national newspaper and on every TV news channel. Then there was the stupid fucking TV chat shows, debating about whether I should be allowed to fight! It nearly drove me mad. I hadn't wanted or expected all the media interest — all I'd wanted was to be able to box on licensed boxing shows in my own country.

I found it all too hard to deal with at first, but I did deal with it, although not without a few fiery tantrums along the way! Who could blame me? There were these so-called boxing experts crawling out of the woodwork to give their pathetic opinions on whether they thought what I wanted to do was acceptable. Fuck me! It was *my choice* of career, and these ex-boxers, managers, promoters and press people, all gobbing off left, right and centre. I wouldn't have minded so much if I had felt that they were real experts, and had some idea what they were talking about. In fact, it was just a lot of inexperienced, uneducated personal opinions — they all thought they had some God-given right to mouth-off to journalists in order to fill a few lines in the newspapers, or some time on the air-waves.

Somehow all this bombastic bullshit brought out an anger in me that made me want to get hold of and batter each one of them, the gobby bastards, until I had really hurt them. Frank Maloney, for instance, will never know how close he got to having his face bashed in at the BBC Radio studios in London.

I kept hearing the same words, 'Oh, no! Women are not

made the same. Women shouldn't be boxing, *it's not feminine.'* Bollocks! Women have been fighting since time began. But still, *'It's OK for men but not for women.'* Not one of these thoughtless pricks could produce an original opinion. It was all words I had heard a thousand times before. They weren't able to accept women's boxing, so they felt entitled to try and influence other, more broad-minded, people.

The people that really lit a fuse in me that would have caused a serious explosion if they had said these words to my face were the ex-champions, who had only fought bums on the way up, and the promoters and managers that had, reportedly, fucked up the lives, physically and financially, of so many male boxers. These people were trying to have a say in *my* life. Not fucking likely. Granddad would try to calm me down. 'Don't let it bother you, it's only words, they can't hurt you.' He was right, but I knew I would never forget those people who had tried to put me down. I thought, What goes around comes around, and it will. It was a thought that helped me sleep.

Despite my distrust of some media people, I began to suss the bad ones out, and I did make some good friends. I actually quite liked Colin Hart. He really did know boxing and could use the same language as me. Steve Holdsworth was always great to me and supportive, as was David Passmore of BBC TV West, and David Smith and Richard Hunt of the Fleetwood papers, keeping all the Fleeties in touch with what I was doing. It wasn't easy for me, at first, meeting so many people, all of them from a very different background from me. After the massive publicity I had in the papers, and a lot of appearances on television, people started wanting to help me. All wanting to help themselves more like. One dickhead after another promising to do this or that for me. I'm not joking, there were loads of them, and me, being new to it all, believed everything I was told. Granddad, being the cynical old bastard he was, didn't believe a word. He would say, 'Jane, don't believe it until you see it.' As usual, he was right.

After a while I started to learn. People would ring up, or visit the farm, and talk about putting on fights, sponsorship, making films or documentaries. Granddad and me just sat listening and smiling to ourselves. When they had finished telling us what they were going to do for me, we would look at each other and think to ourselves, 'More like, what are we going to do for them?' It was great fun, listening to all the bullshit.

One guy I got involved with, before Granddad started organising my business as well as my boxing, was another of those 'You will be a millionaire within a year' types but he didn't really understand the boxing world. He had tried to get Glyn Leach, Editor of *Boxing Monthly*, to do an article about me. Glyn was quite interested, but when he was told he would have to pay for the interview, a hairdresser, a make-up artist and that he couldn't have any boxing pictures, he quickly lost interest. I went mental, I couldn't believe it. For fuck's sake, it was for a boxing magazine, not *Vogue*. Luckily, Tex had to talk to Glyn about something else, and he asked why *Boxing Monthly* hadn't done an article on me. When Glyn told him, he soon put that straight: 'We don't want any money or make-up, we shall just be pleased to see you in the gym.'

Hey, I didn't respect a lot of writers, but Glyn was one of the tops. I liked the way he wrote about what he saw and what he thought — he didn't kiss ass. When he finally came to see me I didn't really know what to expect — I thought he would be arrogant and cocky, and I was nervous about meeting someone as knowledgeable about boxing as him. I thought he would hate women's boxing and give me a hard time. Talk about never judge a book by its cover. Glyn was one of the nicest, most honest guys I had ever met. What really surprised me was how down to earth he was. He made me feel comfortable in his company, and he had actually come to see me and he listened to what I had to say. He didn't just write a story from bits he had read in the newspapers, or seen on TV, like a lot of other reporters. He told me he wasn't really for or against women's boxing, and in the article he put both sides across honestly, and that's something that I discovered was a bit rare in the boxing world.

One smart-ass reporter wanted to know if I was managed or trained by a woman. I can remember thinking to myself, I wonder why they would think that. In all honesty, I never considered being managed by a woman. I suppose that sounds a bit strange, as I expect some women would feel more comfortable with a woman manager or trainer, but me — definitely not. I've spent more time around men than women, so I expect that has something to do with it. Anyway, I think it would have looked a bit corny having an all-female team. It was hard enough being a female boxer and listening to all the media's comments about that, without having all the rubbish about feminism and 'girl power' shoved down my throat. I was brought up in the tradition that men are men and women are women, and that's how I've always been — just because I was a boxer that didn't change! Some women weren't like me, though, and they couldn't accept what I was doing without making snidey remarks.

I can remember reading in a newspaper one day and there was an article about a woman becoming a boxing manager. I was thinking Well done, and all that — it's not easy going into a male-dominated sport. As I read further, it said, 'I was approached by Jane Couch, but I told her I wouldn't manage her, there's a place for women in boxing but it's not in the ring.' Well! I can't remember *meeting* this woman, never mind having such a conversation. I rang Granddad immediately. I was screaming down the phone to him, 'Who is this fucking woman? Is she trying to flatter herself or what?' I was raving mad.

If women are going to get respect in the boxing world, they want to get in the ring and box, not flaunt around pretending to understand how it feels to get smacked in the face with a boxing glove, or guessing at what a boxer goes through mentally and physically. You can have all the paper qualifications in the world but the only way to know what a fighter has to go through is by doing it, or at least by being close to a boxer for a long, long time. For fuck's sake, this girl was only in her twenties. Granddad, in his usual calm manner, was just laughing, and the madder I got the more he laughed. 'Calm down, don't get excited, it's just another one trying to jump on the bandwagon and get herself a bit of publicity.' After a while, I saw the funny side of it, and we both laughed. I told him that I wouldn't want any other manager, only him. You couldn't buy experience like Granddad's, and as long as we both knew that, it was all that mattered. I was still cross about that woman manager, though.

19

MISSISSIPPI, OCTOBER 1997

My eighth fight was in the Lady Luck Rhythm and Blues Casino in Lula, Mississippi. My opponent: veteran American tough-woman fighter Dora Webber. Sandra 'the Midget' Rouse couldn't make it on this trip, so Tex had asked his old school chum, now a Doctor of Acupuncture, Tony Evans, to take her place. Tony looked a bit like Oliver Hardy in the Laurel and Hardy films, and he was just as funny — and believe me, we needed a sense of humour in Lula!

Any optimistic ideas of a casino among the bright lights of an exciting town disappeared. We drove, mile after mile along a straight road, taking us further and further away from the comparatively densely built-up area near the airport. The vast acreage of cotton fields on each side of the road seemed to get larger, and the number of houses much smaller, often vanishing for miles at a time. As we drove along, parallel to the Mississippi, we would see the odd casino on the banks of the river, but far more frequently we would see churches and chapels.

Jerry, the driver of the casino's ultra-modern 'space cruiser', that had collected us from the airport, was an interesting chap. He was a part-time driver, a full-time policeman and, as often as he could manage, a guide to deer-shooting parties. As he drove us at the American legally restricted crawl through the cotton fields, Tex enquired about the crops growing on both sides of the road. 'I know the plants with the white buds are cotton, but what are the ones on the other side of the road with pink buds?'

Jerry was totally bemused. 'They're not pink, they're white.' Tex thought, This is all we need, a colour-blind driver.

I soon solved the problem. 'The windows are tinted on that side, you stupid grey-haired old bastard.'

One of the infrequent clusters of buildings we passed must have been Lula, but it didn't register. We turned down a long, open drive, through a massive car park, towards the famous river. There, sprawling before us, was a large ranch-style building. The huge illuminated guitar and saxophone looming over the entrance accentuated the theme of the Rhythm and Blues Casino.

We booked into large en-suite bedrooms that were bigger than the gymnasium. We quickly found the gym with, of course, the obligatory scales. My weight was never a serious problem, but with the wonderful assortment of free food in the casino's restaurant it may well have become one. We had time to kill before fight night, to get over jet-lag but it soon began to drag. The Rhythm and Blues complex was self-contained — it had to be, as it was quite a few miles to the nearest small town. As well as a large amount of slot machines and black jack tables shrewdly placed between the accommodation and the restaurant, there was a cinema and a concert hall. The film we watched, *G I Jane* was reasonable and seemed appropriate, featuring another female fighting her way into a male-dominated environment.

The concert hall wasn't quite as entertaining. I quite like country and western music, but this was a bit slow and drawn out, so much so that halfway through the show, Tony, he of infinite patience and good manners in his surgery, said, 'If I didn't know what was outside, I'd fuck off out of here!' There was *nothing* outside, the highlight of an earlier short stroll along the uncared-for banks of the Mississippi, being a string of barges packed with bales of cotton, slowly being tugged along the river.

Boredom was a problem, especially for an active, restless person like me, waiting to fight. I would keep flitting from place to place, talking to anyone who had time, *and* was willing to listen to me, *and* could understand my broad accent. Then I would go back and tell Tex, Tony, or both of them what stories I'd heard. They would only believe half of what I said, because they had this idea that I sort of embroidered each tale to make it more interesting. I didn't — well, maybe a bit, but only to make it more interesting. Honest! One story I heard was really good. I told them, 'Do you know that nice black lady in the office, she gave us the tickets for food?'

'Yes.'

'She killed her husband! She told me he was abusing her children, so she got a big knife, stuck it in his stomach, and slit him right up to his chest. She said there was blood everywhere, all over her hands, up her arms, and she really enjoyed doing it.' She told me the story with great amusement and enthusiasm. Scary!

Weigh-in time, the evening before the show that was advertised as 'Female Fistic Frenzy', couldn't come quickly enough. When it arrived, it brought together the largest and most able group of female boxers we had seen at any one time, all boxing on the same bill, under the rules of the International Female Boxing Association, the youngest of the female boxing governing bodies at the time. The IFBA had secured the services of one of professional boxing's most famous women, Jackie Kallan, as its Commissioner. Jackie, an attractive mature Barbie doll, accompanied by a young, eager-to-please muscle-man, had already earned her place in boxing's history books for her work with Thomas Hearns and James Toney.

After the rigours, trauma and waiting time of the weigh-in and medical at Foxwoods Casino, Connecticut, the laid-back Lula doctor and scales official were so casual as to be almost unbelievable. 'You've got your medical papers? Good. Give me your hand, I'll just check your pulse. That's OK. How do you feel? That's good, you'll be OK. How much do you weigh? That's right, good.' The only close attention paid by all the chaps was when a curvaceous female stepped on the scales wearing nothing but a mini-mini-bra and a G-string. Somehow it seemed to take longer to weigh her, while the cameras flashed.

Certainly the most obtrusive part of the event was the voice of my opponent, Dora Webber, a tough-looking, sturdily built woman in her late thirties, who seemed intent on making her presence known to anyone in earshot — and with her voice, that was quite a distance. Dora, accompanied by her equally hard-looking boxing sister Cora, certainly made an impression on me. I took one look at my opponent and said, 'Fuckin' hell! It's a swamp monster.' The name stuck. Dora Webber was the Swamp Monster from then on.

Unlike the rest of the female boxers that night who had made every effort to dress up for the weigh-in, or in the case of the G-string girl dress down, Dora dressed as if she had come straight from work on a building site. She caused a certain amount of conjecture as she stepped on to the scales wearing what appeared to me, from where I stood, to be a pair of men's knee-length flannel underpants. Like everyone else, she made the weight.

Fight day always has its problems, especially with a fit, hyperactive, boxer who doesn't know how to rest the body and relax the mind. I, in many ways a young teenager trapped in an adult body, had no intention of doing either. As I became more restless, Tex suggested we go and check out the hall where the boxing was being held. By this time, late afternoon, everything should be in place and we could familiarise ourselves with the layout. He liked to know the corner we were in, what sort of corner steps there were, what type of stool we had and how easy it was to get the stool through the ropes, was there a bucket of water and spit-bowl or tray? Of course, he would have his own sponge, towel, water bottle, adrenalin and all the other essentials necessary for corner work, but there was one very important item missing which we could not have foreseen. There was no boxing ring!

The seating was neatly laid out but there in the centre of it all was a space. With the boxing being shown live on pay-per-view TV in a couple of hours' time, panic was about to set in. We began to visualise a chalk square, or four coats down for posts. We left.

When we returned there was a ring. It looked OK, but the thickly padded floor was more like a wrestling ring. The backstage dressing rooms may have been adequate for the previous night's country and western singers, but for myriad officials, male and female boxers, trainers and reporters, they were totally inadequate. Space was limited, privacy virtually impossible, and I had to change screened only by a towel. Bandaging and taping a boxer's hands while people jostle around you is irritating to say the least, but we got it done. Warm-up time, gloves on, more warm-up and it was time for a six-round battle with the loudest-voiced opponent I had met.

'The ring's a bit wobbly,' I said as I danced in the corner waiting for the bell to start the fight. Still, we were lucky to *have* a ring after the earlier panic. Dora Webber was stamping around the ring, presumably psyching herself up. If she was trying to look menacing, she was making a good job of it. I hardly noticed her, though, as Tex was giving me last-minute advice, and for once I was looking at him.

The fight started and ended in much the same pattern, me moving directly forwards, Dora counter-punching with hooks, swings and uppercuts from all angles, some missing but enough landing to pinch the first half of the fight. In the interval before the fourth round Tex told me, 'You have lost the first three rounds, you must be much sharper, get busy, busy, busy — in, out, get your left hand working. Punch in combinations, ones and twos won't do.' At the time I didn't believe him when he said I was behind on points.

The fight wasn't a classic to watch; as Dora, a cagey, rough-house old fighter, got more tired, there was more mauling, wrestling and danger of head clashes. I was standing my ground, or pushing relentlessly straight forward. A dangerous tactic, and for the first time in my boxing career I had a cut eye. It wasn't too bad — the doctor had a quick look but I brushed him away with, 'I'm fine.' I was eager to get back into battle, so I back-handed the adrenalin bottle into the front row of spectators before Tex could make use of the coagulant liquid. We didn't see it again, but luckily the eye didn't get worse.

The last two rounds continued in the same manner, but with Dora Webber tiring, my fitness brought me back into the fight. Unfortunately, two of the judges didn't think I'd fought back strongly enough. There was a very disappointed English corner. I was convinced the main reason I had lost was because I was the visiting boxer. Also, because it was only a six-round fight, being the fitter, I was coming into my own towards the end of the fight. Tex's main concern was not so much that I had lost a fight some people thought I had won, but the fact that I wasn't even breathing heavily in the corner at the end. He thought this was a sign that I could have been capable of working just that much harder, which may well have resulted in a clear win.

Losing was a new experience for me — I found it traumatic and embarrassing. When you have been previously unbeaten, and think you are unbeatable, how do you explain a loss to your friends? I was gutted. I felt like I had let everyone down. It was going to be a long, long time before I could clear my mind of the thought that losing made me a less desirable person to know. I suppose in a way it did. Everyone loves a winner, and it's easy to offer praise and congratulations. What do you say to a loser? It's easier to say nothing, just keep out of their way.

I was really pissed off. Although I was convinced it was a bad decision, everyone thinks you are making excuses for losing. It did play on my mind for weeks, and while I can never say I'm glad it happened, what it *did* do was make me realise that, while you are winning everyone wants to know you; when you lose it's only your real friends and family that are supportive.

Going into the fight with Dora I was undefeated, and in my mind I thought I just had to do what I always did to win. I hadn't realised that the top girls in America were training just as hard as me, and those like Dora Webber had a lot more ring experience. That night I hadn't given all I'd got. The spark just didn't seem to be there, and it made me realise, that if I was going to keep boxing, the spark would have to be rekindled.

Everyone should know how lonely a loser's dressing room is, and ours was much quieter than usual that night. Even the customary after-fight drinking in the casino was low key for us, with just a small group gathered in the casino bar. One of the gathering was the judge who scored for a Couch win — he was popular!

The doctor was there, and he looked, dressed and acted like an ultra-polite 1940s film star. He had already become good pals with Tony Evans. Tony in his usual, quiet, unassuming manner had earlier been acting as deputy medical officer for the show, as the other appointed doctor hadn't turned up. As it was obligatory for two doctors to be in attendance, Tony had saved the show, and got paid for it! I was quite happy for him to do this, as long as he took time out to help Tex in the corner.

We left the Rhythm and Blues Casino with mixed feelings, in a mini-bus driven by a somewhat more dour driver than Jerry. Tex was quite relieved that this vehicle had no tinted windows.

Gracelands, home of Elvis Presley in Memphis, was not too far from the airport, but a diversion of a few miles would be needed, and the driver didn't appear to be listening to the suggestions that we could pay a visit there. Even the wheedling from the lady boxer with the taped-up eye seemed to be having no effect. Suddenly, a massive sign, 'Gracelands', appeared; the driver had been playing games. I was astounded. 'I didn't realise it was so big!'

'You ain't seen nuttin' 'til you go inside,' the driver informed us. 'He only got one kid, and she don't know what to do with the money.'

We drove past Elvis's first car, parked on a large brick plinth on the side of the road — it was big, open-topped and pale green! We stopped outside the estate with its long stone walls, every stone covered with signatures of visitors. I rubbed my hand along the wall and said laughingly, 'It's amazing. Just think, when I die they might come to me mum's flat and sign the walls.'

There was no time to go inside — we had a plane to catch.

20

ANYONE, ANY TIME, ANYWHERE...

An American guy called Eddie Glyn phoned Tex and asked him if I was interested in a rematch with Dora Webber at the Tropicana Casino, Atlantic City on an all-female show that he and his partner, Diane Fischer, were promoting. Tex said, 'Yes' before he spoke to me about it. He was going along with the phrase we had adopted about opponents: 'Anyone, any time, anywhere.' This reflected our confidence in my fitness and ability and would, hopefully, get me enough fights to gain in experience and income. Also, I wanted to prove that I was the best boxer at my weight in the world. Yet, when he told me about the fight, I had a bad feeling about it. 'I don't want to fight her.'

Tex was really taken aback. 'Jane, this is your chance to put the record straight and beat the only woman to take a decision off you.'

'*I don't want to fight her.*'

'Jane, you are a professional boxer, it's your job. You thought you had beaten Dora last time and got a bad decision, now is your chance to prove it was wrong.'

'Well, OK but I don't want to. I have a really bad feeling about this fight.' Tex should have listened to my hunch — I was going to have more problems outside the ring than in it on that occasion.

The Tropicana Casino was in an exciting building, the accommodation was good, Diane and Eddie, our hosts, were pleasant, friendly and helpful. The one drawback was that we were eating in the staff canteen. The food was just about adequate for the workers but not me. After the sumptuous variety of food we had had at the Rhythm and Blues Casino in Mississippi, this was a disaster. I stopped going to the canteen. 'I'm not eating that stuff in there!' Most of the time I didn't — I relied on Tex to bring me back bananas and any other tasty snacks he could stuff in his track suit pockets. He kept that up until my brother, Tom, and Steve Presnail arrived. They had flown out to watch me box and they took me to eat in all the enticing eating houses around the casino.

The day before the weigh-in, all the girls who were fighting had to be completely medically examined — we were to discover that the rules in New Jersey were seriously more stringent than in Mississippi! Tex, me and several others of the girls fighting on the bill travelled to the medical centre in a mini-bus. It was an eighty-mile round trip. Come on! That was ridiculous, especially the way they drive so slowly over there. In a way though, it was interesting, as being that close to the other fighters for such a long time meant that they began to relax and lose some of their hostile rivalry and aggressive attitudes, and reveal their more normal personalities. Even the loud-mouthed 'Swamp Monster', Dora Webber, became a quite pleasant mother of two teenage boys. Give her her due, she could match me for being foul-mouthed, and some of the things she had done, outside the ring, equalled me for lawlessness. Nevertheless, she came over as a much nicer person than I had thought her to be.

Kathy Collins, one of the other top fighters at my weight, was OK. She had neat, plaited hair and was friendly, but had less to say for herself than me and Dora, probably because we were trying to wind her up to fight us!

One of the passengers I really took to, and have kept in touch with, and that was a bubbly black girl called Eva Young. Eva was fun and had a super sense of humour. She was also a very good fighter. She told us she mainly made her living as a window cleaner, often working on very high-rise buildings without the luxury of a cradle — just hanging on a rope! We met Eva's husband later, he was a quiet white man who was as reserved as Eva was vivacious. Her spent most of his time in the background looking after their young baby daughter.

As usual, the weigh-in was the day before the show. Running parallel to the weigh-in was the licensing procedures. All American licences were checked, and those not valid in New Jersey had to be replaced and paid for. This meant long queues of boxers, trainers, and managers having to line up and fill in application forms. I don't like queues and the one I was in didn't seem to be moving. By the time I got to the head of the line I was like a keg of gunpowder, waiting to explode.

The black woman clerk lit the touch paper. I had been tut-tutting and muttering about the long wait, and had got more indignant as time went on. To be told the licence I had obtained in Mississippi was no good and would have to be replaced was the last straw! I banged my application form down, the clerk looked at it and said, 'You've got blue eyes.'

'No, I've got green eyes.'

'This licence isn't valid.'

'I've got another in my room, I'll go and get it.'

I started to do just that only to be told, 'Sit down, white honky.'

I never like being told what to do, and to order me about the day before a fight, when the nerves were a bit taut, was a particularly bad idea. As for being called a 'white honky', I didn't know what it meant but I knew it wasn't complimentary. I leant over the table and grabbed the black girl by the throat and said, 'Who the fuck do you think you are talking to?' My intended next move was to knock her out. Andrea DeShong and Dora Webber were right behind me in the queue. They grabbed me and pulled me away. Sam Jones, Andrea's trainer, then pulled me away to a chair and held me down until I cooled off, which took a while. Sam told me, 'You mustn't, Jane, they will get the police and you won't be able to fight.' He was still holding me down, which was just as well, when a black male official came and told me I was being fined $100 for 'creating a disturbance'. Luckily the fine wasn't increased when I told him, in no uncertain terms, to 'stick the money up your ass!' Then it hit me, Oh my God, what have I done? I wasn't regretting my words or actions in any way, it was just that I was at the back of the queue again!

Luckily, the weigh-in itself was free from controversy — well, almost. I, as usual, was comfortably inside the 140lb limit. Well, I would be, wouldn't I, with Tex watching me like a hawk? Dora Webber, however, was almost a pound overweight. Granddad, the great scale-watcher, was there. 'She will have to take it off.' He was told that New Jersey rules say the weight can be 'give or take a pound'. Granddad's getting stubborn. 'I went through all this when the match was made. I've got a contract here that says 140lb, and 140lb it must be.' He produced the contract from his pocket, it was studied and Dora had to take the pound off. She disappeared and came back a short time later. Three of the other girls draped towels round her — presumably she had stripped naked. She made the weight. I couldn't wait to get out of that fucking room and get some food, drinks and fresh air in.

My brother Tom and Steve Presnail came with me, and we went for a walk along the famous Boardwalk. It ran along the beach edge, and with the waves of the Atlantic Ocean splashing on the beach it was like getting out of jail all over again. I just needed to move, and strode away, Tom and Steve having to stretch their legs to keep up with me.

That evening I was alone in my hotel room when the phone rang. It was John Bentham, Chris Webb's partner at Outlaw Films, the company putting together the documentary on me. The film was nearly finished, and John invited me for a night-cap to discuss signing the release contract, and the advance they would pay me on the sale of the film. Tex had already been negotiating with John and was holding out for £5,000. He thought that amount was reasonable and would have taken away the constant worry I had of having no money.

I enjoyed the drink and chat with John. He was from Fleetwood and had managed my brother's band, so we had a lot in common to chat about. John pointed out to me the problems involved in selling the documentary, and how he thought $1,500 would be a reasonable and fair payment for both sides of the deal. I was a bit disappointed at first, but when he offered me money there and then I thought, great, I can get round the shops and buy some good gear and lots of presents to take home.

I signed the contract but I had to have a witness. John and I went back to my room and I rang Tex and told him John Bentham had a contract for him to sign. He didn't take long finding his way around the maze of corridors. I thrust the paperwork at him when he came in, and said, 'Sign it.' I should have known he wouldn't sign anything without studying it. He took the contract from me, read a couple of paragraphs and started shaking his head. 'Look, it's late, it's time you were in bed, you've got to fight tomorrow and you need your sleep. I'm tired. I'll look this through in the morning.'

'Sign it now!'

'No, I'll sort it out tomorrow.'

'*Sign it now!* I want the money.' What I was going to do with money at that time of night I don't know, but I wanted it. Tex wasn't the only one who was tired. I had had a long day, some of it so fucking irritating I could just have run away. Now I was getting this stupid hassle when I should have been in bed resting for my fight with Dora.

I flipped, exploded, went berserk. I don't know *what* I did, it was all a wild blur, but I wanted to be out of there and go home. I was shouting and screaming, and I grabbed a suitcase and started stuffing my clothes in it. 'I'm going home, I'm not going to fight. Nobody helps me. You're all trying to get what you can out of me. You're a lot of phoney bastards. You're only here for a holiday. None of your care about me.'

John Bentham couldn't get out of the room fast enough — he knew more about my history of violence than Tex. Tex was sat on the edge of the bed, speaking quietly, trying to calm me down. It didn't calm me down, it just pissed me off. What did he care? He had an income, a nice place to live, money to spend. He didn't give a fuck. Well let him have a taste of what life's *really* about. I grabbed a massive armchair and hurled it towards him. Luckily for him, it missed. How I had the strength to pick it up, God knows. I couldn't move it next day!

When I saw the chair had missed I launched myself at him in a frenzy of hate. Tex might have been old, but he wasn't frail — we had had plenty of playfights together and he had developed some techniques of controlling me. The most effective was to grab a bunch of my thick, crinkly hair and force me to my knees. That's just what he did. Gone was 'Mr Cool'; he raised his right fist and I thought he was going to smash it into my face. 'What is it with you? The more I try to help you and guide you, the more ingratitude and foul language I get?' He just held me down on my knees until I began to calm down, but I couldn't stop crying and still wanted the money.

Tex knew the only way to shut me up was to let me have

the money. He told me to ring John Bentham and get him to come back with the contract and the cash. He was back in no time. He gave Tex the contract to sign and me the money. Tex signed the contract, without even reading the second page. By this time it could have been a death sentence he was signing but so what? What he *did* notice was that he was only signing as a witness to my signature. This time *he* exploded, 'What's up with you two, have you no sense? Why didn't you tell me you only wanted me to sign as a witness? Anybody could have done that and this whole pantomime could have been avoided!'

Later, days later, Tex said to me, 'I've seen some things in my time but I have never seen anyone behave like you did in Atlantic City. It was just like one of those psycho-thriller films I enjoy watching, when the subject changes into a demon or is possessed by the devil. I never thought I would see it in real life.'

Tex kept out of my way as much as he could next day. Luckily I had Tom and Steve to keep me company. It was a relief for all of us when we finally made our way to the boxing arena, but there was still a tension among us that wasn't usually there. The pre-fight dressing room procedure was carried out professionally and with no problems — except one. I changed into my boxing strip, shorts, groin protector and sports bra top, my dressing gown was on, hands bandaged, gloves on and signed by the official in charge, warm-up completed, and then it happened. I wanted a wee!

There was no way I had time to get my gloves off, on again, and signed before it was time to fight. And there was no way I could manage to go to the toilet on my own *and* manage to pull my shorts and protector down with gloves on. I needed some help — it was a bit embarrassing. I couldn't ask a bloke! I hovered around outside the loo getting more and more frantic until I spotted Cora Webber, Dora's sister, who was also boxing on the bill. She didn't have her gloves on and I pleaded for help.

Cora wasn't over-enthusiastic at first, but in the end agreed saying, 'Well, OK, but don't expect me to wipe you!' I was saved in the nick of time, but somehow I'd managed to wet the tassles on my shorts — I couldn't go in the ring like that. Luckily there was a hair-dryer in the washroom, and that solved the damp problem.

Back in the dressing room, and there was just time for a re-run over tactics. This time Tex wanted me to box more carefully, using the skills I had been practising in the gym, and not walking face first into Dora's swinging counter-punches. It worked pretty well in the first round. There was no doubt I was the classier boxer. I was using my left lead well, moving in and out but occasionally not getting out of range quickly enough to avoid some of Dora's thudding swings. She caught me with one or two but they didn't hurt me much. When the bell ended the first round and I was back in the corner, Tex said, 'That's good, you are giving her a boxing lesson, but I want you to be sharper and more dominating.' Each round was much the same, me boxing with an orthodox style, Dora plodding backwards, slugging away as I came in. I suppose the fight was always close: it was Dora's crude power against my skills. I didn't think I had any problems. But Tex, not wanting it to be too close a decision, urged me to up my workrate in the last four rounds. It was hard to change my rhythm, it had been working well in the first six rounds and I felt comfortable with it.

In the interval before the tenth and last round, Tex told me he felt a last round onslaught would make me certain of victory. To fire me up to make that last extra effort, he said, 'You must punch non-stop for two minutes now, if you don't, you lose.' He didn't really believe that, but a grandstand finish is always impressive.

The last round finished, or should have, with the sound of the final bell, but Dora and me put in a bit of overtime, both looking to land the last punch — at least I got that satisfaction before the referee parted us!

When the MC, Ed Derian, started to announce the result, saying, 'All the judges have scored 98-92 for...', we all relaxed in the corner. With a score like that there could be only one winner — me! The MC continued, 'the new IWBF welterweight champion, Dora 'The Destroyer' Webber!' None of us could believe it. The crowd were booing and whistling. I couldn't handle it, I had to get out of that ring and out of the arena as fast as I could. I ran back to my hotel room, threw myself on the bed, and sobbed with anger.

I gradually controlled myself, changed and went back to the arena. I had my wages to collect, minus my fine, licence fees and whatever else they took out of my purse. I kept well away from Tex. I couldn't speak to him; I felt it was all his fault, he knew I didn't want to take the fight. Nevertheless, he was still trying to help me by querying the decision. Dennis Diaz, the new owner of the WIBF, was there with his lawyer. Tex wanted to know what their opinion of the decision was. They both thought I had won and promised to lodge a legal complaint.

Promises! Tex still wasn't satisfied, so he button-holed State Commissioner Larry Hazzard in his seat against the ring apron. 'Please may I see the score cards, Mr Hazzard, and what did you think of the decision?'

The answer? 'I wasn't watching!' What he *was* watching, sitting so close to the action, who knows...

If there is a moral to this story, it is, Don't go to America and take on a tough fighter in their own State with hometown judges. If you have to, don't upset the local officials before the fight starts.

We all ended up at the after-fight party. I stayed with Tom and Steve and set about drowning my sorrows. I tried to forget the fight for a while but it was impossible, everyone had an opinion. Roy Foreman, brother of George Foreman the ex-World Heavyweight Champion, said, 'Yeah! They did the same to George when he boxed Shannon Briggs here — the only difference was that it cost him millions of dollars.' Perhaps the sole consolation of the evening was the fact that Dennis Diaz had not sanctioned the fight to be for the WIBF World Title, so I could still, justifiably, claim to be the WIBF World Welterweight Champion.

As we were waiting for the taxi to take us to the airport next morning, Tex was chatting to James Condon, who had refereed my fight with Dora. He was completely sympathetic towards me, and said, 'If I had had to make that decision alone, Jane would have won!'

21

LAS VEGAS

If there is one place in the world I really wanted to box, it was Las Vegas, half because I wanted to actually box on one of the top shows at a big-name venue, but also because of the world-famous bright lights, the casinos, the glamorous people, the night life, the pure excitement of mixing with the gamblers, the stars, the gangsters, the indescribable. That chance came at 2 a.m. one Tuesday morning in a dreary, drizzly, autumnal October. The sun-soaked city of Las Vegas beckoned like a jewel glistening in a sand-surrounded crown.

Rick Kulas, Head of Event Entertainment, Los Angeles,

California, was promoting a show at the Tropicana Casino, Las Vegas. His star female fighter, Hannah 'The Vegas' Fox, was due to shine on this show and was expected to extend her unbeaten record of eight wins against Marischa Sjauw from Holland. It wasn't to be — Marischa withdrew from the fight with an injury.

Now, everybody in the boxing world knows the problems of getting a suitable last-minute opponent for an unbeaten fighter. It's not easy. The opponent mustn't be too good or the money-spinning star may be stopped from shining. Equally, if the opponent only comes along for the ride, as so often happens, and goes out in the first round, nobody benefits and the promoter gets a lot of bad press. Those Yanks must have been really desperate to ring for me. Rick Kulas had seen me box and must have known I would be a handful, and would be coming to win and not just to be cannon fodder for Hannah Fox. If they had a list of fighters they were going to ask, I'll bet my name was a long way down the list. I can just imagine the aching heads and fraught tempers at Event Entertainment as they ticked off the names above me. I wonder how many American coaches, managers, matchmakers were approached before, in desperation, Rick Kulas rang Tex.

I had put a challenge on the Internet, suggesting that all the American women fighters were trying to avoid me as they didn't want a hard night's work. They must have known I was confident, but were gambling on me not being fit at short notice. They were probably thinking, Jane's not been in the ring, competitively, for almost a year. Hannah is well-prepared, match-fit, with a good recent victory over Diane Dutra, the Canadian ex-WIBF World Champion. Jane will have all the problems of travelling and jet-lag. What they *didn't* know was that during the months since my last visit to the States, I had spent most of that time on the farm training twice a day, and on some days playing squash as well.

Tex coached squash most days, and I really wanted to have a go but I was a bit embarrassed to try as I had never played —

I thought it was a bit of a 'cissy' game for posh bastards. In fact, I had never heard of the game before I started training with Tex. The first time we played, Granddad showed me how to hit the ball, then he knocked it around the court and I chased after it for about fifteen minutes. 'That's enough,' he says, with that silly grin on his face. It wasn't enough — I was beginning to enjoy hitting the ball all over the place and I was certainly fit enough to wear out my old-age-pensioner, coach. The more I ran the more Tex grinned. 'I should stop now if I were you.' No chance! He was only saying that because he was tired — at least that's what I thought. 'You will regret this!'

'No, I won't!' After half an hour or so I was beginning to feel the pace and told Tex we had better stop as he was beginning to look tired. He wasn't, though, and the grin had turned to laughter — he was almost creased up. Silly old bastard, I thought, what does he think's so funny? Next day I knew. I could hardly move, my legs were stiff and sore, and my ass, it was agony, I could hardly sit on it. I never wanted to hear the word 'squash' again, but I did. 'Get your kit, we're off for another game of squash.'

'No! No! No! I'm never going on a squash court again.'
'Yes, you are!'
'No, I'm not!' Why wasn't *he* suffering? 'Yes, you are. Remember what I told you, what gave you the pain will take it away.' Granddad was right, *again*. I got back on court regularly, the pain went, and I even got good enough to be offered a place in a local ladies' team.

It was a real break from gym work and speeded up my reactions and footwork, but I wouldn't have liked any of my friends from Fleetwood watching me dashing round the court in a little white skirt, waving a squash racket. My street-cred would have disappeared faster than a rat up a drainpipe.

Apart from squash, my life was taken up with boxing. I trained, practised skills, read boxing books. I couldn't wait for Friday's fight with Tex over who read the *Boxing News* first. He usually won because he got up earlier than me, but I would snatch it off him before he had finished it! I watched videos of my fights over and over again, often alone in my room. Sometimes one of my sparring partners, often Mike Loveridge and occasionally the Midget, would keep me company. Other times I would watch fights on TV with Tex and we would discuss for hours whatever was going on in the boxing world.

Amazingly I almost stopped drinking, our trips to The Fox in Easter Compton becoming less and less frequent. I liked being a world champion boxer, and I was determined to stay champion as long as I could. To do that, I had to keep training and learning. Tex would say, 'You musn't be satisfied with your ability, you must get better. You can't stay at a level, because if you don't improve you will go backwards.' So, living in this almost total boxing environment, it was no wonder I was fit and ready to take a fight at short notice.

Las Vegas is a city of gamblers, and this time it was Rick Kula's turn to roll the dice. He rang Tex; so what if it was 2 a.m. in the UK and Granddad needed his beauty sleep — Event Entertainment needed an opponent for their star. 'Hi Tex! How ya doin'?' Tex told him he was 'doin' all right'. He managed to stop himself saying he would have been doin' a lot better if Rick had rung a few hours earlier, or later, and not disturbed his sleep. 'How's Jane Couch?'

'She is fit and well and ready to fight.'

'Will she fight Hannah Fox on Saturday?'

Tex went through the routine questions, 'At what weight? How many rounds? How much?'

He finished the call with, 'Yes, that should be OK. I'll talk to Jane and ring you back.'

Before he spoke to me he went through the 'logistics', as he calls them, in his mind. The length of travelling time to Las Vegas, could we get flights in time? We would have to leave next day. Which airport? How do we travel to the airport? Jet-lag? Now that part was important. OK, Jane has to get up, confirm she wants the fight and if so, we must immediately change our life-pattern, eating, drinking, training and sleeping to American time, to help counter-act jet-lag.

Surprisingly, I woke up at 2.30 a.m. easier than my normal 10 a.m. Tex could hardly believe it, no verbal abuse from me, no violence! The words Las Vegas had sharply penetrated my usual reluctance to open my eyes! I said, 'You're kidding, what at this time of night?'

'Get up, we'll talk about this, and if we agree you should fight we travel tomorrow.'

It was probably the fastest I have ever got out of bed. I brewed some tea and then talked with Tex about the fight. As always, he was cautious. I wasn't — I was impetuous, as usual. 'Take it, I'll beat her.' We knew Hannah Fox had an unbeaten record but we didn't know the standard of her opposition. Maybe she was just another protected star with a padded record of low-ability opponents. Tex decided she must be checked out before a final decision was made, so he rang Tom Eaton, an American guy who was very involved in women's boxing and the Internet. We had met Tom in America and Tex had kept in touch.

When Tom answered the phone it was, 'Hi Tex! What are you doing up at this time of night?'

'Hannah Fox, what do you know about her?'

'Hey, she's good, she has the best left hand in the business and follows it with a good straight right. She's really sharp and match-fit, and she's just beaten Diana Dutra.'

'Jane has been offered a chance to box her on Saturday. What do you think?'

'Thinking as a manager, I wouldn't take the fight. Jane's been out of the ring too long, she has to be a bit rusty and this girl is sharp.' Tex told him that I was really fit right now and had been sparring a lot. 'Yeah,' says Tom, 'but sparring's not the same — when they get hurt and bruised in a contest they wonder what's going on.'

Tom could be forgiven for that thought, since he had not seen the men I sparred with! Dean Cooper, Darren Dorrington, Simon Stowell, Eddie Hedges and several other good male fighters. Pain, blood — they had all experienced it regularly, and so had I! Tom's reasons for not taking the fight had influenced Tex, though. He said, 'Jane, I think Tom's right. It is very short notice and if the fight is close you won't get a points victory. Anyway the purse is too small. $1,500 is not enough to risk your WIBF title for. What's more, you have your first BBB of C licensed fight booked for Streatham, London, in just four weeks, and any injury might spoil that!' We went over the 'fors' and 'againsts' many times, Tex insisting it was a bit pointless asking someone who is better informed on a subject for advice and then not taking it. I didn't care. I told him again, 'I want the fight.' He always said it's the boxer who employs the manager, not the other way round as most people think, so now I was telling him. 'OK, you have given me your advice, but I am going to take the fight.' Tex phoned Tom back and told him of my decision. He wasn't surprised, he had experienced my headstrong actions first hand in the USA!

The decision made, we were into the gym, which conveniently was just ten yards from my room in the farmhouse. It was just after 3 a.m., and after a warm-up Tex put me through a fast and furious ten by two-minute rounds workout, just to see how fit and sharp I looked. He was surprised and impressed. It may have been an early hour, but I had to prove I was ready for a fight, and I wasn't going to miss Las Vegas! I'd proved my point, so Tex rang Event Entertainment, confirming the fight. Details were discussed, and the travel arrangements would be worked out next day.

Wednesday came and went, food, drink and sleep on American time. The early hours of Thursday approached, and the last training session echoed around in an otherwise, empty gym. Back in the house for supper time, and the trans-Atlantic calls started again. Wide awake, this time, Tex discussed details with Event Entertainment's matchmaker Brian Allen — we had met him in Mississippi. Tex thought he was a pleasant chap. All details sorted out and the fight was *on*!

We were packing our cases when the phone rang again.

Tex took the call. It was another American voice. 'Hey, is that Tex? This is Gerry Coulton, I'm looking for a 140lb girl to box in Vegas on Saturday. Is Jane Couch fit?'

'Yes, Gerry, she's fit, who do you want her to box?' It was no surprise when the answer came, 'Hannah Fox.' 'That's interesting, when did you get the call, asking for a boxer?'

'About twenty minutes ago.'

'Who was it from?'

'Someone at Event Entertainment.'

The alarm bells started ringing. Brian Allen had said he would ring back within the hour. He didn't. We stopped packing, and the phone still didn't ring. Tex called Brian Allan. 'Hello Brian, what's happening? What's your game? Why am I getting a call from another matchmaker?'

'Oh! That was someone else rang him by mistake.'

That was a load of bollocks! Tex kept on, as he does. 'So! What's going on?'

Brian said, 'Hannah doesn't want the fight...' His voice trailed off, and Tex distinctly heard another voice in the background say, 'Don't say that! Say she's ill.' Brian's voice again, 'Hannah's got the 'flu, she won't be boxing Saturday.'

Tex was calm — he knew the ways of the boxing world and that it is hard to be certain a fight will take place until you see the two boxers enter the ring. He couldn't resist one parting shot at Brian before he hung up. It was polite but pointed: 'I think you got it right the first time, Brian. Hannah doesn't want the fight. Goodbye.'

We slumped in our chairs, looking at each other, disappointment tinged with relief, or was it relief tinged with disappointment? The glittering lights of Las Vegas had been temporarily extinguished in our minds, but at least we could go to our beds and get back on English time.

For the next two days we had jet-lag without having been anywhere!

PART THREE

ANOTHER KIND OF FIGHTING

22

A BBB OF C BOXER'S LICENCE

In March 1997, Steve Presnail was still managing the business side of my boxing career, helping to finance my almost permanent stay at Spaniorum Farm. He would visit at weekends and watch me train. When I was sparring, he would stand well away from the ring, sometimes reading the cuttings and posters on the walls. I guess he didn't like seeing the only boxer he admired more than Chris Eubank getting hit.

Occasionally the trips would be reversed and Steve would take me home for the weekend. On one of these breaks from training we took Tex with us — not, I hasten to add, to let loose the old grey one on the Fleetwood nightlife, but to attend a business meeting we had arranged with John Hyland, the Liverpool professional boxing manager and promoter.

John, an ex-England amateur boxer, was now making a success of the administrative side of pro-boxing, and had professed an interest in meeting me with the prospect of letting me box on one of his shows. This, of course, was unlikely to be approved of by the British Boxing Board of Control, as the Board, mostly through their General Secretary, John Morris, were giving the impression that, although they knew women's boxing was taking place, they wanted no part of it. Tex knew this only too well, as he had attended a meeting, some months before at the BBB of C's office in Borough High Street, London.

He had been there with Barbara Buttrick and Jimmy Finn, all of them in their Women's International Boxing Federation governing roles. John Morris had been, as usual, polite, and not without a certain amount of encouragement, despite Jimmy Finn's fiery behaviour. The outcome of the meeting was as written to Tex by John Morris on January 1st 1994: 'the Board would not seek to approve or disapprove of your organisation [WIBF] but would simply be aware that it is now in existence with the aims you have outlined...'

A lot of help that was! Either back women's boxing or go against it. Don't sit on the fence!

The meeting with John Hyland was held in the Morton Suite of the Moathouse Hotel, Liverpool. It was a pleasant meeting, the strong scouser accents and hospitality a pleasure after some of the southern indifference I was having to get used to. Steve and Tex had little to say, which wasn't unusual when I was holding forth and trying to impress someone with my wit, charm and good looks! John went the way of most men. He was hooked! When I come to think of it though, it probably wasn't just me, but the business potential around me. Jane Couch. Make-up: Revlon, Max Factor? Clothes: Calvin Klein? Shoes: Gucci? Sports outfitters: Nike, Adidas? An attractive woman who can box well and is an entertainer. What a ticket-seller! What a prospect for drawing a whole new type of sponsor and spectator from those usually involved in the blood-and-guts scene of male pro-boxing. I couldn't read John's mind *exactly*, but he looked to have £ signs in his eyes!

Tex had been quiet for a long time as he listened to me and John creating our dreams. 'Don't get too carried away. Jane must get a boxer's licence from the Board first.'

John Hyland's reaction was positive. 'I will back you, and if needs be we will take the BBB of C to court.' It wasn't long, though, before John Hyland seemed to lose interest in my career as a BBB of C licensed boxer, but fortunately Tex hadn't! John's statement that he would have been willing to take the Board to court to contest my application on the grounds of sex discrimination stuck in his mind. It resurfaced when one of the many journalists who visited the farm to interview me and watch me train said he knew a barrister, Barbara Hewson, who specialised in sex discrimination. He was sure she would be interested in representing me in any forthcoming legal battle with the Boxing Board.

Tex mentally stored this information. It was retrieved at our first visit to Morris Rosen's home in Kensington, London. We had all been chatting away — me, Sandra, Morris — when Tex suddenly comes out with, 'I have been thinking, Morris. If we applied to the BBB of C for a boxer's licence for Jane, and she got it, we would make history and possibly a lot of money. If she got turned down, we would, at least, create a great deal of publicity for her.'

Straight away Morris picked up his telephone and called his solicitor, Andrew Brecher. When he had said why he was calling he handed the phone to Tex, who then spoke to Andrew and outlined his scheme. The seed of the idea he had had was now well planted and ready to grow.

The next move: an application to the BBB of C, on their official Form 4 for a boxer's licence for Jane Couch. It was no surprise that, two weeks later, a letter from the Board, addressed to me at Morris Rosen's Kensington address, said, 'The Board has decided that it would not be possible to grant you a hearing of this application at the present time, and the Stewards are sure you appreciate that there is considerable research being conducted into the medical aspects generally of women's boxing.' There was more but it all meant just one thing. The BBB of C were not prepared to accept a woman boxer into their ranks. I thought, Right you bastards, you are going to find out what I 'appreciate', and it's not being fobbed off by a lot of old codgers who have got no idea what a good boxer I am.

It was back to Barbara Hewson, ready for legal battle to commence. For some reason, she didn't continue with the case, which meant that barrister, Dinah Rose, took her place. I didn't get to know Barbara but I am sure no one could have done a better job than Dinah. I thought she was the nicest, cleverest barrister in the world. Backing up Dinah, and what a brilliant back-up it was, was solicitor Sara Leslie of Irwin Mitchell, in London.

For the next nine months there were meetings in London and at the farm, faxes, telephone calls buzzing backwards and forwards, letters, all building up to my historic Industrial Tribunal case of sex discrimination. Me, Jane Couch, versus the might of the Boxing Board for the right to box on BBB of C licensed boxing shows.

The long-awaited Industrial Tribunal case to decide whether the British Boxing Board of Control should grant me a licence to box on professional boxing shows, under their jurisdiction, was held in Croydon. The date of the hearing had already been postponed and the venue changed from Bristol. It did appear, at that time, that the BBB of C were dragging their heels. Maybe if they closed their eyes and waited, the case would go away, and I would become too old to be a boxer.

The case wasn't going to go away. I had a powerful, proficient legal team representing me, and strong backing from the Equal Opportunities Commission. Nothing in life can ever be a foregone conclusion, but I had, from the start of the application, expected it all to be settled out of court. I was wrong.

The Montague Court building at Croydon was like a rabbit warren of corridors, waiting rooms and court rooms. We were shown to our room, the BBB of C team being guided elsewhere. The similarity of being in separate dressing rooms before a fight was hard to get out of my mind, but on this occasion Tex wasn't bandaging my hands or warming me up. That was being done, metaphorically, by my legal team, barrister Dinah Rose, an attractive dark-haired young lady with a twinkle in her eye — a twinkle I was to recognise over the next two days as she waited for a witness to fall into a trap she had laid, or to dig themselves even deeper into a hole of their own making. She was brilliant, and very early in the case she had said, 'If we don't win this case, I will eat my wig!' Solicitor Sara Leslie of Irwin Mitchell, who had been working closely with me and Tex for many weeks, excelled in her own right — another young lady, whose smart grey costume, glasses and cropped hair, presented a severe image that belied the pleasant and caring person she was. Young and female, my legal team may have been, but middle-aged Barry Butler, the BBB of C's barrister, didn't seem so sparky.

The preparatory work Sara Leslie and Dinah Rose had done was phenomenal. A 385-page bundle of documents was produced to substantiate my application, in addition to their personal files. Every court has its jester and as usual I was playing my favourite role. Periodic horrified outbursts when I disagreed with some statement earned me a critical look over the rims of the Chairman of the Tribunal's glasses, a stern look and mouthed warnings from Sara Leslie, disapproval from the BBB of C's representatives and a 'shush, shush' combined with a dig in the ribs from Tex.

Superstar of the Board's defence was Dr Adrian Whiteson, OBE, whose initial shining and confidence was slowly but surely extinguished by direct questions from Dinah Rose. She received indirect answers, or in some cases no answers at all, leading to the regular request, 'Will you please answer the question, Dr Whiteson.' The replies suggested that the Doctor didn't *have* an answer.

Dr Whiteson was finding it increasingly difficult to remain calm and polite while being determinedly and cleverly cross-examined by this woman who, just a short while ago, knew little of the boxing world and nothing at all of Dr Whiteson. For a man whose medical work on the side of boxing had previously earned a great deal of respect, to have his statements and opinions queried and questioned must have been a very irritating experience.

John Morris, the Board's General Secretary, was his usual pleasantly amiable self. Leonard 'Nipper' Read, QPM President and Chairman of the BBB of C, the ex-police Superintendent whose claim to fame was for his work in apprehending the Kray brothers, should have been used to courts and giving evidence. But on this occasion he looked distinctly uncomfortable and had nothing memorable to contribute.

One elderley Board official spent the two days nodding in agreement, apparently with both sets of witnesses. Surprisingly, Tex didn't have much to say, probably as they didn't let him. He answered the questions carefully, trying not to offend either side — something he found difficult when talking about Jimmy Finn. He thought Jimmy had tried hard to negotiate with the BBB of C, but that the Irishman's bull-at-a-gate approach had done more harm than good to women's boxing.

Commander Rod Robertson, Chairman of the Amateur Boxing Association of England, was an unlikely ally for a woman who wanted to become a professional boxer. Nevertheless he took time off from his usually over-filled schedule to support my rights to earn a living as a boxer. Commander Robertson had been through the whole experience before, at International Amateur Boxing level. As a supporter of morale and provider of useful information to Sara Leslie and Dinah Rose he could not have been better. For some reason he wasn't called to give evidence, but he was at the hotel when the case was over and we all had an optimistic, celebratory drink.

During the two days the case was heard, media interest had flourished, the majority of national newspapers and most TV news stations covering the proceedings. A press conference was held at a Croydon hotel after which Imogen Lee, PR Secretary for Irwin Mitchell, arranged for me to attend a photo-shoot in London. A national newspaper had overcome my reluctance to pose in poncy dresses by offering me a four-figure fee. Not bad for a couple of hours' work! Yet, as always in my life, nothing is that simple. The taxi driver found his way from Croydon to the East End without much difficulty, which wasn't exactly surprising. What *was* surprising was the fact that he couldn't find his way back to Croydon.

The photographic studio was interesting, and the photographer a pleasant, down-to-earth chap, who had left the wilds of Wiltshire, but had not left his country charm behind. He had converted the ground floor of what appeared to be an old cottage into his studio and office. Holding pride of place at one end was the photographic backdrop, at the other end a pine table on which various bottles of alcohol, glasses and bowls of sweets suggested a party may be going on.

We didn't see a party, but we *did* see off our fair share of alcohol. Sandra and Tex tried to pass away the hours as I donned and discarded various outfits with equal disgust. I was enjoying the drinks, if not the dresses. The photo-shoot over, the photographer gave me £20 for the taxi saying, 'Don't give him any more.' Then we were off. Three-quarters of an hour later, the bright lights of London behind us, the street lights getting ever rarer, a heavy fog around us, and we were lost. I had been biting my tongue for a while, as I was sure we were going the wrong way — but this was a London taxi driver, surely he had the 'knowledge'.

I was even more convinced when I saw a road sign saying, 'Gatwick Airport 3 miles'. Even then we had to get closer to Gatwick before a roundabout appeared and we could finally head in the right direction. When we found Croydon he had difficulty finding the hotel. As we left the taxi, with great relief, I remembered the photographer's words, 'Don't give him more than twenty pounds.' Twenty pounds? I was tempted to give him nothing. It was a bad end to an interesting two days, but worse was to follow. The newspaper did not pay its promised four-figure sum. I had given my time and energy for nothing.

It was a long six weeks before the Industrial Tribunal announced their findings in the Couch v BBB of C case. From the middle of February to the middle of March, as the days got longer, the tension and speculation grew. Despite training twice a day, going to watch amateur boxing shows, presenting prizes, appearing on TV news and chat shows, I couldn't fill my mind enough to stop the endless pondering. Will I get the licence? What if I don't? I'll go to America and box there. No, I won't, it's too far from home. I want my licence. I want to box in England. I'll pack in boxing, I'd at least have money to spend if I got a job — and I wouldn't have all the hard training to do. I could get back to a real fucking life!

Of all the places to be when the result finally came through, Tex and I were in a queue at the local vehicle licensing office, where Tex was renewing the tax on his car. My new mobile phone rang and I went outside to take the call. It was Sara Leslie, my super solicitor. 'Jane, we've won. The Industrial Tribunal ruled in your favour. The BBB of C are going to have to let you have a boxer's licence. You must come to London this afternoon for a press conference.' I thought, Got the bastards!

I ran back into the office, where Tex was nearing the head of the queue. I was so excited I could hardly get the words out: 'I've won, I've won! Come on, we've got to go to London.

Come on! We've got to go! The Board have got to give me a licence and we have to go to a press conference.' Tex looked quite relieved, not just because of the news, but because he thought I'd gone even crazier than usual, my eyes blazing, ranting and raving, throwing my arms about as if I'd really flipped. Pleased he may have been, but he wasn't going anywhere until he'd taxed his car. 'Jane, I'm not leaving the queue and dashing off. I came here to tax my car, and that's what I'm going to do.'

We did manage to make the Press Conference on time despite Tex 'dashing about' at his own leisurely pace. It was held at the impressive London Law Courts building. Sara Leslie made the official announcement to a well-filled room of hastily gathered TV and newspaper reporters. The cameras, the questions, the regularly rehearsed answers, were all noted down and ready to be printed out in the next day's papers, ready to pack my already bulky scrapbook.

Now, legally given the right to apply for a professional boxer's licence, I had to fulfil the criteria demanded by the BBB of C before it issues a licence to any boxer. My boxing ability was not queried, as the Board have every right to do in the case of a boxer's previous experience in the ring being questionable. Having won the WIBF World Welterweight title, and defended it successfully twice in America, I was obviously a competent boxer. For most boxers applying for a licence, proving their skill is the easy part — passing the serious medical tests can be much more difficult.

A BBB of C approved doctor has to carry out a comprehensive physical examination. An MR angiogram brain scan must be carried out at one of the Board's nine approved hospital units, to make sure that the boxer's brain has no abnormalities that may enhance the possibility of serious brain damage from a blow to the head. The thought of this scan alone caused me to panic: 'I can't do it! I don't want it done! I'm going to give up boxing, I can't go through with it.'

Tex drove me to the hospital, the Bristol Royal Infirmary.

He dropped me off, and luckily for him he couldn't find anywhere to park — at least that's what he told me, so he kept driving around until I came out. He had to suffer, though — he wasn't getting away with it that easy after what I had been through. 'Where have you been? Why weren't you there? They were trying to find you because I wouldn't get in the fucking machine. I was screaming and shouting. I threatened to hit one of them! When I did get in it was like torture, with a great hum throbbing through my head. I'm not going to do that again!'

'Come on, Jane, it can't be that bad. All the boxers have to have it done and I've never heard anyone complain before.'

'I didn't like it, I get claustrophobia and I'm not doing it again!'

'We'll see. You're OK, and it's one more step towards your licence.'

Worse was to come. Tex made an appointment for me to have the compulsory AIDS test at a clinic which was attached to the BRI. This time I made him park and come in with me and thank fuck he did. It was like going in to another world. What a weird variety of people there were. Seedy, sordid, dodgy, dirty and the odd person clean and smartly dressed. Most of them looked like drug addicts or prostitutes. All of them had serious, apprehensive looks on their faces.

'I know you, you're that lady boxer.' That was just what I needed, to be recognised in a place like that. It was a smart, friendly, young Welsh girl who had come in with an extremely unpleasant-looking 'drugged-up' boyfriend. I signed my autograph for her, looked at Tex and said, 'That's it. I'm off. I'm not staying here to be recognised by this lot, they will all think I've got AIDS.'

'Calm down, we'll soon be out of here.' He didn't tell me that he couldn't wait to get out of the place either.

We stood as far away as we could from the crowded benches. I was definitely feeling uncomfortable, more out of a guilty conscience because I was fit and well and here to prove that, rather than being there because I thought I may have a disease. Before the AIDS test came the counselling. It must have been light relief for the very polite and helpful young lady consultant. 'No, I'm not pregnant; no, I haven't got AIDS, I had a test in America a few weeks ago. No, I don't need any consultation or humouring. Just get it done. I don't like fuckin' needles!' All that was before the poor woman had said, 'Good afternoon, Jane...'

Tex held me down on the treatment table — he had to or I would have been off when I saw the needle coming, or whacked out at the person holding it. I hardly felt anything, though, and the test was over. It must have been the fastest and noisiest she had ever done! I needn't have worried — I was OK. I had another certificate for the Boxing Board, and one more hurdle cleared.

Each new applicant for the BBB of C licence has to be interviewed by the Area Council. As I was living on the farm whilst I was in training I appeared before the Western Area Council. Tex wasn't allowed into the interview room with me and he gave me severe instructions before I went in: 'Just answer the questions. Don't get aggressive, don't swear at anyone or call them tossers. Just bite your tongue and ooze that charm that comes to order when you are trying to con somebody.'

It was a good job I got that lecture. Bite my tongue? I nearly bit it off and pulled some face muscles forcing myself to smile. To call them tossers would have been a compliment! Here was me, in all my ignorance, expecting to come before an Area Council made up of well-dressed, intelligent business men and what did I see? A right motley crew, with hardly a suit amongst them. Luckily John Morris, who was in attendance, presumably because it was an important and historic occasion, was suited and looked the part. As for the rest, well when they asked me if I had a criminal record, I looked around the room and thought, I wouldn't be on my own if I said 'Yes!'

Then the question came, 'Who is going to manage you?

You can't have a licence unless you have a licensed manager.'

'I've got one.'

'Who?'

'Tex Woodward'

'He hasn't got a licence.'

I smiled at them. They thought they had me, but I knew something they didn't...

Earlier in Tex's career, he had held a BBB of C licence as a boxer, manager, promoter and MC but he had let it expire. When it became apparent that I would need a manager with a licence, he didn't have one!

There were foreseeable problems for Tex renewing his manager's licence. His relationship with the Western Area Council was not of the friendliest — calling the Area Secretary, Jim Paull, a 'silly old woman' had not been one of his best moves. Then, to add fuel to the flames, he was reported to the Board for seconding Mike Barratt's Ugandan light middleweight, Richard Okumu, who he had been training when his trainer's/second's licence had run out. He had to appear before the Area Council and be interviewed before they would renew his licence. He was not impressed! He was even less impressed with what he thought were questions designed for a first-time applicant, not an experienced coach. Tex ended his interview a bit quicker than the Board had expected when he stood up and said, 'I'm not answering stupid questions like those.' It was no surprise he was refused his trainer's/second's licence. He was told he could re-apply the following year! That really got his back up! 'Oh, so I need some more experience?'

'No,' Jim Paull said, 'if you become more servile you will get your licence!' Tex? *Servile*? What a laugh! He just withdrew, quite happily, into his own world and didn't even bother renewing his manager's licence. Now he needed one, there were going to be problems!

Dai Corp, an ex-boxer for Wales, had taken over from Jim Paull as Western Area Secretary. Tex thought this was a good omen — he had always got on with Welsh people and he had never offended Dai, as far as he knew. He must have offended someone, though; a letter from Dai, dated June 5th 1996, said, 'Dear Sir, With reference to your fax dated 18th May '96, which was read and discussed at the last meeting of the Council on 21st April '96, I regret to inform you, that after due consideration, the Council have agreed it would not be in the best interest of boxing to re-instate your licence. D. Corp. Western Area Secretary.' That got Granddad's back up! He wanted some answers. 'Why isn't it in the best interest of boxing to re-instate my licence? Is it to do with me, or the fact I am involved in women's boxing?'

He didn't get an answer so he applied directly to the main Boxing Board of Control in London. He was granted an interview on Wednesday, July 10th 1996 and was treated politely, fairly and questioned sensibly. I had travelled with Tex to the Board's offices in Borough High Street in South London. I didn't get involved. I stayed in the waiting area of the office while Tex was interviewed. Lots of Board members passed me, speaking politely and friendly. I was hoping they were being as pleasant to Granddad, otherwise he would be sharing his thoughts with them! Before he left the interview room, Tex made a point of saying that he was involved in women's boxing, as if they didn't know.

The fact was accepted, his licence application approved, and when a short while later he applied to renew his manager's licence it was processed without query. I now had an official manager. I didn't have to start training one all over again from scratch!

So you can imagine how satisfying it was when the Council told me he didn't have a licence, and I, quite calmly, smiled back, 'Yes, he has.' They looked at each other, perplexed, and the meeting was held up while John Morris went into the next room to speak to Tex.

'Your manager's licence, Tex. Have you renewed it?'

A pause. 'Yes, John. I have.'

What a pantomime. The next hurdle was my eyes. 'Jane's

eyes, there has been a report that she has an eye problem.'

'No, John. Her eyes are fine.'

'Well, you'd better get them checked again.'

They had tried hard, but couldn't find a valid reason to stop me having a licence. I had the requested eye test and, at long last, all the BBB of C's comprehensive criteria were complete. It was only a matter of time before my licence was processed.

Standing just outside the door to the farmhouse was an old-fashioned, white, enamel bread bin with a lid. The postman and the milkman took turns to put their deliveries inside it. My room was near the door. If I heard the lid of the bin rattle I would be out in a flash, always hoping that someone had written to me. It was junk mail mostly, and bills for Tex, but one spring morning I got to the bin first and there was a brown envelope addressed to Jane Couch, Spaniorum Farm Gymnasium. It felt as if it contained a video cassette. I opened it with only a little interest until I saw what it was. There, in my hand, lay my sporting history, the small, brown, stiff-backed BBB of C Professional Boxer's Licence, the first one ever to be issued to a woman. After months of endeavour, anticipation, expectation, rejection, dejection and frustration, I finally had it in my hands.

It was three years from the time I had first met Tex, when my boxing career was only a passing daydream, one of my periodic whims: 'I want to be a ballerina!' (some hope with my lack of grace); 'I want to be an astronaut!' (come to think of it I wasn't far off, I had my head in the clouds, so much; 'I want to be a singer!' (with my voice!?) Now I really was something — a professional boxer!

23

TRAIL BLAZER

One of the things people kept saying to me when I got my BBB of C licence was, 'It's really brilliant what you have done for other women who want to follow in your footsteps.' Those women's rights types and feminists got on my tits. What I had done with my battle against the BBB of C was get myself in the position to be able to box on the BBB of C's licensed shows. I wasn't trying to be Joan of Arc or Emmy Parkhurst, or whatever her fucking name was, fighting for other women. I was only fighting for me. Yes, I know I was a selfish bitch, but what had anyone done for me except try to rip me off?

Gradually, as I met and chatted to lots of girls who had been watching my progress, and were excited for themselves and me at what I had achieved, I began to feel really proud of myself, and gradually more kindly disposed to these women who mostly never expected to get as far as me but just wanted to have a go anyway.

There were still one or two loud-mouthed tossers who thought they were the bees knees. One or two of these came down from London to spar with me, thinking they were going to knock me about. What a hope! I'd think, Don't come in my gym shouting your mouth off, or you'll get a spanking. Probably more would have done, as I felt I had to prove a point, if it hadn't been for Tex. He would be in the ring saying, 'Take it easy, Jane, pull your punches.' I pulled some of them, but let the odd one or two go. It was a bit late Tex shouting then!

One Londoner that came down really made my day. She had her own personal trainer, wealthy sponsor, boyfriend or whatever he was. Before she came into the gym she was in the dressing room tarting herself up and putting make-up on. I made up my mind to get her almost at once, but Tex watched her move about for a minute or so and said to her trainer, 'Don't let her spar with Jane.' Why don't people listen? She still wanted to spar with me.

Eventually, after I had done ten or so really hard rounds, and she had been poncing about, Tex thought I might have had some of the steam taken out of me and he gave in to the sparring request. He got me on one side and said, 'Don't hit her hard, Jane, she isn't very strong. Just move around and make her miss.' I said, 'All right,' and I sort of meant it. Anyway, the bell goes, I move towards her, jab out a straight left and she really surprised me by sticking her nose hard on my glove — and her nose broke. Tex was really mad with me: 'You're not supposed to do that with novices, you ought to be ashamed of yourself.' I was a bit, but she was cocky! We never saw, or heard, anything from that little team again!

I would get these silly challenges from time to time —
people just didn't understand the level I was boxing at. Tex
would take the phone calls and be all encouraging to all the
wannabees. 'Yes, come down, by all means. Yes, you can train
with Jane.' One came down, from London again, with her
manager or whatever he was. She was a Moroccan or
something, quite strong but no skills. She was a cocky,
miserable cow who really fancied her chances. She was bigger
than me as well, and supposed to be a world Thai-boxing
champion, so Tex didn't mind me whacking her!

As time went by, though, and I polished my skills, I
stopped hitting people hard, well, the girls and novice men.
Not *really* hard, that is. I'd still get shouted at by Tex from time
to time.

Gradually, as I came to spend more and more time in Tex's
gym, I came to regard it as *my* gym. I was proud of it. When
the cleaners weren't doing their job as well as I would have
liked, I would clean the many mirrors, wipe down the punch
bags, scrub the sauna and showers. We got lots of visiting
boxers and I wanted *my* gym to be admired, not criticised like
some of the shitholes I had been in. I would show the visitors,
and new customers, around and explain the apparatus and how
to use it. I especially helped all the young boys and girls who
wanted to become boxers. Tex said I was a natural coach and
should do more of it when I stopped boxing. Really, I didn't
think I had enough patience, but I did like to see the kids
improving even if some of the best were cheeky little bastards. I
suppose that's why they were the best — and they didn't get
cheeky with me.

In the rare moments I stop to think about what the
boxing licence has done for me (and they are rare moments
because my mind flits about like the Midge does when we're
sparring), I know it has changed me and my life. It's turned me
into someone who now cares for, and wants to help, those
people who, like me, had a disadvantaged start to their lives or
have fallen on bad times. I have pressed a £5 note into the

hand of a homeless person, when it was probably the last one I had. Also, I gave every encouragement I could to deserving charities by attending functions, or donating signed items to be auctioned, or making personal appearances. I often found it a very humbling experience and very gratifying that I could help people just because I was now doing legally what had got me into so much trouble when I was doing it illegally — FIGHTING!

Of all the promoters in the country to promote my first BBB of C fight, it turned out to be Roy Cameron, Morris Rosen's friend. When Tex told me he had been talking to Roy, I said, 'You can fuck off, I am *not* boxing for that lot.' So, one of our regular battles started. 'Roy's a nice guy, he has done you no harm.'

'They are all phoney bastards, he is only using me to make money!'

'Of course he is, Jane, that's what promoters are supposed to do. If they don't make money the boxers don't get any fights.'

'Well, he isn't making any money out of me!'

'Jane, you are a professional boxer, you just box and I will take care of the business.'

'Fuck the business, I am *not* boxing for those London bastards!'

'Listen to me!' Tex was getting stroppy. He waffled on and on about me needing to get my first fight booked so that I would be seen fighting in this country and impress everyone. How much easier it would be, travelling to London instead of thousands of miles to America, and then he hit me where it hurts. Money! Like always, I didn't have any, and the chance of a few hundred pounds to spend eventually convinced me I should fight. I was going to have the last word, though. 'I'm only going to fight. I'm not going to talk to any of them!'

I had been ticking-over training, for what seemed like for ever, but now I had a specific training schedule of work times:

weight training, circuit, boxing skills and sparring. The sparring brought with it the irritation of having to wear a headguard. Something I would not previously do, much to Tex's annoyance. I learnt my lesson the hard way, though, in the build-up to a fight in Atlantic City, where I was going to defend my WIBF title against Leah Mellinger.

I had been sparring with Simon Stowell, a powerful, very useful, but reckless, amateur boxer. We always had wars. We would start off listening to Tex's instructions, 'Now, just practise your skills, fast and light punching.' OK, but it didn't last long before we were at it. Simon was ducking and rolling his head around my face when suddenly there was a clash of heads and my eyebrow turned into a red gash. It was a cut that sent shivers through everyone who saw it, Simon especially. Tex, who was in the ring with us, threw his hands to his head and said, 'Oh, my God!' He mopped my eye and then the lecture started. 'I have told you so many times about wearing a headguard, now perhaps you will listen. You will *not* spar with *anyone* again without wearing a headguard.' Needless to say, I had to pull out of my fight with Mellinger.

Now, with the cut well healed, Tex had arranged for me to fight at Caesars Palace Casino, Streatham, against a German girl, Simone Lukic, on November 25th 1998. The promoter — Roy Cameron! This time, in my preparations for the fight, I wore a headguard and I survived dozens of rounds of sparring with good male boxers, Dean Cooper, Mike Loveridge, Eddie Hedges, Darren Dorrington, ultra-tough Thai-boxer Martin Hurd and even 'Crazy Head' Simon. The men provided some heavy sparring for me, while eight-stoner Sandra 'the Midget' Rouse, my friend, sparring partner and Tex's corner assistant provided the speed work, and the occasional surprisingly hard right-hand punch.

The final training session over, I stood looking at myself in one of the many gym mirrors — not an unusual thing for me to do but on this occasion it was more of an assessment of my fitness, than my regular admiration of my looks. I looked like a super-fit athlete. I was hot and sweaty, my biceps and abdominal muscles glistening with sweat, showing their definition. My hated headguard had been discarded and thrown on to the ringside leaving my black ringlets stuck to my forehead with perspiration. I didn't know how good this Kraut boxer would be, but she was going to be in for a hard night's work.

Just three days to go before the fight. Three days to relax, away from the clanging sound of weight machines, the grunting, groaning and gasping as I forced myself around the circuit trying to beat the stopwatch. All I had to do was relax and let all my energy rebuild for my fight. Relax? That was harder than training! I had no problem with my weight and as I kept eating my energy built up. I had to be doing something. I'd clean my room, over and over again. I'd tidy up the gym. I would get to the local giant shopping centre as much as I could, wandering around spending the last of my money on hair lotions, trendy outfits, chocolates, food, a bottle of martini for Tex.

It was great to be away from the gym and have time to spend on myself, but Tex didn't like me walking around shopping so much. 'It is one of the worst things you can do, it will take all the energy out of your legs. Now we have to have a plan to keep you mentally occupied.' So he tried — it was supposed to go something like this: Monday 10.00 a.m. Get up, breakfast; 11.30 BBC West TV interview, followed by them filming me going through the motions of a training session without using any energy. David Passmore, who came to interview me, was early, so Tex invited him into the house for a cup of tea. I thought, Great! I'll sneak off into the gym and have a workout while they are chatting.

I'd been punching the bag for a while when Tex came storming in. He had suddenly realised that everything was quiet and peaceful in the house and that meant I wasn't around. So where was I and what was I up to? He needed to find out. When he did, he exploded. 'What on earth do you think you are doing?'

'I was just practising.'

'What were you practising?' I couldn't answer. He touched my bare shoulders, they were dripping with sweat. 'You don't sweat like that "practising" — you have been working hard. I told you you should be resting!' He was sensible enough not to make a big issue out of it. It didn't take much for us to have a row with each other at the best of times. With me in the taut, nervous state many boxers experience before a fight, a real argument could have had me flipping and catching the next train home.

From that moment onwards things went according to plan: 11.30 David Passmore's TV interview. I was now in fine fettle. I liked David, we had got on really well together since I had met him two years before at the BBC Sports Awards dinner, in the absence of a bottle opener, I had taken the cap off a bottle of beer with my teeth for him.

12.15 Shower time, lunch time, and last-minute packing to leave the farm. 2.30 We put our bags into a luxurious BMW and were whisked away to the TV Studios in Manchester where we appeared on the *Here and Now* programme, hosted by Juliet Morris. We weren't the sole representatives from the boxing world. Two young, female amateur boxers shadow-boxed in a boxing ring, a third punched the pads, held by a woman coach, all this overlooked by three lads, who were supposed to be punching bags suspended on a balcony overlooking the ring. It wasn't a bad little show, but I didn't have much to say — or rather they didn't give me enough time to say a lot. I enjoyed chatting to the girls, backstage, who were hoping to become boxers. They were nice girls. After the recording it was back to a hotel.

Tuesday 8 a.m. Breakfast! A luxury few boxers have on the day of a weigh-in. I had been consistently weighing 10 stone and I knew I would make the weight in comfort. At 9.30 a.m. a pleasant, Scottish taxi driver arrived to take us to Manchester Airport for our flight to Heathrow, London. It was our quickest flight anywhere, and I had hardly finished my cup of tea when we were touching down to be met by yet another talkative driver who seemed to know how to miss all the traffic. He dropped us with time to spare before the weigh-in at our Streatham hotel.

I had booked several rooms in this hotel for myself, Sandra, Tex and my family and some friends. It was clean and tidy, if a bit sparse. There were no shelves in the shower room, and you had to squeeze round the toilet to get in the shower and be a contortionist to dry yourself afterwards. The room where meals were served was something else. Tex said it reminded him of an RAF dining hall. All its tables and chairs were exactly in line, mostly unoccupied. As eating time ran out the door to the room was locked, a bit worrying at first if you were on the inside, and hard luck if you were on the outside!

There was little time to kill before starting the few hundred yards' walk to Caesars Palace for the 1.30 p.m. weigh-in. We arrived an hour early, expecting a certain amount of media attention, but were surprised at how much there was. The hour slipped away, my mind occupied with non-stop interviews and camera shots. It was then we first saw Simone Lukic. My first feeling was relief that an opponent had turned up — I had been let down that many times in the past that I wouldn't have been surprised if it had all been some stupid bastard's idea of a publicity stunt. I was called to the scales. Tex almost dragged me away from the non-stop attention of the journalists. I stripped to shorts and crop-top. As I stepped on the scales there must have been dozens of camera flashes, and the dim surroundings of the casino were lit up like daylight.

The clerk of the scales glanced at the dial and said, 'Jane Couch, ten stone!' I wasn't, I was 9 stone 13½lb. Old watch-everything-very-carefully Tex, noted that down but said nothing: it was not important enough to ask for a correction. Simone stepped on the scales and weighed 10 stone ½lb. The announcement came 'Simone Lukic, 10 stone.' Either the clerk couldn't see in the dim light, had left his glasses at home, or had a 10 stone fixation. Whatever, it didn't matter. If it had been a title fight Tex would have been saying, in his best voice, 'She will have to take it off!'

Simone was a tall, slim, pale-complexioned, good-looking girl who seemed to be about four inches taller than me. We both had dark hair, but that was about all. My biceps were much bigger, and my abdominal muscles were not quite washboard, but you could tell I liked my sit-ups almost as much as I liked my sun-bed suntan. There was such a difference in our appearance that Dave Smith, of the London *Evening Standard*, headlined his article, BEAUTY AND THE BEAST. I wasn't too chuffed about that, and I told him so. I always considered myself a bit bonny and attractive, and although she wasn't bad looking, she wasn't brilliant.

Tex wasn't bothered about beauty — he was weighing up Lukic's possible fighting ability. 'Simone has had eight fights. Now with the fresh, unmarked face she has got, it means she hasn't been hit hard, or often. Now that could mean one of several things. She has a good defence, the opponents can't get past her long reach or she hasn't fought anybody capable of punishing her. We'll soon find out!' Me and Simone both passed the doctor's examination and I managed to get away from the photographers when they all dashed off to where she was posing like a model on a rug. I thought, Silly cow, you won't be lying about quite so comfortably tomorrow night.

I never looked forward to the day of a fight. The fight itself, yes! Let me get in that ring in front of a big crowd and show them what I can do. But it's a long day before that first bell rings. Nevertheless I was up early the next day. Tex had arranged two TV interviews for me — left to that grey-haired old bastard I wasn't going to have much time to sit around and think. He knew I would take ages preening myself, as he called it, especially if I was going to face a camera. I would comb my hair, wet my hair, check my hair, moisturise my skin, draw my lips back and admire my shining white and gold teeth. In fact, I'd admire my whole reflection!

Another taxi, another trip, this time to the ITN Studios in London. I did one good TV interview, one not-so-good, a radio phone-in, got lots of good wishes, and then it was back to Streatham.

Almost within minutes of getting back to the hotel the Midge was with us. She had driven, alone, from Bristol, and despite a bit of unexpected and unplanned sight-seeing around South London, had time to relax and swap gym gossip before we took the short walk to Caesars Palace and into sporting history. As we neared the Palace with its life-size replica of chariot and horses above the door, a shiver went through my body as I realised *I* was one of the gladiators tonight. Thankfully I only had to fight a German, not a lion!

Once in the dressing room, it's time to clear the mind from all the pre-fight chatter, all the good wishes, and concentrate on the job in hand, or in a boxer's case, both hands. There was one more visitor before the dressing room was cleared, Kevin Leushing, the ex-British Welterweight Champion. He gave me a kiss and was really nice as he wished me luck for the fight. Next day in the press he is criticising me!

What really pissed me off was that it wasn't as if he hadn't had his fair share of easy fights on the way up, and then when he did get a world title fight against a good boxer, Felix Trinidad, he got stopped in the third round, cheeky bastard! I was already a world champion and had defended my title, successfully, twice in America!

Kevin Leushing wasn't on his own as a critic — there were loads of the bastards, at first. Most of them hadn't even done a fraction of what Leushing had done. What they *had* done was kiss a load of asses along the way, and still not made it to the top. Then they saw all the publicity I was getting, without kissing anybody's ass, not fucking one, and they didn't like it. To them I was the new kid on the block. I was a world champion that hadn't been protected all the way, or had my career path smoothed out for me. I had challenged Sandra Geiger for the world title when I was almost unknown, and been accepted as a passable opponent. Didn't that cause an upset when a four-fight novice beat the favourite! All my fights had been hard, in fact it was hard for me to *get* a fight — I was too tough! It was easier and cheaper for the new governing bodies, like the International Females Boxing Association, and the older International Women's Boxing Federation, to set up 'World' title fights and produce their own 'champions'.

My fight was the second of the evening's entertainment, and we had about an hour to get ready. Tex's first job was always to prepare the tape and bandages for my hands. He did it the way you often see in the old-fashioned films. One-inch zinc oxide, adhesive tape cut in strips and stuck on the wall, the long strips, the shorter strips, and thin strips to secure between the fingers. The two-inch gauze bandage opened, and thumb holes cut at the starting end, ready to wrap the hand before applying the tape. Sandra was buzzing about, filling the ice-bag, helping me tie my hair back tightly so that it wouldn't get in my eyes. Me getting into my boxing gear, mentally going through my boxing skills and trying to focus my mind now I was away from outside distractions. Then it was the important warm-up time.

Tex had been quiet as he changed into his corner outfit and prepared his equipment, and thoughts, for the fight. Now it was action time and he was alive, and he was making me even more alive. Gentle shadow-boxing, faster shadow-boxing, stretching, bending, fast combination punching, and finally rehearsing the aggressive body language I was to show when leaving the corner at the start of the first round. Tex told me to stand in the corner of the dressing room and then turn as if I was coming out to fight with blazing eyes and menacing attitude. He believed this gave an initial psychological advantage to me: he needn't have bothered. I was going to frighten the Kraut out of her wits anyway!

The rap on the dressing room door caught us by surprise. It was Ernie, the whip, a man who had probably called more boxers to the ring than anyone else in the country. I liked

Ernie, he was really nice to us. He said, 'Two minutes.' The Midge helped me on with my dressing gown. I had been given a new boxing kit by a firm called BeG. Black and red satin gown, ribboned shorts and a black crop-top — I looked amazing!

After some of the massive halls I had boxed in in America, the ring was very close. My entrance music, 'My Way' by the Sex Pistols, started, and after what seemed like just a few steps I was in the ring. Simone Lukic was waiting in her corner, she looked even taller, with her dark hair, like mine, tightly drawn back. She looked thoughtful as she leaned, arms resting on the ropes, in the red corner, and watched me dancing, shadow-boxing, waving to the crowd.

Simon Goodall, who had previously erected the ring but was now a smart, formally dressed Master of Ceremonies, introduced us to the crowd. There was a sporting cheer for the German girl, but I had the best reception I had ever had — there were a lot of people who had come to see me box. Referee Richie Davis called the two of us to the centre of the ring for final instructions, a quick touch of our gloves, and all the hype, the legal battles, the debates and discussions, the thousands of miles travelling abroad to fight the home-town girl, were over. Now I was the home-town girl! When the bell started the first round, I came out of that corner with all the aggressive body language Tex could have wished for.

Before the echoes of the bell had faded away I was in the middle of the ring, I feinted with a straight left and followed it with a straight right. In the first ten seconds I threw fourteen punches — luckily for Simone most of them were a little out of range, but the pattern was set. She backed off, jabbing with her long left hand. I was bobbing, weaving, blocking and counter-punching with both hands. The bell went and I walked slowly back to my corner. Tex was waiting for me: 'Sit down, relax.' Gumshield out and rinsed, a gentle sponging, the vital drink. 'That's fine, you're just a little tense. Relax, breathe deeply. Now, keep your hands up and keep working.'

Gumshield in, the bell for the second round sounded, and it was back into action. Lukic's left jab was becoming more accurate, she was moving better and I was feeling a bit awkward trying to work my way inside her long reach. I got close, backed her up against the ropes and whacked her with two right hands to the head, followed by a right uppercut, before she slid off the ropes and backed away. I worked my way in again behind five straight lefts.

Once in range, I threw one right then another right, and was about to finish her off with another big punch when the referee rushed in to save her further punishment. He cradled her against the ropes and I couldn't resist one last swing to her ribs — sadly I hit her elbow. It didn't matter, what I had done was enough, and I had won quickly and everybody was pleased. Really I would have liked it to have been a much harder fight, so that I could have shown the crowd just how good I was. Nevertheless, it was a good result and I jogged happily around the ring enjoying every last clap, cheer and whistle I could get. Simone was slumped on her stool probably wondering what had hit her. It was me! It was great! 'That will teach them for bombing me Granny's fish and chip shop in the war.' It was a joke, but it didn't go down well with the Germans!

Silke Weickenmein and Greg Steene, Simone Lukic's seconds, revived and consoled her under the watchful eye of John Morris, the General Secretary of the BBB of C, and a Board female doctor. She recovered quickly enough. The fight result was announced, and as the excitement died away I was quickly back in the dressing room with a pint of Guinness in my hand. Gloves off, my breathing and heart rate slowing down, and it was time to face a press conference. The number of cameras working overtime had probably never been seen before in Caesars Palace, Streatham and would have more than held its own at Caesars Palace, Las Vegas!

The media attention at the fight had been phenomenal. It was later described by Claude Abrams, Editor of *Boxing News*, as having 'exceeded interest shown in either Lennox Lewis or Naseem Hamed, when they made their professional débuts in this country'. So many questions, so many answers. 'Look this way, Jane!' 'Here, Jane!' 'Smile, Jane!' 'Pose, Jane!' So many camera flashes it was like I was hypnotised. I couldn't remember anything I had said. It must have been all right, with no bad language, because Tex said the interview was good.

If my mind was in a blur trying to keep up with the journalists, it got even more blurred when we got back to the hotel. I changed and we went to the bar for a drink or two. We had been escorted back from Caesars Palace by a group of security men who were horrified at the thought of us walking through Streatham on our own late at night. So we reached the hotel safely but slowly, and there were still autograph hunters looking for me!

In the bar someone had organised a video cassette player, so we watched the video of the fight which, like thousands of other fights before it, had been rapidly produced by Steve Holdsworth. There was quite a group of watchers, Sandra, Tex, family, friends and a few hotel workers. I enjoyed watching myself and listening to the praise, and I enjoyed the first glass of whisky I had drunk for what seemed like ages and ages. In fact I think more than one — things were getting even more blurred.

Tex held out till 3 a.m. before he left us to go to bed. Me and Sandra still had some life left in us, high on adrenalin and alcohol. I was in a fine flirtatious mood, chatting up a butcher from Brecon called Paddy! He had travelled from Wales just to watch me box! 'What a shame we don't live closer together.' I wondered what was coming. 'I could help you out and provide free steaks!'

Next day, with my family and friends, I started the long train journey back to Fleetwood. Me, I had suffered more from being in the bar the night before than I had in the fight. We had all tried to hide our smiles in the dressing room after I had won so quickly when the lady doctor said, 'Now, don't drink

231 / FLEETWOOD ASSASSIN

any alcohol tonight!' I wish I had listened. Not for the first time, nor I expect the last time, I said, 'Ooooh! Ooooh! I'm never going to drink again.'

Back home in Fleetwood, things were crazy. I had been very well known before I had started boxing, but now, with all the massive publicity I had been having in almost every newspaper, and on telly, it was mental. I was mobbed everywhere I went. If people didn't speak, they would point at me and whisper to each other. I felt like shouting out, 'It's all right, it's only me, I haven't got seven heads!' Mum couldn't stand it: we'd have to go home because the pressure was getting too much for her. Telephone calls, questions, criticisms of me in the press, it was all making her snappy and irritable. She had snapped at Tex after my fight saying that I was giving the press too much time. She just didn't understand that, at this time, I was very newsworthy, well known across the country, and that media attention was all part of the job. I don't know how my Dad dealt with it — he wasn't seen for a couple of days after we got home.

Being back at home, and seeing all the problems I was causing, even though it wasn't *really* my fault, put me back into worrying mode. Was it right that I cause my family troubles? If I was making them unhappy, perhaps it would be better to stop boxing. I had to be on my own to think this out. I managed to get down to Memorial Park without too much hassle. I had played there so much as a kid that the familiar surroundings instantly eased my frantic thoughts.

I stepped over the fence around the small lake and sat watching the ducks swimming, and others exploring the grass with their beaks, looking for food. I found some bits of bread to throw to them, and I relaxed even more as I watched them race each other to get each bit. For once my mind wasn't in a turmoil, but I knew I must sort out where my life was going from here. To box or not to box, that was the question. It made me think of something I had learned at school, or heard somewhere, but I couldn't remember what it was.

I don't know how long I sat there, but it was time well spent. I decided I wasn't going to live my life around other people's thoughts. I was going to do what I wanted to do, be a brilliant boxer, even if it did mean going back to the farm, and literally working my tits off.

It always makes me laugh when mostly female journalists say, 'Doesn't it hurt when you get hit in the...' They make signs with their hands.

'You mean my tits? I haven't got any. If you trained as hard as me, you wouldn't have any either.' Anyway under some rules you have to wear breast protectors, but most girls don't like them. I've only worn them once and I felt more exposed as they stop you pulling in your elbows for a good guard.

Decision made, I was on my way to Bristol Parkway next day. I was only kidding myself that I wanted to get back into hard training though. Even Tex said I should rest a while. The main reason for returning to the farm was that Tex and I had been invited to the West Country BBC TV and Radio Sports Awards dinner at The Swallow Hotel, Bristol. I'd been to the same dinner the year before, and I had made a big impression that night on a few of the male guests: I was getting phone calls for days from the most unlikely faces!

This year's do had a different atmosphere, in some ways more enjoyable as I knew more people, and certainly more people knew me. The food was great and there was plenty of wine. I had a right argument with Tex about that. He had insisted on driving his car and wouldn't have a drink. I said he was too mean to pay a taxi fare, he said it was more convenient to have the car with him. Lying bastard — he enjoyed a drink.

I got cross with him again when the Sportswoman of the Year award nominations were announced. I was one of three names. Tex said, 'That's really good you being nominated, and you're not even from this area.' I told him, 'I don't want to be a nominee, I want to win it.' I don't know who was the most surprised when I did win it, Tex or me. It was brilliant and when I made my speech everyone thought it was hilarious, especially when I told off the Bristol RFC coach, Australian Bob Dwyer, for knocking our cricket team. I told him I was going to knock him out later. Everyone loved that.

The person that got the best clap of the evening was John Ward, the ex-Bristol City FC manager, who, like me, came to Bristol from the North of England. John had recently left his job as City manager, but everyone in the room would have reinstated him on the spot if they could have. The clapping went on and on. I suppose I shouldn't have said it in Bristol, but it sort of came out — as things tend to do when I am talking, when I mentioned in my speech how good it was that two Northerners got trophies!

It was definitely a really good end to 1998, a year that certainly had its ups and downs for me.

24

MIDDLESBROUGH

1 999. A new year, a new promoter — Jonathan Feld of the World Sports Organisation — and a new venue, the Thornaby Pavilion, Middlesbrough. The bare brick walls of a run-of-the-mill leisure centre, were a stark contrast to the dimly lit, nightclub atmosphere of Caesars Palace, Streatham.

Equally contrasting was the ability of the opponent selected for me. Marischa Sjauw, a Dutch girl of Surinamese origin, who had been honing her boxing skills in Florida, USA, under the tutelage of top-class American trainer Jessie Reid. Marischa's boxing record was good, and the more I researched about her, the more impressed I was. I scanned the Internet to glean as much information as possible. The Dutch girl was favourite to win; she, her husband and an American trainer had come to England for the formality of collecting my world title, the belt and the prestige that went with it. A feeling of *déja vu* crept over me. It was like Denmark all over again, when I had been taken as an opponent for Sandra Geiger — but this time they would have to deal with a more experienced Jane Couch.

It had taken almost as long travelling to Middlesbrough as it had to Denmark, and we arrived at the Marton Hotel reception desk immediately behind Marischa and her team. Introductions were friendly, and we chatted briefly before getting into the lift to go to our rooms. As the lift doors closed, I exploded with laughter: 'She's got a little fuckin' monkey face, she had her jaw stuck out and she was looking me up and down.'

'Yes Jane, I think you won the first round of the psychological battle,' said Tex, laughing.

Luggage ensconced in our respective rooms, it was time to locate the scales and make a precautionary weight check. Through years of experience in gaining access to the scales before the weigh-in, it didn't take Tex long to locate them. When he did he smiled at the ingenuity of the boxer, or his manager, who had secreted them in his bathroom! My weight was no problem, low enough to eat a good meal.

Somehow we couldn't avoid meeting Marischa, Marcel, her husband, and Jason, her American trainer. We chatted a lot, had a drink together, and the little monkey face changed to a quite attractive, pleasant young woman who I got to like.

On the morning of the weigh-in, scheduled for three o'clock in the afternoon, we again made the obligatory pilgrimage to the scales. They were gone! So were the occupants of the room. It was no disaster — Tex had the ability to find scales like a homing pigeon finds its loft. The official weigh-in was in the sun-lounge, a large room next to the hotel ballroom with windows the length of one side. There, hidden under a sheet, with a large cardboard box over the top, were the electronic scales. Plugged in, switched on, the scales weighed me well inside the limit — time to eat again. With the scales carefully re-sheeted and boxed, it was away to the restaurant.

At the official weigh-in Marischa and I both made the weight comfortably inside the limit, both wearing clothes, which is more than can be said for some of the men boxers weighing in nude. Judith Rollestone, the BBB of C representative, carefully averted her eyes and pretended not to notice a tattooed bottom! I did!

For once, waiting for fight time didn't drag at first. With all the officials, trainers and boxers all staying at the Marton Hotel and Country Club, there was always someone to talk to, and I talked to almost everyone, with my usual mixture of charm and cheek. Calling Larry O'Connell, one of the judges for my fight, a 'fat bastard' probably wasn't the cleverest thing I'd ever done, though. John Coyle, the referee, didn't escape comment either, his receding hairline deteriorating to 'bald' in my eyes. Luckily Larry and John were nice guys with a sense of humour and there was no $100 fine, as there had been in Atlantic City.

It was a long wait in the dressing room. People came and people went, fans, friends, family and officials. Gradually they all faded away with the exception of an ex-athlete, Lorraine Johnson, who was now working for the Sports Council Anti-doping Directorate. Lorraine had to take a urine sample from me and then stay watching me closely to make sure I took nothing that could be a performance-enhancing drug before or during the fight. I did not take kindly to providing a sample, but it had to be done, and at least Lorraine didn't appear to have had a similar authoritarian training to her counterpart in Connecticut!

At last, Tex could start to bandage and tape my hands. Time began to drag, and the show started an hour late. During the lulls in the warming-up session we listened to the distant sound of the referee, counting over a knocked-down boxer, hoping the count would get to ten. It wasn't that we wanted anybody to be hurt, or even knew who was on the canvas, it was just that an early finish to a fight meant getting the battle that meant most to us started.

Then there was the interval. I was on first in the second half. It was the longest time we had ever had to wait to get in the ring, nearly four hours in the dressing room. Somehow it passed and even more miraculously I, normally a hotbed of impatience, had kept my mind focused on the task I had in front of me.

At last we headed for the ring, team Couch, for once, without a familiar corner assistant. Sandra Rouse and Tony Evans had both, unfortunately, booked holidays abroad. Substitute assistant, Tony Brown, a good ex-boxer from Liverpool, filled the slot excellently, even if his strong scouser accent did leave us wondering what he was talking about at times. Boxing in the North of England for the first time since my early days as a novice fighter in Fleetwood, I was given a tremendous reception by the crowd. Marischa was also given an encouraging, sporty welcome and we rewarded the crowd with ten rounds of non-stop action, described by Srikumar Sen, reporting for the *Times* newspaper as, 'the most entertaining of the evening'. The headline of his article: CROWD OF 1,200 GRIPPED BY TEN-ROUND ENCOUNTER, was followed by, 'Women's boxing came under the spotlights again and passed with flying colours.' Nick Halling, writing in the *Independent*, was also supportive, including in his article, 'Many of the crowd had come to experience the novelty of female boxing. In the end they showed their appreciation of two, highly motivated, well-trained athletes.' Praise indeed for two female fighters who had set a standard that would be very difficult to follow in the UK. Unfortunately, Daniel Herbert, writing in *Boxing News*, could not match his more illustrious journalistic colleagues for enthusiasm about the efforts of

Marischa and me. Perhaps he was following in the footsteps of *Boxing News* editor Claude Abrams, and previous editor Harry Mullan, in portraying his own dislike for women's boxing. Whatever the reason was for his negative report, it certainly didn't reflect the crowd's enjoyment of the contest.

The judges' scores for the fight, which was originally a defence of my WIBF welterweight title but surprisingly had the World Boxing Federation title up for grabs as well, were: Terry O'Connor 98-93, Paul Thomas 97-93 and Larry O'Connell making me the winner by just one point — I knew I shouldn't have called him a fat bastard! Still, he obviously knew what he was doing as he scored me to win!

The fight started well for me — I even knocked Marischa down in the first round and she had the compulsory 8 count. It's just as well I did, because I would have lost that round otherwise, and Larry O'Connell with his scoring would have made the fight a draw! The only other round I might have lost was the last one when I went out and traded blows instead of jabbing and moving as I should have done. 'Go out and box behind your jab, you have easily won this, just keep out of trouble.' Ah, well! One day I'll learn to do as I'm told — maybe! The only momentary shock was when blood started running down my face from a cut, high on my head, in the eighth round. There was no panic in the corner, Granddad had the adrenalin and swabs ready. There was just one problem — he couldn't find the cut! My tight sweat-matted Afro-type curls were completely hiding the damage. He just dabbed the adrenalin around at random, hoping to be lucky, wiped away what blood he could, and was grateful there were only two rounds to go. The blood didn't bother me, I'd had worse for no wages.

Back in the dressing room, after all the well-wishers and relatives had been cleared out (except my mum), the BBB of C doctor, Dr Kipling, examined me for the cut on my head. What a search, it must have lasted more than an hour — no wonder Tex couldn't find it. He was enjoying it all: 'Shave a patch of her head, doctor, so you can see it.' Like hell I was going to have my head shaved. I screamed, cursed, threatened and all the doctor said was, 'She is an amusing girl, isn't she?' If he thought *that* was amusing, he must have thought it was hilarious when he found the cut at last and said, 'I think three stitches should do,' and proceeded to bend two needles on my scalp. I really gave him some verbal. He took it all in his stride — what a nice man. If any of the Board's doctors were awarded a commendation for patience and tolerance, he would get my vote. I'll forgive him for missing with one of the stitches and just tying it around the thick roots of my hair!

Showered, changed and sewn up, it was time to head back to the Marton Hotel and the party there. We got a lift from the son-in-law of the man who had seconded Granddad in his last amateur fight. It was in 1956, before he was even a Dad! They hadn't met for forty-three years, but I'd heard a lot about Geordie Walton, and he turned out to be a super chap, as was his son-in-law Norman. Nice as they were though, they didn't party like the Midget and Tony Evans!

25

AN EVENING WITH PRETTY BOY

It could have been the Annual General Meeting of the London underworld. Actually it was a professional boxing dinner at a London hotel, a charity fund-raiser that I had been asked to attend, I thought, to add some glamour to the occasion. Glamour? Fuck me! There were birds there dressed to kill, most of them with older blokes, dressed in traditional black dinner suits and bow ties, who greeted their mates with more kisses and hugs than they gave the women.

I should have been warned about what we were getting into, when we shared the lift with a Londoner with a heavily scarred face who was heading for the function room where the boxing was being held. Me, what am I like? I said, 'How did you get those scars, mate?' He told me, and I shuddered. Tex wasn't going to be outdone. He put on his 'hard' face and said, 'How about these?' He pointed to a large scar on the top of his nose and a few minor lines around his face. (He didn't bother to mention that I had inflicted the large scar, accidentally, with my racket when we had been playing squash.) We got out of the lift, apprehensive but still unharmed, and walked into the bar which was swarming with black suits, bow ties, and plenty of faces whose features had been enhanced with plenty of time inside and a good deal of violence.

The boxing world is comparatively small, and once you get on the circuit the same faces appear over and over again: the often maligned and criticised referees; the smooth, and not-so-smooth managers and promoters; the usually cynical, often jaded, trainers, and cornermen. It was one of these faces that greeted us warmly as we tried to blend in to the pre-fight festivities. As we chatted we were told, 'There must be a million years of bird (prison time) in here tonight, and at least twelve shooters.' If that was supposed to make us feel at home and relaxed, it *didn't* have the desired effect. Granddad, looking the part in the Italian-style, striped suit, with the four-button jacket I had bought him, evoked the comment from pig-tailed giant Jim Fielder, 'He looks like something out of a *Rocky* film.' Tex wasn't sure if that was a compliment or a criticism!

Muhammad Ali would have been proud of me. He used to say he 'floated like a butterfly and stung like a bee'. I was doing the butterfly bit, and flitting everywhere, but I wasn't stinging like a bee, I was dishing out the honey. They all loved me and treated me like one of their own, and that wasn't just the men: the wives were brilliant, and dead supportive of me boxing. They were really disappointed I wasn't boxing on the show that night, but I made up for it by teaching some of them a few moves. I thought, God, I hope they don't go home and thump their husbands or I'll really be in trouble.

I sat still long enough to eat the starter and the main course, but that was long enough. Everyone seemed to want to talk to me, have photos taken with me, or get my autograph. What a night!! It must have been one of the best of my life, I felt like a really big star. I got back to the table, ready for my dessert, only to find some black guy had eaten it, *and* his own, *and* he'd tried to pinch Tex's as well — some hope!

The boxing was ordinary, but it didn't matter — I had plenty of people chatting to me, some getting really enthusiastic. Fred 'Nosher' Powell, ex-professional heavyweight boxer and famous stuntman, cornered me and took me through some of the rougher moves of boxing that would have had the Marquis of Queensbury tut-tutting over his glass of port. I played along but thought, Come off it, Nosher, I was playing these games in the pubs long before I ever got into the boxing ring! Still, it was nice of him to try and help me.

Fuckin' hell! There were some names and faces there that night! I couldn't remember all of them, or even how to say some of them. Tony Lambrianou, that was a mouthful I just couldn't get my tongue around — well, the surname that is, Tony was easy enough. He was a really good-looking chap; shame he was too old for me.

The one guy there I just had to meet was Roy 'Pretty Boy' Shaw. I hadn't long finished reading his book — what a life he had led. No one deserved to be treated the way he had been in Broadmoor Hospital for the Criminally Insane. Five years of hell, not all of his own making. No wonder he had that blank, wooden look on his face when I introduced myself! He probably thought, Who the fuck's this grinning bitch? *My* first thoughts were, Where on earth did he get the name 'Pretty Boy'? He was all right with me, though, when he found out who I was, and with Tex. It broke the ice with Roy when he discovered we all had a mutual friend Bob Vodden. Bob, a good amateur boxer from London who had boxed in the same team as Tex in the RAF, had actually beaten Roy Shaw on points, over three rounds, at the Hornsey Town Hall in the early fifties — he lived not only to tell the tale, but to be a good friend of Roy.

I had never been a particularly enthusiastic autograph hunter, but to be talking to this legend of a street-fighter, I had to have a souvenir. I pushed a pen and paper towards him. He looked at it without expression. I thought he was going to ignore my request. He reached for his inside pocket, and I had a nervous thought that maybe it was time I was somewhere else. It was with great relief that I saw him pull out a solid gold pen. I was impressed, and I asked to handle it and get a closer look at it. No chance, he wasn't letting go of that little treasure! I didn't know why he had any worries about losing it — I certainly wasn't going to do a runner with Roy Shaw's pen in my hand... He took a long time writing a little message to me and signing his autograph, and then Peter Richardson took a photograph of us. The pen then quickly disappeared into Roy Shaw's inside pocket. I knew, at that moment, the memories of that evening that I would have in the future would not be of the boxing, but of the intriguing characters I had met.

I got my own computer! So what? A lot of people had computers, but with me — no technical skills, and more comfortable hitting a punchbag than a keyboard — it wasn't exactly what anyone would expect. It became another obsession, like boxing. Really it was the same obsession, as I could now communicate with the world and become familiar with all the female and male boxers. Who they were, where they came from, what weight they were, and even more importantly get the results of fights and how they boxed. I was trapped by the Internet.

As I delved deeper and deeper into my new and fascinating hobby, I began to get mixed emotions. People were saying things about me on the websites and chat rooms they would never say to my face. Marcel, Marischa Sjauw's husband, who had been so charming to me and Tex when I beat her in Middlesbrough, was saying I was lucky to win, and I was frightened to have a re-match — bollocks! I always said I would fight any female fighter: anyone, any time, anywhere!

God! Tex had faxed Don King enough times challenging

Christie Martin. He even contacted Christie by telephone and suggested we fight. Stan Hoffman was phoned several times so that I could challenge Lucia Rijker. Somehow these challenges were never accepted, and all the time I was being criticised on the Net for picking my fights and avoiding re-matches. I found it so annoying and discouraging that I threatened to get rid of my computer. How could people be so unkind and critical when they probably hadn't even seen me fight? If they had, they were probably useless judges of boxing anyway. I knew it shouldn't depress me, but it did, particularly the waffle about return fights — so I had given someone the opportunity to beat me and take my title, and I won the fight. Why should I need to do it again? Going over old ground didn't interest me, I wanted new challenges.

After winning and retaining my WIBF world title, as well as gaining the WBF world title on April Fool's Day 1999 in Middlesbrough against Marischa Sjauw, my next new challenge was against Sharon Anyos, from Australia, in Raynes Park, London. This time it was Hallowe'en! Could it be symbolic? In one of those rare quiet moments before the ritual building up to the fight, I got Tex on his own. I hung my head forward and whispered to him, 'I'm frightened!' I felt embarrassed. I never thought I could have said those words.

Tex tried to be understanding. 'Jane, you are boxing better than you have ever boxed. You're fit and have the best mental preparation for this fight you could have. This girl may be strong and can hit hard but she is *not* going to beat you.'

'No, it's not her I'm frightened of, it's the atmosphere, the whole occasion.' More calming words from Tex, but the apprehension was still lurking in my mind — what of, I didn't know.

The first time I saw Sharon Anyos was at the weigh-in. She looked taller than I expected — until I found out she was wearing high-heeled shoes. I was first on the scales, always a bit of a heart-stopping moment, even though I had checked my weight on those scales not long before. I had weighed in then at 9 stone 8½lb. The lightweight limit: 9 stone 9lb. This was the first time I had boxed at lightweight, something Tex and I had often discussed. He would say, 'You are always whingeing about giving weight away. I think it is much better for a boxer to box at their natural weight. Anyway, I am not sure you can discipline your eating and drinking habits to lose that extra couple of pounds.'

As it turned out, for the Anyos fight I didn't need to discipline my food intake. I was scoffing ice-cream and chocolate right up to the day of the weigh-in. I should have been really pleased. We had made a slight change in my weight-training programme, which must have burned off some of the small amount of fat on me. As my weight gradually dropped I found it worrying. What if it wasn't the training I was doing? What if I had cancer and it was eating me away? Tex was despairing for me. 'Jane, you are a nutcase. You whinge about giving weight away. When you are trained down naturally, you think you are ill! How could you train like you do if you were ill? It's just a case of burning up more energy than you take in with your food.'

On the morning of the weigh-in, at twelve o'clock in the Marriott Hotel, Heathrow, London, we found the official scales before anyone else was about and a check weigh-in had me a pound and a half under the limit. I could eat! I ate under the watchful eye of Tex, who wasn't slow in reminding me that it didn't take much food and drink to put on a couple of pounds. Another check later, still a bit light, and I was supping at my water bottle. I didn't want to be under the limit at all, I thought it wasn't professional, even though Granddad kept muttering, 'It's better to be a pound under than a pound over.' I weighed in at 9 stone 8½lb, wearing my shorts and bra top.

Sharon Anyos stepped out of her high heels, and practically everything else, getting on the scales wearing just a skimpy bra and a G-string. She weighed 9 stone 8lb, turned around and posed on the scales like a cross between a body-builder and a bird out of a strip-joint. I thought, What a woman, big mouth, big ass, and an attitude bigger than Blackpool Tower. It wasn't hard for *me* to take a dislike to the loud-mouthed Aussie bird — after all I was fighting her.

One good thing about the Australians, from my point of view, was that they had refused to stay in the same hotel as us. If I had kept bumping into her I'm sure I would have been tempted to beat her cocky head in before we entered the ring. I wouldn't have given much for her chances in a street-style fight with me.

The rest of the boxing people staying at the Marriott Hotel were great. As always, I got on well with the Welsh trainers and boxers — they had seen me box before, and treated me as another professional and not as some curiosity. We had a few drinks and a lot of laughs together, and it took away a lot of the pre-fight tension — probably for all of us.

On the day of the fight it became even more of a social gathering as my friends and my dad arrived at the hotel. He, Graham 'Gesh' Webster, and Ray 'Fred' Hutchinson, had driven down from Fleetwood. Louise Raines, a winning contestant on *Gladiators*, had made the big trip from Preston with her husband. Claire Cooper, my protégé from Spaniorum Farm Gym, who I had hopes would follow in my boxing footsteps, was there along with Mike Loveridge, one of my sparring partners. Ronnie Butler and his son, Mark, minders and training partners, had come to escort me to the ring. Shaney, the receptionist from the gym who had become my friend and agony aunt, was there. Sandra, the Midget, had managed to avoid choosing this time for her overseas holiday and was there to work with Tex in the corner. In fact, when this lot had all managed to get into the dressing room it felt like a training night at the farm.

When I was changed, my hands taped, my gloves on, Ronnie let me belt him in the stomach for a few minutes, to warm me up. I then did some light sparring with the Midget to sharpen my reactions, occasionally hearing words that I had heard a thousand times from my nagging old trainer, 'Keep your hands up, chin down, snap that left hand out.' It really was like being back in the gym, with Ronnie's last minute technical advice, 'Knock her fuckin' head off, listen to Tex, listen to him and you will win, batter the cow!' My apprehension was disappearing as I got warmed-up, but as always when it came time to walk to the ring, the butterflies started.

Les Anyos led his daughter to the ring accompanied by the music 'Are You Ready'. Sharon was trying to look hard, her face stony under the baseball cap she was wearing. Les was probably trying *not* to look hard, but neither of them having much success. The daughter's blonde hair was braided into a plait down to her shoulders, the father's greying locks, even thicker and longer, tied back in an oversized ponytail. His gnarled features were emphasised, more than disguised, by the heavy moustache and stringy beard. Looking at him I thought, Boxing trainer? He would have more chance of passing an audition for an 'Old Man Of The Mountains' film.

Sharon Anyos ducked through the ropes, and threw her baseball cap into the crowd before dancing around the ring, backing into the ropes on all four sides, as if to check ring erector Mike Goodall's handiwork. Ronnie and Mark led me to my corner — they looked hard without trying. Me? I was doing what I liked best, being cheered in by the big crowd and dancing to the music of Michael Jackson's 'Thriller'. I was all smiles, the nerves gone and replaced by the adrenalin of excitement.

As John McDonald, the Master of Ceremonies, made the introductions, Anyos stamped towards our corner with a threatening look on her face. Me and Tex just grinned back at her. She probably thought we were nuts but it wasn't time to get too serious — the bell hadn't rung yet. It didn't ring for quite a while.

The MC introduced Sharon Anyos as 'The Wild Thing', the current undefeated Australian lightweight champion, the light-weight champion and the Oceanic Boxing Association lightweight champion. She tried to look even more vicious as she banged her gloves together and waved aggressively to the large crowd, many of them returning from the bars to watch me fight. I laughed and waved to all my supporters, as if I had already won.

Then the pantomime started. The Boxing Board rules were that all women must wear a chest guard and groin protector. Both these items were shown to the Board Inspector in the dressing room, but for some reason Sharon had not worn either into the ring. Jonathan Feld, the promoter, got into the ring to talk to the Australian corner, quickly followed by Ron Scalf, the WBF Official in Charge. Richie Davies, the referee, and Simon Block, the BBB of C's senior official at the show, consulted. They all ruled that Anyos must put her protective guards on. She left the ring, shaking her head in defiance, as the crowd booed.

So there I was, waiting in the ring, while she went back to the dressing room to get herself organised. It would have blown the minds of most boxers, to be left in the ring waiting for fifteen minutes, or however long it was, for an opponent to come in and the fight to start. Not me though. I wandered around, chatting to people, leaning over the ropes talking to anyone I knew, and some I didn't. Occasionally I would do some shadow-boxing to keep warm or, more to the point, loose, as it was so warm in the arena that it melted the ice in the ice-bag. I went back to the corner from time to time to talk to Tex — he was even more relaxed than me, leaning on the ropes saying, 'Enjoy yourself, keep cool, don't let the wait bother you. This is going to stress her out more than you.'

John McDonald, the MC, was doing his best to keep the crowd interested by introducing some of the large amount of celebrities in the audience. John H Stracey, Julius Francis, Steve Collins, Duke McKenzie, Charlie Magri, Colin McMillan. The girls acting as the national flag carriers, the Union Jack and the Australian flag, must have been praying to give one last wave and let their arms rest. More shadow-boxing, and finally Anyos was back in the ring. Last-minute instructions from Richie Davies, who was refereeing his tenth world title fight, and at long last it was time for the first bell.

Tex had warned, 'After the long delay she will probably be all worked up, and come out and try to take your head off.' He was right. She had certainly come to fight, and came looking for me. She found me, behind my left hand. For once I was using my boxing skills and she found it hard to get past my longer punches. It was a close round. Back on my stool in the first interval I listened to Tex. He was satisfied: 'That was a good round, you're boxing well. Just do a little more of the same and don't take any chances.'

The second round was similar, me jabbing away with my left hand, picking up the points, while the 'Wild Thing' lived up to her name and kept coming after me, swinging punches. At the end of the round I said to my casual cornerman, 'She can't half hit!' I got the usual sympathetic response: 'In that case, don't let her hit you.' I thought, It's all right for you, Granddad, she isn't hitting you. I knew what he meant, though, and told myself to keep boxing thoughtfully.

I did, and the pattern was set — Anyos trying to destroy me, and me, often boxing on the retreat, pinching the points with more accurate straight punches. It was close, and I must admit Sharon had some reasonable boxing skills to back up her aggression, but I was confident that I was controlling the contest.

Round four started with an all-out Aussie onslaught. She probably thought that she was going to rough me out of the fight — no chance! I kept working behind my jab, and then the chest protector pantomime started all over again when a pad flew out. Richie Davies picked it up, gave it to the Australian cornerman who stuffed it back in to the sloppy bra top. Another flurry of blows and another pad flew out. The ref picked it up but didn't bother to stop the action. It was a busy round, and we both threw a lot of punches. I felt I had thrown enough to keep ahead on points.

The only changes in the next two rounds were a change of bra top for Anyos, which stopped her chest pads from copying flying saucers. Tex's relaxed corner attitude became a bit more serious, with him saying, 'You are boxing really well. Keep doing the same but you must up your workrate.'

I told him, 'I'm OK. I'm winning every round.'

'No, it's too close, you must up your workrate.'

It was hard work again in round seven, but I scored with some good straight right-hand punches. Anyos was throwing a lot back but they weren't hurting so much now. The one thing that did hurt was a collision of heads which brought up a lump the size of a walnut on my forehead. Back in the corner, Tex got the En-swell out of the ice and ironed the lump flat, 'Ow! It hurts!' No comment from my caring cornerman other than, 'Keep boxing and keep working!'

The eighth round over, and I was happy that I had won it. I sat on the stool, was sponged down, given a drink and then Tex went into his '*Now listen to me!*' routine. 'You have just two rounds to go.'

'Yes, but I'm tired.'

'Think of these two rounds as the last lap of your circuit training — you know what's got to be done, and you know it's got to be done with everything you've got left. The fight's too close. You *must* up your workrate. I told you this in America, you didn't do what I told you, and you lost. Now, *you must listen and up your workrate.*'

Anyos upped her workrate. I expect she was told in her corner that she was behind on points. She kept storming after me, but for once I did as I was told, kept boxing on the retreat and scored with some great, straight, left and right counter-punches, stopping from time to time to throw some combination punches to her head and body. I didn't like Anyos, I thought she was rude, much too cocky and had a little piggy face, but I had to give her credit for being fit, and trying.

I had begun to believe the fight was close and there was no way I was going to lose. The one thing I had been doing all through the battle was making the Wild Thing miss with her swinging punches by ducking and weaving. Now, with my timing getting better, and her slowing up a bit, my counter-punches were scoring even better. I certainly won that round, and it was all down to concentrating on the boxing skills I could do so well in the gym but had never managed to produce in a fight before. Tex often told people, 'You have not seen the best of Jane Couch yet!' This time I was beginning to show it.

In the tenth, and final, round we felt Anyos needed a knock-out to win. Her corner must have thought the same because she certainly came out looking for one. The fight finished like it started, full of action until the final bell. When it rang I was sure I had done enough to win. The crowd gave us a standing ovation.

The score cards were collected from the three judges, the referee, Richie Davies, conferred with the MC before taking his position between Anyos and me, holding our wrists, ready to hoist the arm of the winner in the air. Was it my imagination, or did I feel a reassuring squeeze? The seconds seemed like hours. We all thought I had won but what did the judges think? Then the announcement came from John McDonald. 'All three judges in favour of the *new*,' — it was a heart-sinking moment, I had momentarily forgotten I was fighting for the *vacant* WBF lightweight title — 'WBF Lightweight *champion of the world* — from Fleetwood, England, the Fleetwood Assassin, *Jane Couch*!!!'

I was presented with my new title belt, plus a kiss and a cuddle from Ron Scalf, then back to the corner for a quick cuddle from Tex, a big hug from Ronnie Butler, and a little hug from the Midget. What else could she manage? Then it was my dad's turn for another big cuddle. It had been a hard fight, but I thought I had won it clearly, and I thought everyone else must have thought the same. But there were some 'boos' from the crowd — I put that down to Earls Court Aussies, who had been disappointed in seeing their star beaten. As for Larry O'Connell — he was one of the judges and only had a one point win for me — I made a mental note that I shouldn't call him a 'fat bastard' again!

The MC asked the crowd to show their appreciation for 'Wild Thing' Sharon Annoyus. It was a mistake in pronunciation, but it was very appropriate. She and her team had certainly annoyed a lot of people during their visit.

It was my last fight in 1999, I had ended the year as I had started it — a *world champion*. This time, though, I had three world titles to my credit. It was these three titles that, once again, won me the West Country BBC TV and Radio Sportswoman of the Year award, in December — an early Christmas present. Now I couldn't wait for the millennium year 2000 and its unknown challenges...

Little did I expect that the first challenge to get me back in the news in January 2000 wasn't really anything to do with me, but highlighted the career of Julius Francis.

Julius is a nice enough guy who, like me, had had his life turned around by boxing — from 'unsociable' activities to becoming a popular, and respected, British heavyweight champion. His big moment of fame came when he was selected as a risk-free opponent for Mike Tyson at the MEN Arena in Manchester on January 29th. Mike, arguably the best ever world heavyweight champion when in his prime, was trying to re-establish his career after some dismal, even disgusting, displays of boxing discipline. When losing to Evander Holyfield, he left his mark on Evander, and the spectators, not with his boxing skills, but with the size of the chunk he bit out of Holyfield's ear. Not surprisingly, considering his other brushes with the law and the morose, belligerent attitude Mike often adopted when getting bored with media interviews, the American boxing fans had lost their admiration for his past achievements, and with that went their willingness to buy tickets to watch a once-famous, brilliant fighter trying to re-find his popularity and ability.

Not so in England. The 'event', as it was often referred to in the press rather than the 'fight', was a financial coup for promoter Frank Warren, all the tickets for the show being sold out in a very few hours. It wasn't even expected to be a competitive fight, at least not by anyone outside a psychiatric ward. Even Julius, anticipating how the bout would end, sold advertising space on the soles of his boxing boots! He was right: the fight lasted two rounds and he ended up on the canvas, toes uppermost. The boot adverts were photographed and prominently displayed in a national newspaper.

There was far more excitement outside the ring, with vast crowds of boxing fans trying to get a glimpse of Tyson, from the time he landed at Heathrow until he left the country. It wasn't only the fans that tried to besiege him; a women's group of protestors made themselves irritatingly prominent. They had, unsuccessfully, challenged the belated and dithering decision of Jack Straw, the Home Secretary, to allow Mike Tyson, a convicted rapist, into the country. Then some bright spark in the media thought it a good idea to get my opinion – after all, I was a woman and would surely back the feminist group. 'Will you be supporting women's rights? Will you be trying to stop Mike Tyson fighting?'

For once I didn't say it in my usual forthright manner, but the words going through my mind were, Fuck off you stupid bastards. I like what I know about Tyson: he has been one of the greatest fighters ever, a legend. I can sympathise with him, he has been surrounded by hangers-on, money has been leeched off him, possibly millions of dollars. As for being convicted of rape, what did that silly bitch think she was going up to his room for, a cup of hot chocolate and a peck on the cheek? Come off it, any woman would know what she is likely to get in those circumstances. She probably enjoyed it at the time, anyway. I didn't get to meet Mike, but I did try — I even suggested to my old friend John Lloyd of the *Daily Express* that he might be able to arrange for me to train with Tyson. John thought it was a great idea, but it didn't happen. Even though I didn't get to meet Mike, I was so pleased that those stupid 'women's rights' lot didn't get their way.

Having been, to put it mildly for once, a 'free spirit' all my life, I would get right pissed off at people like those women protestors trying to dictate their thoughts, and how to live, to others, especially me. As soon as I heard the words 'minority group' my back would start to bristle — after all, I was the founder of the smallest minority group in the country: female BBB of C licensed professional boxers. For a long time, I was it! OK, so I had my fans and supporters. I was always surprised how many middle-aged and older women would stop me in the shops, or on the street, and say, 'Well done, love, you show 'em!' Sadly there were others, who would point me out to their friends, whisper and stare as if I had green skin, four heads and a tail!

Then there were the thick bastards who thought that because I was taking part in a male-dominated sport I had to be a lesbian! No way! Now don't get me wrong, while I may be a bit old-fashioned and think that men should be men and women should be women, what other people do is their choice, and doesn't bother me as long as they don't expect me to join in. I must admit, when I first started boxing I too fell into the trap of thinking, as I looked around the dressing rooms, trying to keep myself to myself in a corner, Cor! She looks a bit butch, tattoos, cropped hair — I'll keep away from her.

When I got on the world scene, with my trips to Denmark and the United States, it seemed that nearly all the top-class girls were married, a lot of them with children. Like in all walks of life there was the occasional lesbian, but none of them pushed their sexual preferences on me. In fact I made good (arms distant) friends with one or two of them, just as I did with black people, Asians, Catholics, Jews, male homosexuals and foreigners (or 'scrobs' as we called them in Fleetwood) of all types.

It was dead easy to make friends with black people who, apart from their usually happy, laid-back attitude, would be almost magnetically attracted to me. Tex said it was because my crinkly hair and scrawny lower legs suggested I was of Afro descent. In fact, I was asked to appear on a TV show that had a black camera crew, presenter and audience. The presenter said to me, 'Do you mind if we mention that your father was black?

'But he wasn't.'

'Your mother?'

'No.'

'Oh…' Somehow the atmosphere cooled a bit, but I did the show anyway.

Me? I don't give a fuck who I talk to or make friends with, which is just as well, as in the boxing community its participants and supporters come from all backgrounds and beliefs. I'm just happy to be part of a very exciting world, and hopefully I'll be staying in it for a very long time to come…

JANE'S RECORD

30-10-94 KALPNA SHAH W RSC 2 WIGAN

29-01-95 FOSTERES JOSEPH W Pts 6 FLEETWOOD

18-04-95 JANE JOHNSON W RSC 4 FLEETWOOD

01-07-95 JULIA SHIRLEY W Pts 6 FLEETWOOD

24-05-96 SANDRA GEIGER W Pts 10 COPENHAGEN WIBF
WELTERWEIGHT TITLE

01-03-97 ANDREA DeSHONG W RSC 7 NEW ORLEANS
U.S.A. WIBF TITLE DEFENCE

24-08-97 LEAH MELLINGER W Pts 10 CONNECTICUT
U.S.A. WIBF TITLE DEFENCE

24-10-97 DORA WEBBER L Pts 6 MISSISSIPPI U.S.A.

10-01-98 DORA WEBBER L Pts 10 ATLANTIC CITY U.S.A.

25-11-98 SIMONE LUKIC W RSC 2 STREATHAM
LONDON

20-02-99 MARISCHA SJAUW W Pts 10 THORNABY,
MIDDLESBROUGH DEFENCE of WIBF TITLE
AND FOR THE VACANT WBF WELTERWEIGHT
TITLE

01-04-99 HEIKE NOLLER W Pts 8 ASTON VILLA

31-10-99 SHARON ANYOS W Pts 10 RAYNES PARK,
LONDON FOR VACANT WBF LIGHTWEIGHT
TITLE

13 FIGHTS – WON 11 – LOST 2